Discovering Children's Literature

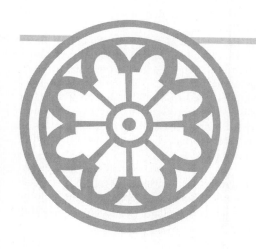

Judith Hillman
Saint Michael's College

Merrill,
an imprint of Prentice Hall
Englewood Cliffs, New Jersey   *Columbus, Ohio*

Library of Congress Cataloging-in-Publication Data

Hillman, Judith.
   Discovering children's literature / Judith Hillman.
      p. cm.
   Includes bibliographical references and index.
   ISBN 0-02-355085-6
   1. Children's literature—History and criticism. I. Title
PN1009.A1H54 1995   94-4319
028.1'62—dc20   CIP

Cover art: Shelly Haas
Editor: Linda James Scharp
Production Editor: Patricia A. Skidmore
Photo Editor: Anne Vega
Text Designer: STELLARViSIONS
Cover Designer: Patti Okuno-Levering
Production Buyer: Deidra M. Schwartz
Electronic Text Management: Marilyn Wilson
   Phelps, Matthew Williams, Jane Lopez, Karen
   L. Bretz

This book was set in Caslon and Swiss by Prentice Hall and was printed and bound by The Book Press. The cover was printed by Phoenix Color Corp.

Credits:

Photo of Judith Hillman by Pete Romanowski.

p. 109: Excerpted from the poem " 'I,' Says the Poem" by Eve Merriam in *A Sky Full of Poems* by Eve Merriam. Copyright © 1964, 1970, 1973 by Eve Merriam. Reprinted by permission of Marian Reiner.

p. 116: "Poem," from *The Dream Keeper and Other Poems* by Langston Hughes. Copyright © 1932 by Alfred A. Knopf, Inc., and renewed 1960 by Langston Hughes. Reprinted by permission of the publisher.

p. 116: Haiku from *More Cricket Songs* Japanese Haiku translated by Harry Behn. Copyright © 1971 by Harry Behn. Used by permission of Marian Reiner.

p. 120: Excerpted from "What In the World?" in *There is No Rhyme for Silver* by Eve Merriam. Copyright © 1962 by Eve Merriam. © renewed 1990 by Eve Merriam. Reprinted by permission of Marian Reiner.

p. 126: "The Falling Star" reprinted with permission of Macmillan Publishing Company from *Collected Poems of Sara Teasdale*. Copyright 1930 by Sara Teasdale, renewed 1958 by Morgan Guaranty Trust of N.Y.

Printed in the United States of America

10 9 8 7 6 5 4 3 2 1

ISBN: 0-02-355085-6

Prentice-Hall International (UK) Limited, *London*
Prentice-Hall of Australia Pty. Limited, *Sydney*
Prentice-Hall of Canada, Inc., *Toronto*
Prentice-Hall Hispanoamericana, S. A., *Mexico*
Prentice-Hall of India Private Limited, *New Delhi*
Prentice-Hall of Japan, Inc., *Tokyo*
Simon & Schuster Asia Pte. Ltd., *Singapore*
Editora Prentice-Hall do Brasil, Ltda., *Rio de Janeiro*

to Donald, with gratitude and love

Preface

This textbook presents an introduction to children's literature. It was built on the premise that the richness and diversity of children's literature can make an immeasurable contribution to children's lives.

Discovering Children's Literature was written for adults who work with children—teachers, prospective teachers, librarians, prospective librarians, and parents. Any adult who is intrigued with children's books and wants to become knowledgeable about children's literature will find this book a helpful resource. This textbook could serve as a primary text in children's literature courses offered to preservice or inservice teachers, or as a supplementary text in reading and language arts teaching methods courses with a strong focus on literature-based instruction, especially those courses where students are required to purchase and read a number of children's trade books. Similar courses offered within an English department or a library science program could also use this text.

The most distinguishing feature of *Discovering Children's Literature* is its deliberately succinct presentation, which highlights only highly significant aspects of children's literature. It serves as a guide, pointing the way to many examples and suggestions rather than providing them. It has been purposefully written as a small, inexpensive text to encourage people to read as many children's books as possible, instead of reading *about* them.

Discovering Children's Literature includes many other special features:

- It is organized systematically to reveal the history, structure, and content of children's literature, providing a foundational knowledge base to which people can add information as they discover new books.

- Evaluating children's books is a major theme in all chapters. Evaluation criteria are clearly articulated and related to the genre that is presented.

- Recently published multicultural books are highlighted in chapters of Traditional Literature (Chapter 4), Poetry (Chapter 6), Realism (Chapter 8) and Biography (Chapter 9).

- A section called "Implications for Instruction," which details questions for reflection, projects for students, and activities for children in primary and intermediate classrooms, concludes each chapter. Therefore, teaching strategies are immediately accessible for those who want them.

- Six literature-based classroom units, appropriate for kindergartners through sixth graders, are described in Chapter 10. This culminating chapter demonstrates several exemplary teaching units for reading and language arts programs.

- A glossary illuminates the specific vocabulary pertinent to children's literature, and an appendix lists books honored by the prestigious Newbery and Caldecott Awards committees.

- Each chapter begins by asking the reader to do something—to categorize, to write, to recall children's books from childhood, or to interact in some way with the chapter's content. This was done so that background knowledge could be tapped in order to provide a framework, or schema, for future learning, thus modeling one effective way to work with children and books.

- Last, I hope a sense of discovery permeates each chapter—a joyous recollection of old favorites coupled with a contemporary zest for new ones.

ACKNOWLEDGMENTS

I want to thank the many teachers and children who tried out my ideas and gave me many of theirs. Also, my colleagues at Saint Michael's College, particularly those in the Education Department who lent me their offices and computers during my sabbatical year, are to be thanked. Their friendship continually sustains and motivates me. Similarly, I am indebted to my friends, especially Virginia Golodetz, who teach children's literature courses in the graduate program with knowledge and dedication. I am also grateful for the support of those who serve with me on the Dorothy Canfield Fisher Book Award Committee.

In addition, I'd like to thank the people at Merrill/Prentice Hall, beginning with sales representative Sylvia Bonadio, who brought my work to the attention of Linda Scharp. As my first editor, Linda has been a guiding light throughout the project, and I am supremely grateful to her. I appreciate the support and encouragement of Jeff Johnston, Publisher, Merrill Education, and the help of production editor Patty Skidmore.

I also thank the reviewers who provided much-needed, informed perspectives: Kathy H. Barclay, Western Illinois University; Catherine J. Coggins, Stetson University; Martha Combs, University of Nevada; Baron D. Conaway, Arkansas State University; Marjorie Hancock, Kansas State University; Virginia Harris, Wayland Baptist University; Anna Heatherly, University of Arkansas at Little Rock; Pose M. Lamb, Purdue University; Eleanor Lofquist, Western Carolina University; Hollis Lowery-Moore, Sam Houston State University; and Patricia McGowan, Bakersfield College.

Last, and best, I thank my family for believing in me—Cara, Rob, Stephanie, Emily, and Don, my husband, who deserves the dedication and much more.

Contents

● ● ● ● ●
CHAPTER FOUR
Once Upon a Time . . . and Tradition Continues   59

● ● ● ● ●
CHAPTER FIVE
Pictures Tell a Story   83

● ● ● ● ●

CHAPTER SIX

Poetry as Sound, Story, and Symbol   109

● ● ● ● ●

CHAPTER SEVEN

Imaginary Worlds of Fantasy   129

● ● ● ● ●

CHAPTER EIGHT

Realism in Present and Past   153

• • • • •

CHAPTER NINE

Literature of Fact: Biography and Information   185

● ● ● ● ●

CHAPTER TEN

The Literacy-Literature Connection: Six Units   209

Chapter One

The Child, the Book, and Literacy

INTRODUCTION AND RESPONSE

What does the phrase *children's literature* mean to you? Does it summon memories of looking at a favorite picture book on a parent's lap, or reading a great story out-doors on a lazy summer day? Mention children's literature to a group of adults and most will smile with a remembered fondness for special books or authors. Do you recall a particular book or incident, such as *Charlotte's Web* (White, 1952), or *Goodnight Moon* (Brown, 1947)?

Children's literature today enjoys unprecedented visibility; children can choose from approximately four thousand books published annually in the United States alone. Worldwide estimates of the total number of children's books in print are as high as seventy-three thousand (Huck, Hepler, & Hickman, 1993). School classrooms and libraries display an abundant selection of literature for all age lev-els because of the popularity of literature-based reading programs (Tompkins & McGee, 1993). The success of specialized children's bookstores proves that the economic climate of this decade will support such ventures.

Children's literature has captured the interest of those in the marketplace and also those in academia who believe that children need quality literature. It has become a legitimate field of study for scholars in literature, and it crosses interdisciplinary lines to education, child development, folklore, and fine arts as well. Truly multidisciplinary and international in scope, today children's literature represents cultural richness and diversity.

In this chapter, your discovery or continued discovery of literature for children begins. Because children's literature is multifaceted and there is much to discover, begin to think about what you would like to know. What are your interests in the field of children's literature? New books? International authors? Multicultural stories? Why are you embarking on this voyage of discovery now? Identify some goals for yourself as you begin to look closely at children's books from today and the past.

This chapter lays the foundation for your study, defining children's literature and suggesting a way to organize this diverse field. The evaluation system is first explained here, then continues through remaining chapters. Understanding children's growth and development helps teachers and parents choose appropriate books and forms the basis for principles of literature-based reading and language arts programs in schools. These principles find expression in projects and activities following each chapter. The last chapter presents integrated activities in thematic units, drawing from examples used throughout the book. A special feature of this introductory chapter, called "How this book is organized," will point you toward information addressing the questions and goals you have identified.

Your discovery has begun. Enjoy a remarkable, thought-provoking journey into children's literature that will not end when you finish this book. Discoveries will continue as each year brings new literature that delights and challenges readers of all ages.

● ● ● ● ●
DEFINING CHILDREN'S LITERATURE

Did you know that there is a difference between children's books and children's literature? Books are concrete, tangible objects, real and heavy. A story or informational book is called a trade book to distinguish it from a textbook. Literature is an abstract concept, a composite of elements or attributes that connote excellence, such as a mesmerizing story that moves the reader to tears or laughter. We can call any work a children's book, but is it literature? Does it have the necessary value, the high quality that the concept *literature* implies? Distinguishing between books and literature is an evaluative judgment based on specific characteristics that define literature.

A definition of children's literature has two parts: one deals with content and the other with quality. The first part, content, is relatively straightforward. Children's literature is material written for infants, children, and adolescents that contains:

1. typical childhood experiences written from a child's perspective;
2. children or childlike characters;
3. simple and direct plots that focus on action;

4. a feeling of optimism and innocence (e.g., happy endings are the norm); and

5. a tendency toward combining reality and fantasy.

In characterizing children's literature, Perry Nodelman (1992) adds that it is often **didactic**, with strong cultural messages inherent in stories designed to teach children how to become adults. Throughout its history, children's literature has been viewed as a socializing agent, a way to inculcate values and norms into following generations.

Both Nodelman and Rebecca Lukens (1990) insist that literature should first of all be pleasurable. The stories in fiction and the prose in nonfiction should be interesting and entertaining while allowing readers to gain new insights and to use their imaginations.

While content is quite easy to describe, the second part, quality, is not. Quality is the subjective dimension of literature, a judgment made as to whether or not a children's book is "good" or "poor." If it is deemed good, then it becomes literature, joining the **canon** with what has been recognized as good or even the best. If the book is "flawed" it is not literature. Some common flaws include stodgy writing, plots that are either too predictable or too illogical, and socially conscious themes that outweigh the slender story that supports them.

Literature can be defined by characteristics that refer to its power to satisfy, explain, invite, and compel. Which books do you know that

- evoke strong emotions while engaging the intellect,

- empower readers with a will to act,

- express a feeling or an act in beautiful language,

- reveal deep and subtle human motives,

- allow readers to experience vicariously a different time, place, and character?

If a book does those things, it can be called literature. In his essay, "Why I Value Literature," Richard Hoggart says that literature "seeks for the meanings in human experience" (Chambers, 1983, p. 8). These meanings allow each of us to explore our humanity. Literature gives us words to describe and explore our thoughts, dreams, and stories.

In *The Snowy Day* (Keats, 1962), text and art work together to create a deeply satisfying aesthetic experience. With Peter, the main character, we share the discovery of a winter world and its unexpected delights. With Peter, we enjoy the rejuvenating power of warmth and food—essentials to our existence as humans. *The Snowy Day,* in its brief thirty-two pages, demonstrates all the characteristics of literature and its elevation to that status has long been recognized.

Similarly, literature of Native Americans finds expression in *Anpao: An American Indian Odyssey* (Highwater, 1977). Moving and engaging stories of shimmering visions, magic, creation, deceit, and trickery allow the reader to become part

From *The Snowy Day* by Ezra
Jack Keats. Copyright © 1962
by Ezra Jack Keats, renewed
© 1990 by Martin Pope. Used
by permission of Viking Penguin, a division of Penguin
Books USA Inc.

— a stick that was just right for
smacking a snow-covered tree.

15

of a tradition, to taste and feel in a dream-time of discovery. Expressive language—
"In the days before the people fled into the water, the wind held leaves aloft in the
sky like dragonflies" (p. 15)—allows the power of this literature to unfold.

Differences Between Children's Literature and Adult Literature

Is children's literature different from adult literature? (Note that there are many
adult books that do not necessarily qualify as literature.) Superficial aspects, such
as fewer characters, simpler plots, and shorter sentences, mark obvious differences when comparing material written for children and that written for adults.
But issues of quality should be the same: the depth and range of emotion, the
profundity of ideas. Many authors, Jill Paton Walsh among them, do not shrink
from expressing a theme or an idea in children's literature in the best comprehensive prose (Hunt, 1991). She does not "write down" to a child audience.
Lukens supports this similarity in quality when she says literature for young readers differs from adult literature in degree but not in kind (Lukens, 1990). Literary quality should be a hallmark of books for every audience: infants, toddlers,
children, adolescents, and adults.

Because our definition of literature hinges on synonymous qualities of adult and
children's literature, we bring the same standards of evaluation to both. In other

words, we do not lower our standards because a book is written especially for children. Lower expectations would be patronizing and condescending to child readers.

● ● ● ● ●
EVALUATION OF CHILDREN'S BOOKS

Most of us have a quick response—"I liked it" or "I liked parts of it" or "It wasn't as good as ____"—when we read a book. Those reactions are honest, and form the basis for a more careful, informed evaluation, particularly when selecting a book for children.

While evaluation can take many forms, three are proposed here:

1. Evaluate the book against your internalized literary criteria: Is the plot coherent? Is it well written? Does it evoke pleasure and understanding? Does it explore the human condition in a unique way?

2. Evaluate the book by comparing it to others you hold in high esteem: Is it as good as . . . *(The Snowy Day, Anpao,* or your own choice)? Does it have the same depth, range of emotion, beautiful language? Using these books as **touchstones** helps to anchor the concept of *literature* in your mind, invites comparison, and sets a standard by which to judge other works. (Matthew Arnold, the noted English poet and critic, first used the term *touchstone* to signify the best and truly excellent, in 1880.)

3. Evaluate the book by identifying a purpose and audience, then determine if that particular book fits. Or, if the book selected does not suit, then search for the best book—the "best" fit.

All three forms of evaluation have their place in book selection, the ultimate evaluative test. With the growing use of literature in school reading programs, the trend has been to move evaluation to the more pragmatic level described in number three above. Finding the best book to fit a specific purpose and audience still rests on the presumption that the evaluator brings literary criteria to the judgment, however. Paul Heins, former editor of the *Horn Book Magazine* and esteemed scholar, suggested that literary criticism was only one way to approach a book, and that other kinds of standards, derived from those who use books with children, were legitimate also (Hunt, 1991). Such standards take into account the match between reader and text, and the personal response a young reader may make in understanding a text.

The kind of evaluation proposed in this text asks you to consider first your personal reaction, then your purposes and audience. Evaluating a book according to your internalized literary criteria is important, but not to the exclusion of judging a book's effectiveness for its audience. There are few books published that are absolutely worthless, but there are many that will not suit a teacher's purposes or children's needs. With the thousands of books available, it is our responsibility to consider carefully what we select and why. Because all children deserve the best, our standards and methods should find the best for them.

• • • • •
ASPECTS OF CHILD DEVELOPMENT

Defining the *child* in children's literature is just about as difficult as determining quality in a literary work. Have children changed in the last generation? Has childhood been redefined? Clearly there are cultural and social influences impinging upon children now that were not present a generation ago. However, psychologists identify stages of development that are predictable, stemming from human biological and psychological imperatives that transcend culture and society.

Although there are several theories about how and why humans develop as they do, these basic characteristics in behavior and language generally typify age groups. The following chart, Figure 1.1, summarizes major points of development, called "psychosocial markers" because their presence marks a unique characteristic in development.

Infancy through Preschool

As infants begin their journey into childhood, their primary tasks are to acquire language, to develop locomotor skills, and to form attachments or bond with a

Figure 1.1   Descriptions of Developmental Characteristics

Ages	Psychosocial Markers
Infancy through Preschool (ages birth – four)	acquiring language forming attachments mastering locomotor skills beginning to learn autonomy enjoying parallel and pretend play
Early Childhood (ages five – eight)	developing language enjoying achievements (learning to read) imitating adult roles using "concrete" thought projecting an optimistic view
Middle Childhood (ages nine – twelve)	becoming more logical and rule-oriented growing increasingly dependent on peer group perfecting skills employing metacognitive thought moving toward independence from parents
Adolescence	maturing biologically establishing sexual identity becoming autonomous while retaining strong attachment to peer group employing abstract thought

Adapted from Hoffman, Paris, Hall, & Schell (1988). *Developmental Psychology Today.*

primary caregiver while at the same time learning the autonomy necessary to function independently. Each of these tasks continues to develop in complexity through the preschool period, forming a foundation for future cognitive, social, and personality development.

As children learn to talk, their language is a window into their minds. A fascinating study of a young child, Anna (Crago & Crago, 1983), responding to literature from the age of twelve months to five years, demonstrated how she learned vocabulary and story structures, used pictures to predict text, and learned to love books. Like Anna, children who are surrounded by a rich language environment, full of experiences with books, can gain linguistic facility through their exposure to stories, poems, songs, and chants.

Developmental theories of Erik Erikson (1963), Jean Piaget (1952), and Lev Vygotsky (1962) have been translated to educational practices particularly relevant to reading and language arts programs. The relationship between language and thought flourishes when pleasurable literature stimulates the senses and the imagination. From pat-a-cake to picture books, young children need to hear language, particularly the connected discourse in story and description, song and poem. Most children are surrounded by snippets of conversation, a quick question or direction from adults, and from that they learn words, phrases, and meanings. But they also need to hear how language extends, to understand how stories begin and end, and to see how the written language symbolizes spoken language.

In addition to language development, emotional and social aspects are enhanced through literature. Developing trust, learning empathy, using imagination, and identifying with role models are all important human traits that can be developed by reading aloud to young children, beginning at birth.

Our basic personality characteristics, cognitive styles, and ideas about the world are formed very early in life. Exposure to children's literature can widen, extend, and enrich that formation.

Early Childhood

Most children ages five through eight participate in a structured educational system. Much of their time and energy is spent learning to read, enjoying achievements, gaining competence, and imitating adult roles. At these ages, children still believe that adults can offer something useful to their lives. There is a general optimism about the world among children whose world is still somewhat carefree and innocent. Family life, school, and community represent the child's wider world. Parents, stepparents, and siblings play a large part in determining the developing values and attitudes of the individual.

In this vital period of beginning formalized instruction, "language not only speeds the acquisition of new concepts, but allows children to reason more effectively as well" (Hoffman, Paris, Hall, & Schell, 1988, p. 278). Language is also fundamental to the development of self-control, aiding necessary socialization in school and family. Thus language development provides the foundation for learning and the control of behavior in primary children.

As the renowned Swiss psychologist Jean Piaget studied the origins of intelligence, his insight led to revolutionary educational practices. He determined that children in this stage learn best by manipulating concrete objects that represent abstract concepts (Flavell, 1985). Particularly in math and science, children profit from describing, sorting, and classifying objects. From this they can learn numerical concepts such as adding and dividing. When language is an integral part of the activity, concepts become entrenched in both long-term and short-term memory.

Because children this age are curious, ready to try new things, and increasingly confident, they should find children's books an ever-widening source of information and pleasure. Learning about other cultures or about scientific topics becomes an exciting project in a primary classroom. Truly soaking up information like sponges, children benefit from exposure to all kinds of books and magazines.

Middle Childhood

Children at this stage—roughly from nine through twelve—are asserting their individuality so much so that generalizations are difficult and rife with error. Perhaps that is the hallmark of this stage—the lack of a stable, consistent way to describe childhood. Richard Louv (1990), a writer and reporter, suggests that the nature of childhood has changed dramatically in one generation due to societal and electronic forces. From new constellations of family definitions to the new television environment, aspects of modern society change preconceived notions of childhood. Clearly, in most middle or junior high schools, a casual observer would notice many changes in learning and social contexts.

Nevertheless, children in this stage are becoming more like adults in logical thought patterns. Piaget referred to the "formal-operations" stage, which most children enter at about age eleven. Manipulation of concrete objects is no longer so necessary; more abstract notions can be internalized without the preliminary movement of physical properties. Also, children gain an ability to reflect on their thought processes, an ability called metacognition. Metacognition is a sophisticated way to monitor one's own language and thought. It is the mental process of becoming aware of how one derives meaning from written and oral language.

Peer group influence grows while parental influence diminishes. As children continue to work on establishing an identity (and this task continues through adolescence) their industriousness is evident. Many children work unhesitatingly on perfecting skills in swimming, basketball, or tennis, or playing a musical instrument, for example. Team play is important, as the team represents identification with a peer group, a marker of growing competence, and the chance to practice governance by rules.

At this time boys and girls express different interests in book selection. Boys select more nonfiction than girls, and the types of fiction vary between genders (Childress, 1985). Boys tend to choose action and adventure, while girls prefer stories that are based on strong interpersonal relationships.

Adolescence

Dramatic changes in adolescence affecting young men and women are most noticeable in physical appearance, but of equal importance is the development in thinking abilities and social-emotional discoveries. Many psychologists feel that the strongest characteristic of adolescence is the quest for autonomy, as the growing urge to define oneself forces shifts in perceptions and attitudes (Hoffman et al., 1988). The emerging sense of self is a hallmark of this period as biological, intellectual, and personality changes work together to establish an adult identity apart from family and friends.

Intellectual development is seen in the capacity to think abstractly and to understand complexities in concepts such as justice, community, and freedom. Teenagers can discuss controversial issues, entertain others' points of view, and forge new opinions. In the social-emotional realm, family roles change as adolescents experiment with new identities.

The inevitable conflicts of adolescence are portrayed realistically in children's literature. The particular interests and needs of this age group are found in a relatively new category called "young adult" literature. Cultural demands, choices (or lack of them), and the risks and joys of emerging independence are all presented in literature as well as other media. Literature such as *Lyddie* (Paterson, 1991) helps young teenagers to reflect, to identify with a time, place, and character, and to reach into their imaginations. Young adult literature fills an important niche between children's and adult literature for many readers, especially when skillful authors create incidents about making decisions and taking responsibility (Nilsen & Donelson, 1993).

A strong call for enhanced language development through literature permeates these periods of child and adolescent development. As language is every person's birthright, so literature is the supreme expression of how humans use this birthright artistically.

● ● ● ● ●

PRINCIPLES OF A LITERATURE-BASED PROGRAM

With appropriate knowledge and selection criteria, teachers can use children's literature to provide the base for the reading and language arts curriculum of any primary or middle school. Reading is defined as "a purposeful, active, strategic search for meaning in which readers use everything they know to make sense of written language" (Wepner & Feeley, 1993, p. 5). Learning how to read effectively is probably the main purpose of attending school, especially in the early years. The overriding goal is to ensure that every child becomes literate and values reading as a lifelong activity.

There are many methods, strategies, techniques, and philosophies of reading instruction, and most include some use of literature. Until the last few years, however, literature has frequently been on the periphery of instruction. A well-known approach, called the basal system or basal approach, includes short stories written with a controlled vocabulary or excerpts from literature in a textbook accompanied by skill pages or workbooks. Other popular approaches recently created for children fall under the umbrella term "whole language." Whole language means that all language processes—reading, writing, speaking, and listening—are working together, holistically, to provide support and confirmation in the challenging task of learning to read (Goodman, 1986). Whole-language approaches elicit the child's oral language and knowledge to initiate reading and writing. "Predictable" books are often an integral part of instruction, with predictable language patterns that most children learn easily. Very often books that are much larger than the typical trade book, called Big Books, allow a teacher to direct the instruction toward a group of children so that the large illustrations and print are easily seen. Children experience the text together and begin to create a community that values literature.

Some other approaches stress skill development, often at the expense of enjoying literature. Still other approaches rely on various combinations of activities organized through learning centers or thematic units. In some reading programs, children are allowed to select their own reading materials, and proceed through them at a self-directed pace. When children feel that they have some investment in the learning process, reading and writing usually become more stimulating and success follows. The transaction between reader and text (Rosenblatt, 1978) takes on more intensity. More will come later about the transactional view and its impact on reading instruction, particularly as it relates to literature-based programs.

For more information about the reading process and current theories, these texts are recommended:

Teaching Reading with Children's Literature, Cox & Zarillo (1993)

Teaching Reading to Every Child, Lapp & Flood (1992)

Teaching Children to Read: From Basals to Books, Reutzel & Cooter (1992)

Moving Forward with Literature: Books, Basals, and Beyond, Wepner & Feeley (1993)

With all the attention focused on literature, there is some concern that it will be ill-used (Goodman, 1988; Silvey, 1989). A major concern is that literature will become the next "basal," merely a vehicle to generate workbook pages of fill-in-the-blank questions, or to spark discussions in which only superficial questions are asked by teachers and children are expected to recall isolated facts. Natalie Babbitt (1990) speaks for other authors when she implores teachers to protect children's literature from vacuous activities. Most people think this is counterproductive to developing a love for literature and reading.

While there is no single correct way to use literature productively, there are suggestions that promote the wise use of literature. The following principles come from many successful classroom literature-based programs and a deeply held belief that literature, if used effectively, has the power to reach and teach all learners.

Principles

1. Teachers must know a wide range of children's literature. They should read extensively, understand how literature works, be familiar with reviewing sources, and enjoy the richness literature offers.

2. In a classroom program, there must be *time* for children to read silently every day, *trust* that each child can choose books appropriately and respond honestly, and a *connection* to a home reading program.

3. Activities based on literature should closely reflect the integrity of the story, the purpose of the teacher, and the children's needs. Music, the visual arts, science, math, and other fields are allied with literature to create meaningful activities, often in a topic-centered or thematic unit approach to learning.

Elaborating briefly on these points will perhaps clarify and extend their practical utility. In the first principle, the responsibility lies with the teacher (or librarian, or parent) to become knowledgeable. Only a secure, comprehensive, and up-to-date knowledge base will equip an adult to make a positive contribution to a child's literacy and love for books.

The second point focuses on classroom organization and an attitude about children's responses. There are many demands on time in a school day, and at home too. But as a major purpose of elementary school is improving reading, writing, and computing, time for literature should not be at risk. Usually class time can be reorganized, allowing more time for discussions and projects and less time for busy work with workbooks. Exciting projects, planned *with* children instead of *for* them, ensure their enthusiasm and trigger the needed support from home. Parents need to be kept well informed about the literature program and how it works, as well as encouraged to become a part of it. Teacher-produced letters or student-produced newsletters can help accomplish this goal. Inviting parents to the classroom to read aloud is also a proven technique.

Helping children to respond to literature has become a fascinating topic as many reconsider what it means to read with depth and understanding. A reconsideration prompted by Louise Rosenblatt's work (1978) pervades many successful classroom programs. She introduced a *transactional* view of reading in which the reader's background, experiences, and view of the world interacted with the text to create meaning. That is, the story does not have one meaning or theme, or a "right" answer to questions about it, but readers may interpret the story for themselves. The transactional view honors a reader's thoughts and gives credence to the ability of children to comprehend what they can from reading material. Children, like adults, can read for different purposes. Teachers who believe in the transactional approach find that discussions are richer because children are not hampered by trying to guess what the teacher wants them to say. All readers gain more control over the reading process, particularly remedial readers who can begin to enjoy making more decisions about what and why they read.

Activities coming from this philosophy of transactive reading may call for discussions about the language, structure, voice, and the reader's experience of the piece of literature (Purves & Monson, 1984). In addition to discussions, activities

Figure 1.2   Integration of Disciplines in STARS: FACT AND FICTION

Discipline	Activities
Literature	listening to and writing legends
	listening to and writing poetry
	reading and selecting books about stars
Science	recognizing constellations
	learning vocabulary and concepts of astronomy
	studying the life cycle of stars
Mathematics	exploring concepts of time and distance
Art	drawing constellations
	constructing models
Social Studies	studying the lives and times of astronomers (past and present)

frequently employ projects with multidisciplinary connections. Thematic units often undergird individual or small-group activities, so that literature is not an isolated subject, but serves as a bridge to other subjects as well. In the study of stars, literature, science, art, and other subjects can be combined to give the topic added depth. For example, the unit STARS: FACT AND FICTION, described in Chapter 10, contains activities that demonstrate connections among disciplines (see Figure 1.2).

In a thematic approach, children are encouraged to respond using several kinds of thinking such as visual, musical, psychomotor, and mathematical. By using these "multiple intelligences," as defined by Howard Gardner (1983), children and adults understand concepts and internalize facts in a more productive way.

The transactional view of the reading process, with its active and multidisciplinary focus in classrooms, is fast gaining adherents. Unlike basal readers, literature provides the substance and complexity that stimulates a transaction between reader and text. Literature-based programs are springing up everywhere; Cox and Zarillo call it an "international phenomenon" (1993, p. 12). But if teachers do not take responsibility to obtain a thorough knowledge of literature, this movement could become just another passing educational fad.

● ● ● ● ●

HOW THIS BOOK IS ORGANIZED

The following chapters are organized so that knowledge proceeds from a historical viewpoint and builds to current practices. In Chapter 2, classic children's books demonstrate attitudes toward children and literature that still influence books and schooling today.

The third chapter gives an explanation of how literature works. Similarities of form and content create categories of literature called **genres.** Genre distinctions and literary elements are described and exemplified through two outstanding books, *Charlotte's Web* (White, 1952) and *Island of the Blue Dolphins* (O'Dell, 1960). After a technical discussion of plot, character development, and other elements, genres are presented in this order:

Traditional Literature (Chapter 4)

Picture Books (Chapter 5)

Poetry (Chapter 6)

Modern Fantasy (Chapter 7)

Realism (Chapter 8)

Literature of Fact (Chapter 9)

Figure 1.3 displays the relationships among genres, with prose, poetry, and picture books identified with fiction or nonfiction. (Numbers after the terms refer to chapters in which the genre is located.)

A rationale for organizing literature this way is presented, along with an invitation to you to discover other organizational patterns. After a short history highlights some important books, each genre, with recommended books, is described. Additional books are listed after each subgenre. Chapters 4 through 9 are replete with suggested books, but part of the responsibility remains with you. It is vital

Figure 1.3 Genres of Children's Literature

Content/form	Picture Books	Prose	Poetry (6)
Fiction	Realism (5) Fantasy (5) Traditional Literature (4) *Alphabet and Counting (5)	Realism (8) Contemporary and Historical (8) Fantasy Modern (7) Traditional (4)	(Poetry can be fiction or
Nonfiction	Concept books *Alphabet and Counting (5)	Information (9) Biography (9)	nonfiction.)
Forms	Nursery rhymes Poetry Stories Essays	Novels Short stories Essays Drama	Lyric Ballad Narrative Haiku and others

*Alphabet and Counting books can be fiction or nonfiction.

that you start a reading list of books, topics, and authors you wish to explore, based on your identified goals from the beginning of this chapter. It is expected that you will search libraries and bookstores for examples, and that you will discuss with colleagues your choices and elicit suggestions from them.

The last chapter contains six units that could be used in elementary classrooms. Based on themes appropriate to grade levels, these units demonstrate a literature-based approach to literacy development. Suitable for kindergarten through grade six, the units were planned to address a wide range of reading abilities found in every classroom. Moreover, they could be used in multiage classrooms in which two grades are included. The units are:

Kindergarten and Grade One: SINGING SONGS AND STORIES

Grades One and Two: WILD THINGS

Grades Two and Three: UNEXPECTED FRIENDS

Grades Three and Four: STARS: FACT AND FICTION

Grades Four and Five: PEOPLE OF DESTINY

Grades Five and Six: JOURNEYS

This text has certain threads running through all chapters, threads that tie the book together and form a web (or net) for you to use to gather information. The first is an evaluation scheme for every genre that (1) asks for your personal response, and (2) asks you to define the purpose and the audience. Selection is easier when you know what you need and for whom.

Second, the pattern of each chapter is similar. The beginning contains an introduction and response section, which is designed to help you recall what you know and decide what you want to find out. The body of each chapter describes genres, an evaluation scheme, and notable books and authors, and provides a summary. An "implications for instruction" section details projects and activities for you and for your young readers. This section also allows you to reflect on issues and controversies. Following the references, additional resources are listed to direct you to other related ideas.

Examples and descriptions of recommended books have been kept brief and to the point. The purpose is to give an introduction to children's literature and to streamline information so that you have time to read the primary sources—the literature itself, not a book about literature. Consequently, many outstanding titles and authors are not mentioned, but you are entrusted to discover them on your own. Also, activities and most examples have been limited to two age groups: primary school children (approximately ages five through eight) and intermediate school children (ages nine through thirteen). Because many school systems are defining a **middle school** population as grades six, seven, and eight (and even five and four, in some cases), activities for children in intermediate and middle schools are grouped together. Essentially, the first activities are for younger children who are emerging as readers and writers, or learning to read; the second group targets those children who have emerged and are now reading to learn.

Multicultural children's books are justifiably establishing an important presence on publishers' lists, in libraries, and in classrooms. Examples from familiar and unfamiliar cultures are included throughout this text, rather than in a separate chapter for multicultural and international children's literature.

SUMMARY

Literature is powerful and pleasurable and has the capacity to entice readers into imaginary kingdoms, realistic stories, or books of fact. Because children's literature is gaining attention as an integral part of reading programs, teachers, librarians, and all adults who deal with children are turning to resources to find out how to best utilize the richness literature offers. This chapter (and, in fact, this book) provides a close look at the field of children's literature and its current strength and diversity.

This chapter began with an introduction that asked for involvement. Identifying needs, recalling background knowledge, and setting purposes were the first responses demanded from this text, and each following chapter opens with a similar invitation to explore different aspects of children's literature.

Children's literature is defined by qualitative statements: it is powerful, mesmerizing, causing readers to think and act. There are many children's books; some of them have the requisite qualities to be considered literature, and some do not. Suggestions for evaluation are considered and stages of child development help to focus on the primary audience and its characteristics that have a special bearing on language and literature.

Principles for a literature-based reading program, derived from developmental and educational axioms, are given. Essentially, principles suggest that adults know the field and read widely; that school organizations support the kind of responses children can make; and that integrated, authentic, and multidisciplinary activities arise from the literature and the needs of the children.

IMPLICATIONS FOR INSTRUCTION

In this section, *Reflections* will allow you to consider some of the ideas presented in the chapter. *Projects* are suggested so that you can actively become engaged with some children's literature, and finally classroom *Activities* are listed for your interaction with primary (ages five through eight) and intermediate and middle school children (ages nine through thirteen).

Reflections

1. What children's book best represents children's literature to you? What qualities does this book have to signify a "touchstone" against which to measure other books?

2. How has your definition of children's literature changed since reading this chapter? List some differences between children's literature and adult literature.

3. What are some advantages and disadvantages of a literature-based reading and language arts program? How can you overcome the disadvantages?

4. Why is it important to get parents involved in their children's reading? Brainstorm some ways to involve parents and the community in literacy efforts.

5. How should adults read children's literature? As they remember in childhood? With a more critical eye? What are some differences you have noted in your own reading process as you reread children's books remembered from childhood?

6. Are there some books, considered children's books, that you think are mislabeled because they seem to be "adult-like," nostalgic, or inappropriate? What are they, and why do you think so?

Projects

1. If you have not already started a reading list, start one now. Also, develop a system that will record your responses to books as you read them. You may want to jot your ideas on small cards, or type them into a computerized data base, or begin a notebook just for this purpose.

2. Research gender differences that become apparent when children select books. Start by looking at children's interests or by consulting the Childress (1985) article to see what boys and girls prefer. Perhaps you'd like to canvas some fourth graders and some eighth graders about their favorites and make generalizations to be tested later in a research study. In October issues of *The Reading Teacher,* published by the International Reading Association, a list of "Children's Choices" gives some indication as to what children like to read. Similarly, November issues of *Journal of Reading,* by the same publisher, lists "Young Adults' Choices," the favorite books of students in middle and junior high schools. With these lists, you can have students mark their favorites and note differences between female and male selections.

3. For a literature-based program, think of a topic suitable for a thematic unit that you would like to develop, and something that would captivate your students' interest. Begin to assemble a bibliography of books on the topic appropriate to the age group that would participate in the unit. Share your ideas with a classroom teacher or try out some of the books in a classroom.

4. Read five new children's books and determine if they are *literature* or not. Evaluate them by the methods suggested in this chapter. What did you discover?

5. Find an author who writes both children's and adult books. Read some of both, and see if there are differences in style, substance, or quality. You could begin with Roald Dahl, Nina Bawden, John Steinbeck, Madeleine L'Engle, or J. R. R. Tolkien, for example.

Activities for the Primary Level

1. Read aloud *The Snowy Day* to a group of six-year-olds. List their responses, and reflect on "what they got" from the literature. Were there surprises? Did the children think of aspects that you did not?

2. Visit a "whole language" classroom and a "basal" classroom. What differences are immediately apparent? How do children respond in each case? What literature is visible in each classroom?

3. Visit a primary classroom and look for the psychosocial markers listed in the stages of development (page 6). Do children manipulate concrete objects for math? Do they seem optimistic about their capabilities and feelings? What oral language patterns are noticeable in children's speech? What kind of activities has the teacher planned that seem to be particularly developmentally appropriate?

4. Talk to some parents of primary children about their attitudes toward a literature-based reading program. What are some parental concerns and hopes? What means of communication about class activities would they appreciate? How often?

5. Visit the children's room of a public library and notice how books are displayed and how posters and other visual aids "sell" books. Find out what kind of programming is done to connect children and books. You may want to ask the children's librarian about book selection, budgets, and other facets of this position.

Activities for the Intermediate and Middle Levels

1. Read aloud a chapter or two of *Anpao: An American Indian Odyssey* to a fourth-, fifth-, or sixth-grade class. How do the children respond? Ask some open-ended questions, or questions beginning with *why* and *how* (rather than *who* and *what*). Continue this approach with the rest of the book on succeeding days if possible.

2. Visit a sixth-, seventh-, or eighth-grade classroom in which literature is the basis for instruction. Perhaps you'll see an integration of literature and social studies, or literature and science. What do you notice? How does the teacher integrate other subjects as an extension of the literature being used for English classes?

3. Discuss with a group of children how they select literature to read. How do they know when a book is too easy or too difficult? What influence does the peer group have?

4. Visit a fourth-grade class and a seventh-grade class to note differences in child development. Can you see instances of "rule-governed" behavior or metacognition? How would you describe the children's language and thought relationships?

5. Construct with children a graph of leisure-time activities and see where reading fits. If children are reading a lot, find out what they are reading. If they are not reading, ask why not.

● ● ● ● ●
REFERENCES

Children's Works Cited

Brown, M. W. (1947). *Goodnight moon.* New York: Harper & Row.

Highwater, J. (1977). *Anpao: An American Indian odyssey* (p. 15). Philadelphia: Lippincott.

Keats, E. J. (1962). *The snowy day.* New York: Viking.

O'Dell, S. (1960). *Island of the blue dolphins.* Boston: Houghton Mifflin.

Paterson, K. (1991). *Lyddie.* New York: Lodestar.

White, E. B. (1952). *Charlotte's web.* New York: Harper & Row.

Professional Works Cited

Babbitt, N. (1990). Protecting children's literature. *The Horn Book Magazine, LXVI,* 696–703.

Chambers, A. (1983). *Introducing books to children* (2nd ed.) (p. 8). Boston: Horn Book.

Childress, G. (1985). Gender gap in the library: Different choices for boys and girls. *Top of the news, 42,* 69–73.

Cox, C., & Zarillo, J. (1993). *Teaching reading with children's literature* (p. 12). New York: Merrill/Macmillan.

Crago, M., & Crago, H. (1983). *Prelude to literacy: A preschool child's encounter with picture and story.* Carbondale, IL: SIU.

Erikson, E. (1963). *Childhood and society.* New York: Norton.

Flavell, J. (1985). *Cognitive development* (2nd ed.). Englewood Cliffs, NJ: Prentice-Hall.

Gardner, H. (1983). *Frames of mind.* New York: Basic.

Goodman, K. S. (1986). *What's whole in whole language.* Portsmouth, NH: Heinemann.

Goodman, K. S. (1988). Look what they've done to Judy Blume!: The basalization of children's literature. *The New Advocate, 1,* 29–41.

Hoffman, L., Paris, S., Hall, E., & Schell, R. (1988). *Developmental psychology today* (5th ed.) (p. 278). New York: McGraw-Hill.

Huck, C., Hepler, S., & Hickman, J. (1993). Children's literature in the elementary school (5th ed.). Fort Worth, TX: Harcourt, Brace, Jovanovich.

Hunt, P. (1991). *Criticism, theory, and children's literature.* Cambridge, MA: Basil Blackwell.

Lapp, D., & Flood, J. (1992). *Teaching reading to every child* (3rd. ed.). New York: Merrill/Macmillan.

Louv, R. (1990). *Childhood's future.* New York: Anchor-Doubleday.

Lukens, R. (1990). *A critical handbook of children's literature* (4th ed.). Glenview, IL: Scott, Foresman/Little, Brown.

Nilsen, A., & Donelson, K. (1993). *Literature for today's young adults* (4th ed.). New York: HarperCollins.

Nodelman, P. (1992). *The pleasures of children's literature.* New York: Longman.

Piaget, J. (1952). *The origins of intelligence in children.* New York: International University Press.

Purves, A., & Monson, D. (1984). *Experiencing children's literature.* Glenview, IL: Scott, Foresman.

Reutzel, D. R., & Cooter, R. B. Jr. (1992). *Teaching children to read from basals to books.* New York: Merrill/Macmillan.

Rosenblatt, L. (1978). *The reader, the text, the poem: The transactional theory of the literary work.* Carbondale, IL: SIU.

Silvey, A. (1989). Editorial: The basalization of trade books. *The Horn Book Magazine, LXV,* 549–550.

Tompkins, G., & McGee, L. (1993). *Teaching reading with literature: Case studies to action plans.* New York: Merrill/Macmillan.

Vygotsky, L. S. (1962). *Thought and language.* Cambridge, MA: MIT.

Wepner, S. B., & Feeley, J. T. (1993). *Moving forward with literature: Basals, books, and beyond* (p. 5). New York: Merrill/Macmillan.

Additional Resources

Cairney, T. H. (1990). *Other worlds: The endless possibilities of literature.* Portsmouth, NH: Heinemann.

A teacher in Australia challenges all teachers to create an environment for literature in elementary classrooms. Providing eleven comprehensive literature units, Cairney is specific and practical.

Glazer, J. T. (1986). *Literature for young children* (2nd ed.). New York: Merrill/Macmillan.

Developmental stages are related to literature in this excellent resource for teachers of primary children. Selecting literature for a curriculum that supports development in language, intelligence, personality, and aesthetic and creative dimensions is the major theme.

Meek, M., Warlow, A., & Barton, G. (Eds.). (1978). *The cool web: The pattern of children's reading.* New York: Atheneum.

This is a collection of outstanding articles that focuses on these themes: The Reader, What the Authors Tell Us, Approaches to Criticism, and Ways Forward. In "The Reader," insights by scholars such as James Britton, Arthur Applebee, and Elaine Moss help us understand how text and reader interact with meaning.

Rudman, M. K. (Ed.). (1993). *Children's literature: Resource for the classroom.* Norwood, MA: Christopher-Gordon.

An up-to-date resource written by well-respected teachers, authors, and librarians, this text also includes a section on selection as a means to diffusing censorship.

Tucker, N. (1981). *The child and the book: A psychological and literary exploration.* Cambridge, England: Cambridge Univ. Press.

These are interesting thoughts about why children at certain ages select and respond to certain literature. For example, children start enjoying fairy tales at age seven, according to Tucker.

Chapter Two

Childhood and History

• • • • •

INTRODUCTION AND RESPONSE

The history of children's literature is one thread in the rich tapestry of human history. If politics, social customs, religion, and economics color the events on the tapestry, then one can see how the thread would be multi-hued as it runs from the beginning of recorded time to the present. These colorful forces become culturally based and shape our lives, as well as our art, our literature, and our commerce. They tell us how to define family life and the roles of men and women, and continue to affect our behavior and attitudes today, just as they have always done. Prevailing attitudes toward children have changed through the centuries, as we shall see, and literature for children has evolved as these fundamental forces—political, social, religious, and economic—began to define a period called **childhood**.

To get a sense of the historical sweep of what is defined as children's literature, match the dates on the left to the classic stories on the right:

___	1484	a. *Valentine and Orson*
___	1504	b. *Robinson Crusoe*
___	1678	c. *Treasure Island*
___	1719	d. *Aesop's Fables*
___	1883	e. *Pilgrim's Progress*

Were there surprises? The first two books, published in the fifteenth and sixteenth centuries, *Aesop's Fables* and *Valentine and Orson*, were not written for children, but were popular stories drawn from the oral tradition of literature. So,

21

actually, they are much older than the dates suggest. The next two books, *Pilgrim's Progress* (published in 1678) and *Robinson Crusoe* (published in 1719), were written for the general reading public, but succeeded phenomenally with young readers because of strong compelling characters, action, and adventure. The last book, *Treasure Island,* brought an unmatched realism to children in the "golden age of children's literature" in the late nineteenth century. From *Aesop's Fables* to *Treasure Island* lie centuries of changing attitudes toward children and toward schooling, reflected in the literature people wrote, published, and read.

● ● ● ● ●

BEFORE THE SIXTEENTH CENTURY

In the medieval world, there was no place for childhood (Aries, 1962). As soon as infants gained physical independence, they were expected to be supporting members of the family. To be sure, the life span of the populace was much shorter, as most individuals had to work for the most basic needs, food and shelter, and socialization into the adult world occurred very quickly for economic reasons. Seven-year-old children were apprenticed to craftsmen or taverners, or into the houses of the aristocracy and landed gentry, if they managed to live through a treacherous childhood vulnerable to disease, the plague, poverty, and sometimes uncaring parents.

Storytellers, Ritual, and Tradition

Most people were nonliterate because they had neither the opportunity nor the means to learn to read. Prior to the fifteenth century, literature for the common people (that is, neither clerics nor nobility) was encased in the oral tradition. A vast repertoire of tales, songs, proverbs, and ditties passed from generation to generation orally. Called traditional literature, or the oral tradition, this repertoire forms the foundation of all literature today. In the next chapter we will examine traditional literature and particular examples from long ago and more modern times.

Traditional literature began as soon as humans could speak. Our ancestors in caves told stories about real and metaphorical beasts as well as drawing pictures of them. Unexplainable forces of nature—lightning, thunder, fire, the sun, and the moon—were explained through stories about their creation and their purpose. This "storying" served many purposes. It bound the tribe together, providing a common body of knowledge. Children were taught what to believe, how to act, and what roles to play. It revealed common psychological impulses, as fears, needs, and universal human problems appeared in stories from geographically distant cultures (see the many versions of "Cinderella," "Snow White," and "Sleeping Beauty," for example, in Bettelheim, 1976). It socialized children into the linguistic and moral practices of the tribe. Traditional literature was the mortar that held communities together; it was an expression for religious, social, and educational beliefs.

Storytelling was a mode of communication, and quite often storytellers were entrusted with the history of the community as well as the tales. This dual role of the storyteller emerged in primitive society: a historian, or person responsible for committing to memory the genealogy and important events of the tribe; and a fantasist, a person who created and/or retold stories to entertain and instruct listeners in the values and mores of society. Storytellers were often transient, traveling from castle to cottage in order to earn their keep. Stories were told and retold, expanded or diminished according to the magical bond between teller and listener. Special names were given to storytellers: bards, troubadours, skalds, and griots.

Illuminated manuscripts, painstakingly drawn and copied by monks in medieval monasteries, and handmade books were available only to a few. Most of the populace had no access to reading material. If books were available, they were enjoyed by everyone who could read, and age was no indicator of reading ability. Chaucer's *Canterbury Tales* (c. 1400) was surely enjoyed by the reading public. There were some manuscripts called "courtesy books" that flourished in the fifteenth century (Townsend, 1987). Very instructive and often in rhyme, these books of lessons exhorted children, and everyone else, to behave properly.

From the Oral Tradition to Print

Traditional literature collided with the invention of the printing press in the middle 1400s. Even this primitive technology, movable type, changed forever the course of language and literature. Social, political, and economic forces soon dictated the need for a literate populace, and the fledgling production of books provided opportunities for more people to learn to read. Schooling became possible for the rising European middle class, and boys (and to some extent, girls) had to have books.

Publication of the first book associated with children's literature is attributed to the Englishman William Caxton, who produced *Aesop's Fables* (1484), *Morte D'Arthur* (1485), and the *History of Reynard the Fox* (1481), among others. These tales came from the oral tradition and so were popular with everyone. But as printed books gained in abundance and popularity, folk literature began to be associated with a new audience, a first-time audience—children.

Beginning in the 1300s and continuing through the 1600s, the Renaissance ushered in new ideas in art, music, and the sciences, but most of all this spirit of rebirth gave dignity to human life and human achievement. From a universe controlled by unseen forces or the divine right of kings, an embryonic belief in the common person emerged, with concepts such as justice, democracy, and the importance of the individual's setting the stage for events soon to come.

● ● ● ● ●
THE SIXTEENTH AND SEVENTEENTH CENTURIES

Throughout the sixteenth century, the demand for all kinds of books continued to grow. Popular subjects were religion, law, medicine, practical manuals, education, arithmetic, astronomy, science, geography, news, and literature (Bingham & Scholt, 1980).

Wynken de Worde had assumed William Caxton's printing business in London, and in 1504 he published the romantic French folktale *Valentine and Orson*. It promptly became popular, finding its audience among young, old, and middle-aged people. Similarly, Robert Whittington translated *A Lytell Book of Good Manners for Children* from the writings of Erasmus, the famous philosopher who influenced Henry VIII, among others. Printed by de Worde in 1532 in Latin and in English, the book exemplifies the "courtesy books" mentioned earlier. It was highly unusual for a scholar of Erasmus's reputation to pay any attention to children, even when the subject was courteous behavior (Bingham & Scholt, 1980).

Religious Didacticism

As literacy became more necessary for men in commerce, so did it also become a focal point in the religious controversies of the sixteenth century. Protestantism, with its emphasis of personal salvation gained apart from the intercession of priests and saints, required each of the "elect," to use Calvinist terminology, to study the Bible and other religious tracts. John Foxe's *Book of Martyrs* (1563), containing horrendous accounts of torture and suffering, was considered highly suitable for children.

From the impetus of the break with Roman Catholicism, literature emerged that typified the personal search for a heavenly end. John Bunyan's *Pilgrim's Progress* (1678) is a prime example. Written in prison, this allegorical, didactic odyssey of a Christian seeking salvation struck a chord in younger readers as an adventurous journey. Didacticism prevailed, however, and most material written and published for children had as its primary purpose the instruction of young souls so that they would be worthy to die. An example of religious didacticism, one of the first books for children published in North America was John Cotton's *Milk for Babes Drawn Out of the Breasts of Both Testaments, chiefly for the Spiritual Nourishment of Boston Babes in Either England, but may be of like use to any Children*, published in England in 1646 and in Boston in 1684 (Rosenbach, 1971).

The first *New England Primer*, known to have been published before 1690, begins

> In Adam's fall
> We sinned all.

thus ensuring that all Pilgrim and Puritan children knew the burden of their sinful beginnings in this life.

This period of didacticism was lightened somewhat by the availability of chapbooks. Analogous to inexpensive paperbacks today, chapbooks were small paper booklets sold by peddlers, or "chapmen" who roamed the countryside and hawked their wares, including humorous and romantic stories. Printed on cheap paper, sometimes with crude woodcuts the only illustrations, these chapbooks were nevertheless available to common people and contained familiar and well-loved stories. For example, a rhymed story of a tiny hero—*Tom Thumb His Life and Death*—was found in a chapbook printed in 1630 (Sutherland & Arbuthnot, 1991).

Photo of a hornbook courtesy
of the Horn Book, Inc., Boston.

Prevalent in the United States and England, hornbooks were small wooden boards shaped like paddles and covered with a very thin layer of transparent horn. Colonial classrooms were replete with these small samplers from which, for example, children chanted the alphabet, then written as *ab, ac, ad,* and so on. The Lord's Prayer and biblical verses were often displayed also.

A Picture Book and Fairy Tales

In 1658, John Comenius wrote and illustrated the first picture book expressly for children, *Orbis Pictus, or The World Illustrated.* Bishop Comenius was a Moravian minister who wrote and printed this little scientific book, as he explained in the preface, "to entice witty children to it" (Sutherland & Arbuthnot, 1991). Woodcuts done by Michael Endter illustrated common plants and animals, accompanied by an explanatory text in German and in Latin. Truly a milestone in publishing for children, this book not only represented a deviation from the religious stories, but also identified an audience heretofore largely ignored.

Although religious material was much more prevalent, another kind of literature made its presence known at the end of the 1600s. Through the efforts of Charles Perrault in France, and later the Brothers Grimm in Germany, old tales common in the oral tradition were collected and frozen in print, to the delight of children, linguists, folklorists, and other scholars. In 1697 Charles Perrault (or possibly his son, Pierre d'Armancourt) published *Mother Goose Tales* in France. These eight tales included "Cinderella," "Puss in Boots," "Sleeping Beauty," and a version of "Little Red Riding Hood," among others.

At the turn of the seventeenth century, the heavy-handedness of religious didacticism was offset somewhat by these ephemeral fairy tales, a welcome addition to literature for children.

A View of Childhood Begins to Emerge

Another event of great importance happened at the turn of this century. When the English philosopher John Locke wrote *Some Thoughts Concerning Education* (c. 1693), a quiet revolution began. Departing from the conventional wisdom, which preached that children were born with the taint of "original sin," Locke argued that infants come into the world with no burden of the sins of the forefathers, but with a **tabula rasa**, or blank slate. Thus, all impressions and experiences were instrumental in forming the personality of human beings. Innocence replaced original sin, and the idea of a formative period, a period of childhood, began to gain acceptance. What an antidote to the stern puritanical views of childhood and education commonly held! These views of the importance of the social environment were also the beginning of nature versus nurture controversies still researched in human psychological development today.

● ● ● ● ●
THE EIGHTEENTH CENTURY

Mother Goose nursery rhymes had been part of the oral tradition in England in another form (not the stories collected by Perrault/d'Armancourt). Short verses, or ditties such as "Humpty Dumpty," "Jack and Jill," "Little Miss Muffet," and so on predate the 1700s, and were enjoyed by adults because many were sometimes thought to be political satires. Humpty Dumpty could have been the king (perhaps Henry VIII?) who fell off the wall (falling away from Roman Catholicism, or failing to keep his wives in place) and "all the King's horses and all the King's men couldn't put Humpty together again" (the kingdom would never be the same). These rhymes provided a way to characterize the nobility as foolish or worse without impugning an aristocrat's name. After all, it was treasonous to speak out, as freedom of speech was only a dream in the minds of a few. To show how a simple rhyme can have wide-ranging interpretations, "Sing a Song of Sixpence" has been described as alluding to the choirs of Tudor monasteries, the printing of the English Bible, the malpractices of the Romish clergy, or the infinite workings of the solar system (Opie & Opie, 1951). Certainly, political satire was not the only interpretation of nursery rhymes, as some were just nonsensical, and some related to the weather, to human traits, or to human folly.

Enduring Legacies of Mother Goose

Mother Goose, whose real identity will never be known, if indeed such a person existed, lends her name to two important contributions to children's literature, verse and fairy tale.

Reasons for linking the name to collections of nursery rhymes or fairy tales have been lost in historical obscurity. But several theories explain why and how the name is so closely associated with children's literature. One of the earliest theories is that the ditties were from the repertoire of medieval storyteller Goose-footed Bertha, who could have been the mother of Charlemagne (742–814) or the wife of Robert II of France (970–1031). Apparently both of these women entertained children with stories and verses while spinning or sewing at court (Gillespie, 1970). It is possible to imagine that a clubfoot, or some other physical impairment contributed to the reason why a "goose-footed" Bertha remained sedentary and delighted listeners as she worked.

One of the later theories suggests that an American in Boston, "Dame Goose," was the true embodiment of the legend. Her tombstone can be found in the Old Granary Burying Ground and properly notes her fame. This claim is supported by the fact that in 1715 her daughter married Thomas Fleet, a publisher who may have published the first American version of *Mother Goose's Melodies* (Gillespie, 1970). Whatever the circumstances and whoever began the tradition makes no difference now. We can enjoy speculating about all the possibilities and imagining even more. The value of the rhymes, their variations, and modern evocations of Mother Goose will be considered further in Chapters 4 and 5.

Adventure and Satire

Two books whose importance cannot be overstated emerged from the puritanical world of the early 1700s. First, *The Life and Strange Surprizing Adventures of Robinson Crusoe* appeared in 1719 at the end of Daniel Defoe's career. The story became immensely popular in the English-speaking world, and was soon translated into other languages. The love of adventure, independence, and ingenuity of the main character, a sailor in the best British tradition, struck a chord in youthful readers and the general public. Defoe's work was instrumental in the development of a new form in literature—the novel.

The second book followed fast and was equally devoured by the reading public. It had an especially compelling storyline for children. Jonathan Swift, writing anonymously because of possible repercussions from his heavy-handed satire, published *Gulliver's Travels* in 1726. As they read of the allegorical journey of the character Lemuel Gulliver, children immediately saw humor and delight in the now-famous Lilliput and Brobdingnag.

Childhood Recognized

John Newbery put his mark on children's literature when he published the first books expressly for children in 1744. John Newbery can be viewed as the father—

Frontispiece of *The Life and Strange Surprizing Adventures of Robinson Crusoe,* courtesy of the Lilly Library, Indiana University, Bloomington, Indiana.

or at least the midwife—of modern children's literature. Newbery published stories written either by himself or by others (Oliver Goldsmith, for one) such as *A Little Pretty Pocket Book* (1744) and *Goody Two Shoes* (1745). Remembered as an energetic entrepreneur who also sold quack medicines, John Newbery can be honored for his vision of providing children with entertaining, as well as instructive, books. The Newbery Medal, awarded each year by the American Library Association to designate the best children's book published in America by an American author, appropriately pays homage to his memory.

According to legend, one of John Newbery's employees invented the battledore, a large piece of cardboard folded in three leaves. It contained alphabets, numerals, and easy reading lessons. Battledores were the only instructional material many children had.

Scientific Didacticism

As the eighteenth century produced more authors and books for children, religious didacticism was replaced with a fervor to instruct children about the natural world, and particularly about good manners. Books were now seen as teaching devices, and were an indispensable part of schools and classrooms. Educational theorists, such as Locke, Rousseau, and Comenius, gave impetus to new ideas about the importance of childhood and the kinds of books that should be available to children.

"The influence of Jean-Jacques Rousseau (1712–78) on English language children's literature is comparable with that of Locke" (Townsend, 1987, p. 25). Another philosopher/reformer, Rousseau wrote *Émile* (1762), and thus provided an example of the child brought up naturally, with the freedom to explore woods, fields, and streams unhampered by direct instruction. Physical activity was important, natural curiosity was encouraged, and "moral" education and even learning to read was postponed until adolescence. (When the intellectual stimulation of reading was approved, the first book Rousseau recommended was *Robinson Crusoe*.) While John Locke's ideas affected educational practices, Jean-Jacques Rousseau invented an entirely different concept of schooling. Even though Rousseau's ideas had widespread interest, and indeed changed some educational practices so that children had more freedom, his new method of schooling remained largely untested. And for the most part, children's literature remained heavily didactic.

Although childhood was now recognized as a developmental period, and education, primarily reading, writing, and arithmetic, was seen as the birthright of many children, the urge to provide thinly disguised moral lessons in story form still characterized most of children's literature. The end of the eighteenth century saw a "stock literary character emerging in books for children—the all-wise and beneficent friend, teacher, or parent, who was constantly available to answer all questions propounded by the children in the books" (Gillespie, 1970, p. 22). This adult figure represented the voice of maturity and common sense, and would inevitably turn a spontaneous question into a sermon on whatever the topic. A child could not just walk in the woods, for example—he had to walk with a purpose, preferably to inspect all the flora and fauna, and ask his adult guide questions that would spark long soliloquies about the natural world. Needless to say, such a character impeded the narrative flow and rendered the story dull and lifeless.

● ● ● ● ●

THE NINETEENTH CENTURY

Collections of Folklore

The first notable spotlight of the nineteenth century focuses on the Brothers Grimm, Jacob and Wilhelm, who collected folktales. Scholars in linguistics, they were interested in how language forms changed, and they used the old tales of their nurse and others to find archaic forms of vocabulary, grammar, and usage. A by-product of their research is of course over two hundred tales and "the inspiration of an entirely new attitude towards the human imagination" (Alderson, 1985, unpaged). The tales were published first in Germany in 1812 as *Kinder und Hausmarchen Gesammelt Durch Die Bruder Grimm* (roughly, *Little Tales for Children and for the Family Collected by the Brothers Grimm*). The English version, published in 1823, was known popularly as *Grimms' Fairy Tales*. It is important to remember that the folktales were of the oral tradition first, and even though the Grimms' title mentions their audience of children, the tales were really for everyone.

At this same time, the "ugly duckling" of Denmark, Hans Christian Andersen, was composing his original fairy tales, which were translated and published in English in 1846 to the wonder of the rest of the world. His tales, such as "The Emperor's New Clothes," "Thumbelina," and "The Steadfast Tin Soldier," speak so clearly with wisdom and insight that it is easy to forget they came from Andersen's imagination instead of the folk culture. Their charm and poignancy come from universal human truths and foibles, but they have a lyrical quality unmatched in any other body of work. "Andersen is unique in his capacity for entering into the very soul of beings and of things" (Hazard, 1944, p. 97).

Children's Literature Enters a "Golden Age"

With the burgeoning industrial revolution and the technology in book design and publishing that sprang from it, children's books began to be plentiful and handsome. There were outstanding books published, books that have become classics and are readily acknowledged as such: *A Christmas Carol* (Charles Dickens, 1843), *Alice's Adventures in Wonderland* (Charles Dodgson writing as Lewis Carroll, 1865), and *Little Women* (Louisa May Alcott, 1868), to list three. Many other books were sentimental, provincial, and didactic: *Tales of Peter Parley* (Samuel Goodrich, 1827 through 1850), *Ragged Dick* (Horatio Alger, 1867), and *Elsie Dinsmore* (Martha Farquharson Finley, 1867).

In *Alice's Adventures in Wonderland* the "wordplay, nonsense, adult-baiting, violence, nightmare, and comedy pushed the whole concept of writing for children light years ahead of the generally safe and sentimental didacticism of the earlier literature" (Frey & Griffith, 1987, p. 116). This book emphatically revolutionized ideas about what was appropriate or permissible for children and still amazes and sometimes unsettles us today. Rich in theme, imagery, and whimsy, "Alice" and its companion, *Through the Looking Glass* (1872), propelled literature for children into a different and wholly new creative dimension.

The Victorian era in England is known for its middle class ethos, an ethos that exalted books, reading, and the innocence and beauty of childhood. A rising middle class wanted their children to have books on manners, morals, and the mores of society. Children were even entertained by some of them. While Mark Twain was writing *The Adventures of Tom Sawyer* (1876) in the United States, Anna Sewell was writing a story from a horse's point of view, *Black Beauty* (1877). An early animal rights activist, she wrote the story to point out harsh and cruel treatment of horses.

Meanwhile, in 1873, Mary Mapes Dodge became editor of one of the most famous magazines for children, *St. Nicholas*. Her interest in and understanding of young people, combined with her literary ability, made it the "outstanding magazine for children of all time" (Gillespie, 1970, p. 73). Other children's magazines also enjoyed unprecedented popularity in this last half of the nineteenth century and provided new outlets for authors and illustrators. Clearly this was a new development in literature for children.

Illustrators Combine Art and Text

The beginning of technical artistry and illustration in this period brought forth a unique art form, the Picture Book, which will be discussed more thoroughly in Chapter 5.

By the turn of the century, children's literature and compulsory education had become firmly established in the fabric of society. Books were plentiful, and in this "Golden Age of Victorian children's books, literature was for pleasure rather than for admonition" (Egoff, 1980, p. 416). Figure 2.1 summarizes milestones in children's literature into the twentieth century, retracing some people and books mentioned previously and adding a few more. Because of the increasing number of notable books, each of the following chapters will include a brief account of the literary development in that genre.

● ● ● ● ●

THE TWENTIETH CENTURY

The early twentieth century was marked by an explosion of picture books, made possible by new technology in photoengraving related to printing in color. A variety of genres became apparent as children began to enjoy the same breadth and depth that characterized all literature. Realistic adventure, animal stories, folklore, fantasy, poetry, family stories, school stories, and so on became readily accessible.

Before World War I, the literary industry in England and Europe dominated, but after the atrocities of war tore apart European nations, leadership in publishing shifted to the United States.

Views of childhood in the 1920s and 1930s were marked by an interest in individual differences, prompted as the new discipline of psychology began to explain human growth and development in intelligence, language, and social behavior. Progressive ideas of schooling advanced by John Dewey and others allowed children much more freedom. Immigrant children filled city schools and literature for children reflected some of the melting-pot philosophy that society then articulated. Generally the literature was optimistic, even during the Great Depression of the early 1930s, as evidenced by a number of happy family stories. Some excellent examples are the Laura Ingalls Wilder "Little House" books, which began to

Figure 2.1   Milestones in Children's Literature

Date	Significance
1454	Gutenberg's printing press initiates the possibility for mass literacy.
1484–1485	William Caxton publishes *Aesop's Fables* and Malory's *Morte D'Arthur*.
1504	*Valentine and Orson* is translated and published by Wynken de Worde in London.
1658	*Orbis Pictus*, the first picture book for children, is written by John Comenius and illustrated by Michael Endter.
1678	*Pilgrim's Progress*, by John Bunyan, enjoys success with a wider audience than anticipated.
1697	Perrault publishes *Tales of Mother Goose*.
1719	*Robinson Crusoe*, by Daniel Defoe, considered one of the first novels in English, appeals to a youthful audience.
1726	*Gulliver's Travels*, by Jonathan Swift, creates new standards for imaginative literature.
1744	John Newbery publishes *A Little Pretty Pocket Book* expressly for children.
1789	William Blake's *Songs of Innocence* initiates poetry for children.
1823	The Grimm collection of fairy tales is translated and published in England.
1846	The unique Danish storyteller Hans Christian Andersen is translated into English.
1865	*Alice's Adventures in Wonderland* creates a new dimension of children's fantasy.
1873	Children's magazines, led by *St. Nicholas*, enjoy a large readership.
1880 and continuing into the twentieth century.	Picture books, animal fantasy (Rudyard Kipling's *Jungle Books*, 1894), and realistic family stories evolve. Children's literature gains variety in genres and becomes less didactic.

be published in 1932. The rise of children's libraries, an influx of talented writers and illustrators from Europe, and advances in medicine, transportation, and communication affected children's book publishing positively (Egoff, Stubbs, & Ashley, 1980).

Though World War II played havoc with all institutions and individuals, the decades of the 1940s and 1950s still saw happy family stories or domestic stories, fantasies, historical fiction, and, indeed, memorable books in all genres. A crisis in education launched by the Russian Sputnik (1957) and the growing interest in the psychological theories of the Swiss psychologist Jean Piaget created a context for educational reform. A host of political changes in the late 1950s and 1960s forced an awareness of social inequity as it became apparent that too many children's books reflected a middle-class, Caucasian, Judeo-Christian, suburban lifestyle unlike that of many of the children for whom the books were written. A new realism, the breaking of taboos in content, permeated children's books of the 1970s, continued through the 1980s and into the 1990s. The shock value of topics previously thought unsuitable for children has lessened and now attention can be directed to the writing and the quality of the storytelling, rather than the topic.

As is evident by now, this historical accounting of the development of a body of literature known as children's literature focused primarily on English-language books and events. Even though England led the world into book publishing, it seems shortsighted, if not prejudicial, to presume that everything of significance happened in England or the United States. However, with rare exceptions, it is difficult to find information about the rise of childhood and children's literature in other parts of the world. This is a very necessary endeavor as we celebrate multicultural differences among all children today.

● ● ● ● ●
SUMMARY

Two themes prevail in this chapter on the historical development of children's literature. The first theme is that children's literature emerged when societal and cultural forces defined a period of childhood. That is, until **childhood** was recognized, there could be no literature for children. The second theme underscores the double nature of children's literature, as it has always had two purposes: to entertain and to instruct. Heavy-handed didacticism, prevalent in religious tracts, then in socially moralistic tomes, is still a concern in children's literature today. This characteristic—using literature to instruct—probably affects children's literature more than any other characteristic. Indeed, when one talks about the unique qualities of a literature for children, this **didacticism** must be considered. Because the audience for whom the books are intended has not fully developed its critical powers nor the communicative abilities to express opinions on a large scale, adult intercession in the form of authorship and critical judgment ensures the imposition of adult values and societal messages. But how much adult intercession in the creation and the opposite force, censorship, can be tolerated, is open to debate.

What are future directions, characteristics, and issues in children's literature as we approach the twenty-first century? We have seen how social, religious, and economic forces play on the tapestry of human history and influence entertainment and instruction for children. How do we define **childhood** in this modern era? Children are expected to be independent at an early age; some say they are hurried into adolescence and adulthood. The definition of childhood will no doubt continue to evolve, and continue to have a remarkable effect on books produced for children of the next century.

● ● ● ● ●

IMPLICATIONS FOR INSTRUCTION

In this section, questions are posed that allow you to reflect on some of the ideas springing from the text. Next, projects are described that encourage you to research in more detail significant events and people who affected the development of children's literature. Last, activities that are relative to classroom participation with primary, intermediate, and middle level children are suggested.

Reflections

1. Are the racial, ethnic, gender, and other stereotypes found in *Little Women* (Alcott, 1987), for example, sufficient to warrant ignoring this book? The question arises, "Should we use books because they are classics even though some of the content is offensive to our twentieth-century awareness?" Mark Twain's *The Adventures of Huckleberry Finn* (1986), and to a lesser extent, *The Adventures of Tom Sawyer* (1989), has been controversial since its first publication, and remains so today. What should we do with these controversies?

2. What will be some characteristics of childhood in the twenty-first century? Are children growing up too fast? What kind of books will be written to celebrate, to entertain, and to instruct that childhood?

3. What are the didactic books today? Do we have modern versions of the religious didacticism or the "good manners" books of past centuries?

4. Many books, events, and authors were not included in this chapter on the history of children's literature because of limitations and focus. What would *you* have included that was not here? Was your favorite classic, such as *The Secret Garden* (Burnett, 1910), or *The Merry Adventures of Robin Hood* (Pyle, l883), or *Treasure Island* (Stevenson, 1883) overlooked? (For modern editions, see Burnett, 1987; Pyle, 1968; and Stevenson, 1981.)

5. Who was Aesop?

Projects

1. John Newbery was an exceptionally talented and quick-thinking person who became financially successful and left a fortune to his descendants. Find out how and why this person was so successful in his time.

2. Since many of the Mother Goose rhymes are politically charged, carry on the precedent by creating some new rhymes that reflect the political situation today.

3. The Opie Collection, over twenty thousand historical children's books, can be found on microfiche at some research universities and library schools. Information is available through University Microfilms International in Ann Arbor, Michigan, as to the nearest location of the collection. If possible, travel to a

location and view chapbooks, battledores, early children's magazines, and other examples of historical interest.

4. *Robinson Crusoe* was such a popular book that it was translated into many languages and spawned many variations, *The Swiss Family Robinson* (Wyss, 1812, and a modern edition, Wyss, 1986) for example. Find out all you can about the storm of literary excitement caused by this book and Daniel Defoe, the author.

5. Why were children's magazines so popular in the United States in the late 1800s? What were some of the titles, and who was the intended audience? Were the magazines organized much like children's magazines today?

Activities for the Primary Level

1. Mother Goose rhymes seem to fit so well into reading and language arts instruction because of their predictable language and appealing content. From a collection of Mother Goose books, select some rhymes for dramatization, or add music for singing or chanting. Many can be grouped into categories: "baby" rhymes, "old man" or "old woman" rhymes, "animal" rhymes, and so on. You can also have the children select their favorite rhymes and their favorite illustrations and tell why.

2. Read aloud Hans Christian Andersen's "Thumbelina", "The Emperor's New Clothes," or "The Snow Queen" (Ehrlich, 1985). Help children to discover this shy, gifted storyteller by telling them about his life in Denmark. Videotapes of the Faerie Tale Theatre productions (Gaylord Production Company: Platypus Productions in association with Lion's Gate Films) of these stories may be rented at most video outlets, and are well done.

3. To celebrate the colonial period, make hornbooks out of construction paper, decorate with poems, counting rhymes, and alphabets, then laminate and fix them with a string through a hole in the handle so that children can wear them around their necks. Create a colonial schoolroom and have a reading lesson there.

4. Many folktales in a collection of *Grimm's Fairy Tales* (for example, the edition illustrated by Rackham, 1973) will be new to modern children and would be enjoyed when read orally. Try some new stories, ones that are unfamiliar to you, as well.

Activities for the Intermediate and Middle Levels

1. Two great survival stories, *Robinson Crusoe* and *Hatchet* (Paulsen, 1987) can be compared; this would be a good way to introduce children to the first novel in English. A teacher can read aloud the part in Crusoe, in which he finds himself truly alone for the first time (p. 66 in the Penguin edition), and have the children compare that paragraph to the part in *Hatchet* in which Brian Robeson

finds himself alone (p. 32). Another point of reference in both books is when the survivors return to their wrecks (Crusoe's ship, Brian's submerged plane) to try to salvage any usable material (see Defoe, page 68, and Paulsen, page 182).

2. Other survival stories beg for comparisons, and *Island of the Blue Dolphins* (O'Dell, 1960) and *Julie of the Wolves* (George, 1972) with their female narrators, would be rich sources of similarities and differences.

3. Children are interested in finding out how printing presses work today. You can build a model of the early Gutenberg press, and explore changes and improvements in printing through the centuries. Printing holds a fascination for many, and it is fun to experiment with different type faces and sizes. Exploring different fonts in a word-processing program is easily done with accessibility to computers. A field trip to a printing establishment would be interesting too.

4. Literature from the latter part of the nineteenth century is easy enough for many children to read independently in the middle grades. Prepare booktalks from modern editions of *Heidi* (Spyri, 1986), *Alice's Adventures in Wonderland* (Carroll, 1985), *Black Beauty* (Sewell, 1990), or *Tom Sawyer* (Twain, 1989), and encourage your students to read these classics.

5. Read aloud *Valentine and Orson* (Burkert, 1989) to acquaint middle-level children with this very old tale. How is it like other folktales they know? How is it different? The Burkert version suggests that the story be acted out, and lists characters. Perhaps the class would enjoy participating in the drama.

● ● ● ● ●
REFERENCES

Children's Works Cited

Alcott, L. M. (1987). *Little women.* New York: Dell Yearling Classics.

Burkert, N. E. (1989). *Valentine and Orson.* New York: Farrar, Strauss & Giroux.

Burnett, F. H. (1987). *The secret garden.* New York: Dell.

Carroll, L. (1985). *Alice's adventures in wonderland.* New York: Puffin.

Defoe, D. (1965). *The life and adventures of Robinson Crusoe.* Baltimore: Penguin Books.

Ehrlich, A. (Adaptor). (1985). *The Random House book of fairy tales.* With an introduction by Bruno Bettelheim and illustrated by Diane Goode. New York: Random House.

George, J. C. (1972). *Julie of the wolves.* New York: HarperCollins.

Grimm's fairy tales: Twenty stories. (1973). Illustrated by Arthur Rackham. New York: Viking Press.

O'Dell, S. (1960). *Island of the blue dolphins.* Boston: Houghton Mifflin.

Paulsen, G. (1987). *Hatchet.* New York: Bradbury.

Pyle, H. (1968). *The merry adventures of Robin Hood.* New York: Dover.

Sewell, A. (1990). *Black Beauty.* New York: Dell Yearling Classics.

Spyri, J. (1986). *Heidi.* Stamford, CT: Longmeadow Press.

Stevenson, R. L. (1981). *Treasure island.* New York: Macmillan Child Group.

Twain, M. (1986). *The Adventures of Huckleberry Finn.* New York: Penguin.

Twain, M. (1989). *The Adventures of Tom Sawyer.* New York: Penguin.

Wyss, J. (1986). *Swiss family Robinson.* New York: Puffin.

Professional Works Cited

Alderson, B. (1985). *Grimm tales in English.* London: British Library Exhibition Notes.

Aries, P. (1962). *Centuries of childhood.* New York: Vintage Books.

Bettelheim, B. (1976). *The uses of enchantment.* New York: Knopf.

Bingham, J., & Scholt, G. (1980). *Fifteen centuries of children's literature.* Westport, CT: Greenwood Press.

Bunyan, J. (1957). *Pilgrim's progress.* New York: Washington Square Press, Inc.

Egoff, S. (1980). Precepts, pleasures, and portents: Changing emphases in children's literature. In Egoff, Stubbs, & Ashley (Eds.), *Only connect* (pp. 405–433, 416). Toronto: Oxford University Press.

Egoff, S., Stubbs, G. T., & Ashley, L. F. (Eds.) (1980). *Only connect* (2nd ed.). Toronto: Oxford University Press.

Frey, C., & Griffith, J. (1987). *The literary heritage of childhood* (p. 116). New York: Greenwood Press.

Gillespie, M. (1970). *History and trends* (pp. 22, 73). Dubuque, IA: Wm. C. Brown.

Hazard, P. (1944). *Books, children, and men* (p. 97). Boston: The Horn Book, Inc.

Opie, I., & Opie, P. (Eds.). (1951). *The Oxford dictionary of nursery rhymes.* Oxford: The Clarendon Press.

Rosenbach, A. S. W. (1971). *Early American children's books.* New York: Dover Publications.

Sutherland, Z., & Arbuthnot, M. H. (1991). *Children and books* (8th ed.). New York: HarperCollins.

Townsend, J. R. (1987). *Written for children* (3rd ed.) (p. 25). New York: Lippincott.

Additional Resources

Carpenter, H. (1985). *Secret gardens: A study of the golden age of children's literature.* Boston: Houghton Mifflin.

Carpenter identifies the period from 1862 to 1930 as the golden age because of the enduring classics coming from that time in England and, to some extent, the United States. He analyzes many classics in order to encourage the reconsideration of childhood favorites.

Darton, F. J. H. (1982). *Children's books in England: Five centuries of social life* (3rd ed.). Cambridge: Cambridge University Press.

This is a complete history of children's literature in England coupled with descriptions of the social milieu of the times. Brian Alderson has updated this highly readable account.

Griffith, J. W., & Frey, C. H. (Eds.). (1987). *Classics of children's literature.* New York: Macmillan.

An anthology of traditional and modern literature, including some of Perrault and Grimm as well as the complete Pinocchio and Treasure Island, this valuable resource also contains a brief introduction to John Newbery, Madame de Beaumont, and others.

Haviland, V. (Ed.). (1973). *Children and literature: Views and reviews.* Glenview, IL: Scott, Foresman.

This is a collection of essays and criticism, many of them classics in the field. The first chapter, "Before the Twentieth Century," includes reviews published before 1900 and two describe the rise of children's magazines. The second chapter, "Of Classics and Golden Ages," discusses Hans Christian Andersen, Alcott's Little Women, and Spyri's Heidi, to name a few.

May, J. P. (Ed.). (1983). *Children and their literature: A readings book.* West Lafayette, IN: Children's Literature Association.

A book of readings by notable contributors; the first chapter, "Classical Tales for the Modern Child," relates specifically to concepts in the history of children's literature.

Meigs, C., Eaton, A., Nesbit, E., & Viguers, R. H. (1953). *A critical history of children's liter-ature.* New York: Macmillan.
   This is the classic history of American children's literature by well-known and entertain-ing writers. This volume particularly sheds light on the nineteenth and early twentieth centuries.
Nodelman, P. (Ed.). (1985). *Touchstones: Reflections on the best in children's literature.* (Volume One). West Lafayette, IN: Children's Literature Association.
   A superb collection of articles, essays, and criticism; many of the writings focus on the classics and their place in children's literature.
Opie, I., & Opie, P. (Eds.). (1980). *A nursery companion.* Oxford: Oxford University Press.
   Historical ditties very much like Mother Goose, but not quite, make this a valuable resource. The Opies, with their meticulous scholarship, include such lesser known rhymes as "Mounseer Nongtongpaw; or the Discoveries of John Bull in a Trip to Paris," and "The Chapter of Kings."

Two periodicals consistently bring thoughtful analysis, criticism, and historical information about children's literature to interested readers. They are:

Children's Literature Association Quarterly, published by Yale University Press. The Children's Literature Association is a nonprofit organization formed to encourage seri-ous scholarship and research in children's literature.
Children's Literature in Education, an international quarterly published by Human Sci-ences Press, Inc.

Chapter Three

Genres and Literary Elements

• • • • •
INTRODUCTION AND RESPONSE

"Correct classification is one of the first steps in a scientific investigation. The accuracy of all further study depends on the accuracy of classification" (Propp, 1968, p. 5). This statement reflects the opinion of a scholar who collected and analyzed Russian folktales in the early part of this century. Then, as now, in literature and in other fields, scientific inquiry began with classification and led to further study and understanding. In this chapter a classification scheme of children's literature will be explored so that this field, with all its rich variety, can be better understood and appreciated. Literature for children covers a wide range of topics, from the realistic to the improbable to the wildly fantastic. Its audience ranges from infancy to adulthood, and many styles, types, and kinds of writing mark its pages. This breadth and depth necessitates schemes of classification so that diversity is recognized, yet function and value remain clear.

The classification, or grouping, of similar traits and structures in literature allows us to study, to evaluate, and to remember. When similar traits form a distinct group, the group is called a **genre**. *Genre* simply means a category, or a family of closely related characteristics based on a single premise. A genre in literature is a category of literature, such as poetry. Even though there are many kinds of poems, they are nevertheless distinguishable from other kinds of literature and hence form a genre.

There are several ways to categorize literary works; the one utilized in this text is based on the content of the literary work and, to some extent, the form. To begin this exploration, compare traits of two well-known books, *Island of the Blue Dolphins* (O'Dell, 1960) and *Charlotte's Web* (White, 1952). These stories are probably familiar to you; if not, a quick perusal might be helpful. (Both are worth more than a quick look, so you may want to take the time to read them unhurriedly and enjoy the fine writing in each.) In order to make genre distinctions, however, think now about the two questions in Figure 3.1, and answer "yes" or "no" in the boxes.

What do your answers tell you about genre? First, if you have any "yes" answers under *Island of the Blue Dolphins,* the book is likely to be nonfiction or historical fiction. Because you know the story could have happened, and that it took place in the past, it is considered historical. *Charlotte's Web,* on the other hand, could not have happened because animals do not talk. It is a fantasy, and it takes place in the present. The basis for categorizing into these genres rests on questions of probability (can animals talk? can a young girl live alone on an island?) and timeliness (when did events happen?). Probability and timeliness are the root of important questions when classifying literature according to the *content* of narrative prose. How probable the prose is or how truly it conforms to realism categorizes it as a fantasy, as a realistic story, or as a work of nonfiction (information). One can imagine a continuum of probability—from the very probable to the wildly implausible!

A continuum of timeliness too can help to categorize a story as historical realism (set in the past), contemporary realism (set in the present), and science fiction (set in the future).

As we use just these two questions to compare other books, genres of nonfiction or historical fiction and fantasy emerge. Classification is knowing something about the concept, creating questions or statements that allow you to look for similar traits or structures, and, finally, grouping like things together.

Genre distinctions do not always form unbreakable or clearly defined categories; in fact, they can be somewhat fluid because certain traits or elements may not be present when one expects them to be. "Poetic license" in literature gives authors permission to break the rules, create new forms, and bring in the unexpected. In *Charlotte's Web,* for example, the story begins very realistically, with a typical farm family taking part in typical activities. As soon as the point of view shifts to Wilbur and he talks, fantasy takes over.

By designating genres, we classify literature, and our generic expectations are raised. That is, we can study a new text, classify it, and then test it against traits and characteristics of that genre. Through this process, evaluation of new works becomes easier. Critic Peter Hunt says that "knowing what is or what is not per-

Figure 3.1   Comparing Traits of Two Novels

Questions	*Island of the Blue Dolphins*	*Charlotte's Web*
1. Could/Did this story happen?		
2. Did the story take place in the past?		

missible in a certain genre controls our reactions to a text" (Hunt, 1991, p. 136). Our intuitive knowledge of genres gives us cues as we read a text and allows us to decide what is permissible and what is not.

After briefly presenting other classification approaches, this chapter focuses on genres as they are defined in this and in other studies of children's literature. Definitions and examples of each genre follow; then literary elements such as theme, plot, character, and so on are defined and related to the two books used as examples above. Literary elements give us the vocabulary of literary analysis and criticism. With this theoretical framework, you will be better prepared to enjoy, evaluate, remember, and use books effectively in a classroom or a library or at home.

● ● ● ● ●
OTHER APPROACHES TO CLASSIFICATION

Most approaches to the study of children's literature include methods of classifying. Common methods use (1) literary forms, (2) motifs, (3) age distinctions, and (4) topics, in addition to genres based on content. Each method is useful in

From *Island of the Blue Dolphins,* by Scott O'Dell, copyright © 1960. Reproduced by permission of the publisher, Houghton Mifflin Company.

certain instances, and gives another perspective to the many children's books being published today.

Literary forms such as novel, drama, poetry, novella, and short story are sometimes the basis for classifying literary works. All of the prose forms mentioned have a distinct length, as well as other sharply defined characteristics. The visual appearance of a literary work determines whether it is a poem, a play, or a novel. A classification by literary form does not take into account how realistic or fanciful a story is.

Another kind of classification was proposed by the eminent Canadian critic Northrop Frye. He identified four forms of fiction: novel, anatomy, confession, and romance (1957). Of these four forms, novel and romance, as he defined them, are much more prevalent in fiction written for children than are anatomy and confession. While many of Frye's ideas are germane to a careful study of children's literature, particularly in the genres Realism and Fantasy, they do not quite provide the widely based foundation necessary to understand the many different kinds of fiction and nonfiction.

Motifs are structural patterns that recur among many works. They can be: (1) a small person's journey from home to isolation away from home; (2) a small person's or a hero's journey from home to a confrontation with a monster; (3) a helpless figure's rescue from a harsh home and the miraculous creation of a secure home; and (4) conflict between a wise beast and a foolish beast (Cullinan, 1971). These motifs seem to be particularly suited to traditional literature, as many folktales, fairy tales, and fables contain these motifs or significant aspects of them, but they have limited value when applied to other genres.

Age distinctions refer to grouping by the age of the intended audience; that is, books for infants from birth to two; books for toddlers; books for preschoolers; and so on, continuing through adolescence. This approach is helpful for school-related use.

Topical categories allow a focus on current issues, a subject area, or a cultural group. For example, in *Shadow and Substance,* Rudine Sims (1982) reports on analysis and evaluation of realistic books depicting the African-American experience. Similarly, current issues such as gender roles, heritage, special needs, old age, and so on form the basis for annotated bibliographies with selection criteria in *Children's Literature: An Issues Approach* (Rudman, 1984).

Other classification schemes are defined by scholars and critics who write, edit, or review children's books, depending upon their purposes and interests. These examples of form, motif, and so on present different models for you to use as you classify and organize children's books.

● ● ● ● ●
A RATIONALE FOR GENRES

When we consider that one definition of *literature* is "the whole body of valued writing in society" (Eagleton, 1983, p. 17) we again see the necessity to categorize. Arbitrarily starting with distinctions of "poetry" and "prose," we see that both of these terms represent large bodies of writing containing many differences. Because poetry, perhaps the oldest example of valued writing, usually presents a clearer distinction (see Chapter 8), it forms a genre all its own. Prose, on the other hand, covers a wide range of forms, subject matter, and style. It can be narrative or expository, fiction or nonfiction. Thus, more specificity is needed.

If we concentrate on the content of prose and ask the questions "could it happen?" and "when?" we find that the two genres of **Realism** and **Fantasy** emerge. Both these genres are fiction. As we add nonfiction, or factual prose, by asking "did it happen?" another genre is created: **Nonfiction**, which includes **Biography** and **Information Books**. **Traditional Literature** forms a genre because it is a definable body of literature that existed before printing presses. Similarly, **Picture Books** form a separate category because of their unique blend of artwork and text. Thus we have the following genres based on content, and, in the case of picture books, on the appearance of the literary work.

> **Poetry** — Words and sentences that conform to certain definitions of length, rhyme, and meter;
>
> **Traditional Literature** — Anonymous stories, wise sayings, and rhymes coming from the oral tradition;
>
> **Picture Books** — Books usually intended for a young audience, that use art as well as text to convey meaning;
>
> **Fantasy** — A story with at least one impossible element;
>
> **Realism** — A story mirroring our world as we understand it, or as we understood it to be;
>
> **Biography** and **Autobiography** — A factual account of a person's life;
>
> **Information** — Factual writing of human and natural phenomena.

Notice some of the similar traits and structures among genres: the element of a past, present, or future time, the factual writing in biography and information, and the narrative stories in traditional literature, fantasy, and realism.

Each of these genres, as it has evolved through time and the fertile imaginations of storytellers and scribes, can be expressed in a variety of subgenres. Subgenres are more detailed classifications of literary works based on the basic premise that unites the category. For example, there are several different kinds of fantasy writing. Figure 3.2 details how each genre can be expressed in a variety of subgenres.

Hereafter, in each chapter, a genre will be discussed first within a historical context with classic examples, then further divided into subgenres with definitions and current examples.

Figure 3.2   Genres and Subgenres

Genre	Examples of Subgenres
Poetry	Limericks, sonnets, ballads, haiku, free verse, and others.
Traditional Literature	Rhymes, chants, proverbs, fables, myths, folktales, and legends.
Picture Books	Alphabet and counting books, concept books, picture storybooks of realism and fantasy, and nursery rhymes.
Fantasy	High fantasy, animal tales, science fiction, time fantasies, and others.
Realism	Set in present or past, realistic stories of sports, mysteries, animals, survival, school, and family.
Biography	Historical and contemporary accounts of persons' lives.
Information	Factual writing in content areas such as ecology, psychology, sexuality, technology, and many more.

• • • • •

LITERARY ELEMENTS

Aspects of analysis, as mentioned previously, give all who study literature a vocabulary with which to discuss and evaluate it. Indispensable to any genre is an understanding of theme, plot, character, setting, style, and point of view. Authors decide how each of these will work within a story; their decisions create memorable writings that live on in our literary tradition or dull, lifeless works.

When examples are drawn from *Island of the Blue Dolphins* or *Charlotte's Web*, the abbreviations (IBD) or (CW) are sometimes used for quick reference.

Theme

Descriptors of Theme: Explicit and implicit

Threading through the story is a common idea that ties the story together. The common idea, or thread, is sometimes stated by the author, in which case it is an **explicit theme.** Usually it is not directly stated, but left to the reader to infer. In that case we have an **implied theme.** Whether it is explicitly stated or implicit, the theme can be drawn out of a story or poem by asking "What does the author seem to say?" If, for example, the author seems to convey an idea that "cooperation is better than conflict to solve problems" or "unfortunate circumstances can help to develop self-understanding" then characters, plot, and other elements act in harmony with that idea. Theme is more than an explanation of what the story is about; it is a value-laden statement. Usually, in children's books, themes are "unifying truths," according to Rebecca Lukens (1990), because they embody the meaning of a story.

Themes are sometimes difficult to articulate, because they can be obscure, or inconsistently demonstrated by characters, or meaningless. Because literature is complex, there are also multiple themes and secondary themes. In *Charlotte's Web,* for example, a theme could be "life is precious and worth scheming for" but there is also a powerful theme concerned with the development of true friendship. Multiple themes must be explored when literary works are as complex and thought-provoking as *Charlotte's Web.*

Plot

> **Descriptors of Plot: Linear, cumulative, and episodic, with flashback, foreshadowing, conflict, and cliffhanger**

If you answer the question "What happens in this story?" you are describing the plot. **Plot** is action, the narrative order of events as the story unfolds. Plot usually has a predictable structure. Three basic structural patterns are called linear, cumulative (or circular), and episodic. A **linear** plot has a beginning (introduction and statement of the problem), a middle (rising action, or action and consequence pattern), and an end (climax and resolution). This linear pattern is sometimes referred to as story structure or story grammar.

Cumulative patterns are composed of phrases, sentences, or events repeated with one new aspect added each time. It is almost as if the plot is continuing in ever-widening circles.

Episodic plots are exemplified by those books in which chapters are almost complete stories in themselves. There is an introduction, problem, action and consequence, climax and resolution with each episode.

Diagrams of each pattern can be seen in Figure 3.3. Because the first two patterns figure prominently in traditional literature, they are also addressed in Chapter 4.

Although one of these three basic patterns is found in almost every story, authors can alter a pattern to achieve other purposes. A **flashback** allows the lin-

Figure 3.3 Patterns of Plot Structure

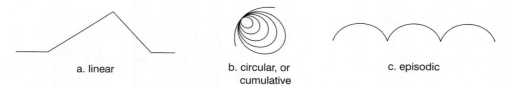

a. linear b. circular, or cumulative c. episodic

ear progression to stop and an earlier event to be interjected. This creates suspense and excitement, and adds another dimension to the story. The opposite dimension, **foreshadowing**, is used by authors to allow readers to anticipate and to look forward to events. The forthcoming event, character, or action is hinted at in the text. Karana's eventual rescue is foreshadowed when a ship visits her island *(IBD)*. Even though she fails to contact it, her sighting of the ship leads us to believe she will be rescued.

Conflict, a term that refers to the interaction of plot and character, is necessary so that a literary work has some tension. Tension derived from conflict provides motivation for characters and it keeps readers interested in the story. Four types of conflict occur in most stories:

person against self,

person against other,

person against society,

person against nature.

It may be helpful to think of examples. In *Charlotte's Web* the conflict is person (Wilbur) against society (represented by society's values that eliminate runt pigs). Tension springs from Wilbur's desire to live a long life in spite of his impending death from the slaughterer's knife. This delicate story is rife with conflict as we know from the first sentence (which is also an example of foreshadowing): "Where's Papa going with that ax?" (p. 1). In this sentence E. B. White foreshadows the conflict between life and death.

Authors use a technique to sustain tension when they leave a chapter in the midst of some dangerous or suspenseful action. **Cliffhanger** is the term describing this unresolved, inconclusive ending of a chapter. Cliffhangers keep pages turning, as they add to tension until the final climax resolves it. When Karana *(IBD)* says "I made two more spears from these points and at last was ready to go to the cave of the wild dogs" (p. 90) at the end of Chapter 14, we are anxious to see what will happen when she confronts the wild dogs in their cave.

Character

Descriptors of Character: Round, flat, foil, dynamic,
static, stereotype, protagonist, and antagonist

Characters in literature, as creations of authors' imaginations, can be as real as persons we know or the most impossibly fantastic creatures inhabiting a planet. From ordinary males and females to ghosts, talking animals, and even creatures from outer space, characters form another indispensable element of story. Occasionally, they move the action forward in poetry and nonfiction too. Characters voice or imply theme, they act or react to events, and they enhance setting with their motives and dialogue. Sometimes readers identify with the ideal traits of a character—characteristics of honesty, truth, courage, and intelligence. Identifying with characters is an important aspect of reading and enjoying literature.

While the main character or characters get most of the attention in a story, minor characters have important roles too. Everyone in a story cannot be fully developed; the story would be too long and too complex and plot would suffer. So characters with different functions must be balanced with the demands of a plot.

Different types of characters balance a story. A fully developed, complex character—sometimes called a main or **round** character—has many traits. **Flat** characters, on the other hand, have only a few dimensions, sometimes only one or two. The rat Templeton *(CW)*, a flat character, is greedy and sarcastic from beginning to end. He plays an important part, as he adds humor and provides a **foil** for Wilbur. A foil is a character whose traits are opposite those of the main character; without foils the main character's traits could not be so sharply etched in the story. Foils are usually flat characters.

When characters change, grow, and develop, they are said to be **dynamic**. Dynamic characters make self-discoveries, influence and cause events to happen, and create movement in the plot. Karana *(IBD)* develops as a self-reliant woman, and Wilbur *(CW)* grows and changes dramatically. Contrasting with this dynamism is the term **static**. Static characters do not change. They can be varied and complex, or exhibit very few traits, but they remain essentially the same. Charlotte *(CW)*, a round character, is nevertheless static because essentially she does not change. The wisdom that she reveals throughout the story has always been a part of her.

When a character mirrors traits that society dictates instead of idiosyncratic traits, a **stereotype** is created. Stereotypes can be destructive in literature, because they are derogatory at worst; even at best, they often reveal an author's lack of imagination and sensitivity. When Native American characters are only depicted as "savage Indians" or Asian Americans as bespectacled computer geniuses, readers lose the variety and richness that fully developed characters bring to a story.

The literary terms **protagonist** and **antagonist** refer to main characters who oppose each other. This opposition is frequently found in the "person against person" conflict. Usually the protagonist is the "good" character, while the antagonist is the opposite.

Setting

Descriptors of Setting: Time, place, mood, and symbol

Setting includes both **time** and **place**. A story may be set in the late 1800s (time) on a remote island (place), such as *Island of the Blue Dolphins*. Setting too can range from very realistic—a time and place we readily recognize—to the most abstract—a time and place existing in an imaginary world.

Setting anchors a story, as it provides the backdrop against which the action occurs and the characters speak. It can be much more important than backdrop, however, and establishes the mood of a literary work. **Mood, a subjective emotional state, adds to the tension of a plot and colors everything in the story.** The variety of moods within *Charlotte's Web* relates to setting and, of course, helps to give the book its power. When Wilbur, Charlotte, and the other animals are in the barn, solving problems and exchanging ideas, the mood is generally cheerful even though Wilbur's worry about his fate is an overriding concern. When the setting moves to the fairgrounds as the climax is approaching, the mood shifts to reflect anxiety.

Setting can also be a **symbol** of what the story is about. The symbol harmonizes with theme, character, and plot. The island, in *Island of the Blue Dolphins*, works as a symbol to denote separation; it is a symbol of Karana and her solitude, independence, and completeness. When the setting is the title of a book, as in this one, you can be sure it functions as a major element of the work. In fantasy, setting is especially important because it creates the fantasy world that is crucial to the narrative. In realistic stories that pit person against nature, the setting can be viewed as an antagonist. Thus it also assumes a major function in survival stories.

Style

> **Descriptors of Style:** Figurative language, metaphor, simile, personification, alliteration, tone, archetype, symbol, allusion, irony, and humor

Style refers to the many ways an author uses words to express ideas resulting in prose or poetry. As we read, we take words for granted, but they stand between us and our comprehension of a work. Because words are the building blocks of character, theme, plot, and so on, they must be selected with care and precision. Language patterns, dialects in characters' speech, words used to create alliteration and rhythm, and connotations and denotations are all aspects of style. Style can be described holistically or specifically. We could summarize the style of Scott O'Dell's work by saying the language seems matter-of-fact and even slightly flat as Karana describes her work, her thoughts, and her solitude. The language is unadorned and unemotional, as Karana is. Thus O'Dell's style is seen as a carefully controlled, but powerful, conveyor of a memorable and masterful story. We'll look at specific aspects of style in *Charlotte's Web* by identifying figurative language.

Figurative language encompasses those terms that use words to stand for something else. We have the ability through language to create metaphors, to personify anything, to allude to something indirectly, and to name symbols that connote a host of meanings.

Metaphors and **similes** create images in our minds as they connect what the author is trying to say to a concrete referent we can recognize. Metaphors and similes compare unlike things, and the unlikely comparison helps us see things in a new, fresh way. For example, a passage at the beginning of Chapter 15 in *Charlotte's Web* demonstrates a feast of figurative language. "The crickets sang in the grasses. They sang a song of summer ending, a sad, monotonous song. 'Summer is over and gone,' they sang" (page 113). Crickets singing this song is an example of **personification**, while "sang a song of summer" exemplifies **alliteration**, or using the same sound to begin words in a series. The sad, monotonous song compares to summer's ending, which is a **metaphor,** and last, the **tone** of sadness is created in that passage and in the following one, which speaks of summer as over, gone, and dying. In this beautiful poetic paragraph E. B. White used the rhythm and sounds of language to create imagery and tone.

Even more deeply felt in the passage is the idea that summer is turning into fall—the year is beginning to die. Besides foreshadowing Wilbur's and/or Charlotte's death, White draws on an **archetype** of seasonal change to convey meaning. Archetypes are universal ideas that probably spring from our unconscious. They are images, situations, themes, and characters that stand for universally held beliefs and meanings. They are found in mythology and religious ritual and are depicted in artistic forms all over the world. Archetypes in literature can relate to the seasons: spring is linked with rebirth and beginnings; summer with triumph and celebration; autumn with tragedy; and winter with death and despair (Frye, 1957). Other archetypes are linked with plot and character as the recurring plot of the hero-quest (Odysseus) and also as a miraculous overturning of a helpless maiden's plight (Cinderella). Settings of ancient forests or waterways are archetypal, with forests regarded as places of terror, unknown and dangerous, while waterways are associated with journeys (Anderson and Groff, 1972). Water, by itself, can be an archetype of baptism, conversion, or birth.

As archetypes are universal patterns of form and structure, deeply symbolic of what human beings have regarded as mysterious and wonderful for centuries, **symbols** are more recent and not quite so universal. The American flag, a song, Charlotte's web—all of these can symbolize something quite specific and personal. Although symbols are visible signs of something, they resist total explanation because they "suggest, reveal, and conceal all at the same time" (Cullinan, 1971, p. 69).

Allusions are indirect references to someone or something well known. To allude to something creates an association with a common concept or person; we can allude to the "Midas touch," for example. When Karana names her dog Rontu, she associates him with fox eyes, then continues the allusion by naming his son Rontu-Aru.

Irony and **humor** can be used very effectively in prose or poetry. **Irony** is the juxtaposition of two opposite ideas; it is sometimes the discrepancy between what is stated and what is known to be true. There is an irony in *Charlotte's Web* because Charlotte was saving Wilbur's life at the same time she was preparing for her own death. The juxtaposition of life and death creates the irony. Opposite forces balanced ironically make a story more interesting and more surprising at the conclusion. Irony has a larger reference than simply stylistic use, as it is identified in literary criticism as forming one of the four plots of story (Sloan, 1991).

Humor comes from the double meanings of words to create jokes, puns, riddles, and witty sayings. Humor is difficult to describe, although we recognize it when it tickles us! Writing comedic lines is truly an art—what may be funny to one person may not necessarily be funny to someone else. Figurative language and surprising word choices can provide humor; humorous language patterns in *Charlotte's Web* give us an added dimension of character when the gander says "certainly-ertainly-ertainly" and "poking-oking-oking" *(CW,* p. 45).

Point of View

> **Descriptors of Point of View: First person, omniscient, and limited omniscient**

Point of view suggests a vantage point from which everything in a story or a poem is seen. That is, we can see the action from one character's point of view or from many characters' points of view. When a character is telling the story, and using *I* in the telling, the point of view is **first person**, as in the grammatical first person singular construction. Many children's books have a single narrator telling the story, and Karana *(IBD)* exemplifies this.

In contrast to first person is the **omniscient** point of view. With his or her omniscience, or knowing everything, an author uses all the characters to tell a story. Thoughts, motives, and descriptions unfold from everyone to advance the plot and delineate character. It is as if the author can read everyone's mind; he or she occupies a lofty position from which to regard everything and describe it. E. B. White uses an omniscient point of view in *Charlotte's Web*.

An author may decide to do a combination, such as alternating first person, or **limiting** omniscience to two or three characters. The possibilities are practically limitless. Point of view provides focus to a literary work and allows an easy identification with the first person narrator in many realistic novels.

• • • • •
EVALUATION OF LITERARY ELEMENTS

So many elements, so many decisions an author must make to create a work of literary distinction or a trashy novel! Three principal criteria for evaluating these literary elements seem to be most important in judging quality, and they are vitality, freshness, and balance. **Vitality** is energy, a life-giving force that speaks to a driving current in prose or poetry that keeps us interested, curious, and engaged. **Freshness** refers to the creation of new characters, situations, plots; it is the inventiveness of taking basic themes, motifs, and archetypes that are universal, well loved, but familiar, and generating new stories and new perspectives. It is creating and re-creating. It is not using cliches, the same old tired lines, hackneyed phrases and trite jokes, the same old stereotypical characters. *Freshness* means "new," but it also means building on the enduring truths of traditional literature in modern ways.

Balance is perhaps the most difficult criterion. It is the integration of all literary elements working together. The literary work is an entity with all parts in balance. Plot depends on character development and conflict, theme draws from both plot and character, and everything meshes to create the whole. Setting supports the framework of a story, and style permeates practically every word an author chooses. To have strong characters and a weak plot, or to have a well-developed setting and nothing to put in it, is a tragedy that balance would correct.

Both *Island of the Blue Dolphins* and *Charlotte's Web* exemplify vitality, freshness, and balance in their genres of historical realism and fantasy.

● ● ● ● ●
LITERARY ELEMENTS RELATED TO GENRES

Characterization, point of view, theme, and plot may work differently in certain genres. Although authors impose their best creative efforts on their work, nevertheless generic expectations dictate certain literary conventions that allow readers to understand how a text is constructed and why characters act in predictable ways.

Key differences in realism and fantasy are most pronounced when we consider characterization, which is essentially narrow and static in fantasy and traditional literature. Stylized figures that expand into psychological archetypes are predominant (Frye, 1957). Thus we have Cinderella, the wicked stepmother, and the hero, as well as the sly fox and the trickster coyote as examples of psychological archetypes. In modern fantasy, particularly in the subgenre called high fantasy, flat characters also predominate. With the exception of a dynamic hero and a small number of round characters, high fantasy is full of one-dimensional characters who are either good or bad. This is as it should be, because the purpose of fantasy is to create a mythlike otherworld, an abstraction based on what we know to be true but one that carries the truth into a different dimension. Flat characters allow this abstraction to occur more easily.

Compare this to our expectations when we read realistic prose fiction. We expect fully developed characters like ourselves and our friends. Characters who show conflicting emotions and motives and who are multidimensional give realism its power. This is as it should be, so that identification with characters can occur more easily.

Fantasy, as an abstraction of reality, gives rise to differences in setting as well. In fantasy, setting is a more integral part of the story, because time and place in the fantasy world drives much of the action. For example, in science fiction, a subgenre of fantasy, a spaceship may harbor the community and help to define community boundaries in action and thought.

Theme in fantasy seems to be loftier, as it is often related to the idealized world of truth and goodness created in the setting. Thus we have good and bad characters, firmly on one side or the other, and a predominant theme of "good

Figure 3.4   Generalizations about Realism and Fantasy

Elements	Realism	Fantasy
Theme	Related to contemporary life	Lofty, as in good vs. evil
Plot	Variety of patterns, with flashbacks, etc.	Usually linear
Characterization	Realistic, with multi-dimensional characters	Idealized, often one-dimensional (good or bad)
Setting	Generalized from reality	Integral part of the story (the fantasy world)
Point-of-view	First person and omniscient	Usually omniscient

triumphing over evil in spite of great odds." Again, high fantasy and science fiction seem to articulate this theme more than other subgenres of fantasy.

Realistic plots are more apt to meander and to include flashbacks or other events that impede the resolution; in fantasy plot is usually straightforward, or linear, with few digressions. Point of view is likely to be omniscient in fantasy and traditional literature, while a variety of points of view may be found in realism. First-person narration is common in young adult realistic novels, probably because the reader's identification with an adolescent narrator makes the story more immediate and timely.

Understanding these differences in literary elements helps us classify literature and shows us how the genres work to reveal structure and cohesion. Figure 3.4 summarizes the differences in literary elements between realism and fantasy. Please note that these are generalizations; not all books follow these rules predictably.

SUMMARY

A rationale for classifying and studying literature preceded an explanation of genre theory, definitions of genres, and examples. Providing a theoretical framework for this chapter and others that follow, the genres of Poetry, Traditional Literature, Picture Books, Fantasy, Realism, Biography, and Information were presented.

Next, specific literary elements such as theme, plot, character, setting, style, and point of view were described and related to two well-known children's books, *Island of the Blue Dolphins* and *Charlotte's Web*.

Key attributes of vitality, freshness, and balance were proposed in order to evaluate how literary elements work in story, poem, and factual writing. Finally, this chapter presented differences in characterization, plot, theme, and point of view as they appear in fantasy and realism and relate to our generic expectations.

Knowledge of literature and how literature works is crucial to those who want to guide children toward lifelong reading enjoyment. This is not so that children will be subjected to analysis in a formal, usually lifeless, way, but so this knowledge will allow adults to suggest, find patterns, guide, and promulgate a rich interpretation of meaning. Literature is every child's birthright, and it deserves our best efforts to search for meanings, to understand, and to delight in it.

IMPLICATIONS FOR INSTRUCTION

Because literary theory and criticism was the focus of this chapter, this section asks you to react to theoretical ideas, to find out more about those that interest you, and to apply them. Reflections, in the form of questions, encourage you to think about various topics. Projects will allow you to pursue aspects of genre theory and literary elements; activities relate to teaching some analysis of literature in classrooms.

Reflections

1. Which book more strongly appealed to you, *Island of the Blue Dolphins* or *Charlotte's Web*? Why? Reflect on how the authors used various literary elements to create these stories. Discuss your opinions with a friend.

2. How do libraries classify books? Bookstores?

3. Themes are changing in realistic books written for children. Themes generally are uplifting, positive messages that reflect idealism and hope. However, in the last two decades a growing realism has tempered some of the sweetness and innocence previously found in children's books. Can you think of some examples in which the theme mirrors reality in a pessimistic way?

4. A British scholar of literature, Terry Eagleton, writing about function of criticism (1984), says that most modern criticism is simply a public relations tool, that its purpose is to sell books. After reading some criticism of children's books, do you think this is true?

5. Are Fantasy and Realism always diametrically opposed? Or are they more similar than dissimilar? How would you describe their relationship?

Projects

1. Select five children's books that appeal to you and classify them according to genres identified in this chapter. Then look at plot structures, note conflicts, and anything else that authors use to make the stories compelling. How would you articulate the books' themes?

2. Continue your analysis with selected books above (or choose others) and explore point of view, the importance of setting in each one, and specific styl-

istic language patterns, such as figurative language. Compare your notes with those of a friend.

3. Compare reviews of the same children's book from two sources, such as *The Horn Book Magazine* and *The Bulletin of the Center for Children's Books* (see Additional Resources). Note how descriptive, analytical, or evaluative each review is. Are the reviews similar, or do they focus on different aspects? Which literary elements are mentioned?

4. In a story, character is revealed in many ways. Characters describe themselves and others. A character's speech, dress, and action reveal traits and personality. Select a book and do a character study. How does the character come alive in your imagination?

5. New trends in literary theory include Peter Hunt's "childist criticism" (Hunt, 1991, ch. 11), a term analogous to feminist criticism; Aidan Chambers's "reader-response" (Chambers, 1983); and Louise Rosenblatt's "transactional theory" (Rosenblatt, 1978). Mentioned in Chapter 1, transactional theory was also described by Peggy Whalen-Levitt in "Pursuing the Reader in the Book" (1983). These theories insist on the primacy of the child-reader's interpretation of the meaning of a literary work. Find out all you can about any one of these theories, or compare all three. These theories have influenced how literature is taught in elementary and middle schools.

6. Can you think of other books that reveal the setting in the title, as in *Island of the Blue Dolphins*? In your examples, do settings have a symbolic function? A literary map helps to demonstrate the importance of setting in a story.

Activities for the Primary Level

Instead of separate activities, part of an interdisciplinary unit on "Journeys" is presented, using a reader response mode of teaching. (See also a JOURNEYS unit for grades five and six in Chapter 10.) Children in grades one through three (kindergartners could participate also) are asked to compare the journeys of two main characters. From the information elicited, a teacher can concretize a plot structure. Diagramming the structure of the plot will help children internalize story structure and relate it to many other works.

This discussion can be part of a classroom experience or it could be part of library study group.

Scenario

Before reading aloud to the whole class or a small group, a teacher asks the children to "Remember all you can about the journeys Max and Peter take." Then the teacher reads aloud two books, *Where the Wild Things Are* (Sendak, 1963) and *The Snowy Day* (Keats, 1962). These stories are likely to be familiar, so children can listen and remember in a concentrated way. Then, the teacher might say, "Tell me about Max's journey," and "Tell me about Peter's journey."

Figure 3.5   Journeys of Max and Peter

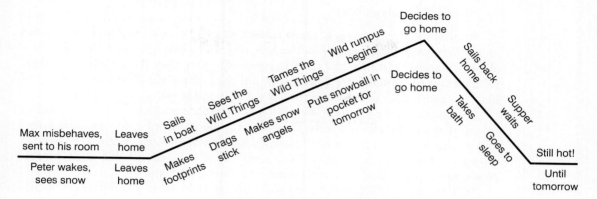

From the children's responses these questions are answered: Did they start at home? Where did they end? What happened to Max? Would you have been scared if you were he? What happened to Peter? and so on. The teacher does not have to ask these questions directly, because the children will likely volunteer everything. From the information elicited, a diagram can be made (see Figure 3.5).

If the parts of the story are on index cards, they can be attached to a big poster board during discussion. Children can later take the cards off and arrange them as they organize the story, or use them to tell their own stories. Teachers can color-code Max (red print on card) and Peter (blue print) for easy identification.

Many other books can be used in this way to teach sequencing and plot structure. These books were chosen because they are excellent and familiar.

Activities for the Intermediate and Middle Levels

Like the primary focus on literature, these activities are based on an interdisciplinary unit called "Islands." Students in grades four through seven may be asked to compare character, setting, and theme of *The Island* (Paulsen, 1988) and *Island of the Blue Dolphins* (O'Dell, 1960). In this part of the unit, students have already chosen which book (or both) to read, and have been introduced to the book appropriately. This discussion could be part of a classroom experience or take place in a library study group.

Note: *The Island* is a contemporary story of fourteen-year-old Wil Neuton, who chooses to go to an island in Wisconsin to escape tensions at home and at school.

Scenario
In a large-group or small-group setting the teacher says,

"We're going to compare Karana and Wil and think about living on an island ourselves."

"Those who read *Island of the Blue Dolphins,* tell me about Karana."

"Now, tell me about Wil."

From students' responses, these questions will be answered and similarities and differences will emerge: Their ages? Did they choose to go? How are they alike? Different? Did they like their islands? Why were they there? What was their relationship to animals? To plants? How did each character change as a result of his/her experience? What would you have done? and so on.

It is the teacher's job to probe, to follow up statements with questions, and to ask students to locate and reread parts of the book in order to draw inferences and to check facts. It is not the teacher's job to acknowledge "right" or "wrong" answers. Charts can be made of character traits, or students can write biographies, autobiographies, or journal entries of Karana and Wil.

"Tell me about the islands" can evoke setting and lead to a comparison of contemporary and historical time periods as well as place. Pictures can be drawn to represent scenes on both islands.

"What do you think the author is trying to say?" should lead to some statements pertaining to theme.

In this way, students make critical evaluations of two books by remembering, discussing, listening, drawing, and writing.

● ● ● ● ●
REFERENCES

Children's Works Cited

Keats, E. J. (1962). *The snowy day.* New York: Viking.
O'Dell, S. (1960). *Island of the blue dolphins* (p. 90). Boston: Houghton Mifflin.
Paulsen, G. (1988). *The island.* New York: Dell.
Sendak, M. (1963). *Where the wild things are.* New York: Harper & Row.
White, E. B. (1952). *Charlotte's Web* (pp. 1, 45, 113). New York: Harper & Row.

Professional Works Cited

Anderson, W., & Groff, P. (1972). *A new look at children's literature.* Belmont, CA: Wadsworth.
Chambers, A. (1983). *Introducing books to children* (2nd ed.). Boston: Horn Book.
Cullinan, B. (1971). *Children's literature: Its discipline and content* (p. 69). Dubuque, IA: Wm. C. Brown.
Eagleton, T. (1983). *Literary theory: An introduction* (p. 17). Minneapolis: University of Minnesota Press.
Eagleton, T. (1984). *The function of criticism from the spectator to post-structuralism.* London: Verso.
Frye, N. (1957). *Anatomy of criticism.* Princeton, NJ: Princeton University Press.
Hunt, P. (1991). *Criticism, theory, and children's literature* (p. 136). Cambridge, MA: Basil Blackwell.
Lukens, R. (1990). *A critical handbook of children's literature* (4th ed.). Glenview, IL: Scott, Foresman/Little, Brown.
Propp, V. (1968). *Morphology of the folktale* (2nd ed.) (p. 5). Austin: University of Texas Press.

Rosenblatt, L. (1978). *The reader, the text, the poem: The transactional theory of the literary work.* Carbondale, IL: Southern Illinois University Press.

Rudman, M. K. (1984). *Children's literature: An issues approach* (2nd ed.). New York: Longman.

Sims, R. (1982). *Shadow and substance.* Urbana, IL: National Council of Teachers of English.

Sloan, G. (1991). *The child as critic* (3rd. ed.). New York: Teachers College Press.

Whalen-Levitt, P. (1983). Pursuing the reader in the book. In J. May. (Ed.), *Children and their literature: A readings book* (pp. 154–159). West Lafayette, IN: Children's Literature Association.

Additional Resources

Bulletin of the Center for Children's Books. Betsy Hearne, Ed. University of Illinois Graduate School of Library and Information Science: University of Illinois Press.

This journal is published monthly (except August) and contains coded reviews of newly published children's books, as well as a "Subject and Use" index grouped by genre, topic, and ethnicity to help in finding books for special uses.

Chester, T. (1989). *Sources of information about children's books.* South Woodchester, England: Thimble Press.

This small volume lists current critical and bibliographical works in England and the United States.

Heins, P. (Ed.). (1977). *Crosscurrents of criticism.* Boston: Horn Book.

Paul Heins has selected essays by noted critics and authors from Horn Book issues pertaining to criticism, translation, classification, and so on.

The Horn Book Magazine. Anita Silvey, Editor-in-chief. Boston: Horn Book, Inc.

Founded in 1924, the Horn Book was the first magazine devoted to theory and criticism of children's books. It is published six times a year and contains articles and reviews.

Hunt, P. (Ed.). (1990). *Children's literature: The development of criticism.* London: Routledge.

Hunt gathered essays to reflect current thoughts on criticism. The last chapter is especially current and insightful, addressing new trends in criticism.

Meek, M., Warlow, A., & Barton, G. (Eds.). (1978). *The cool web: The pattern of children's reading.* New York: Atheneum.

A collection of essays with a section devoted to "Approaches to Criticism."

Stott, J. (1983). Teaching literary criticism in the elementary grades: a symposium. In J. May, (Ed.), *Children and their literature: A readings book* (pp. 160–172). West Lafayette, IN: Children's Literature Association.

Stott, Sonia Landes, Anita Moss, and Norma Bagnall, all professors of children's literature, relate their successful experiences teaching literature to second, fourth, and fifth graders.

Chapter Four

Once Upon a Time . . .
and Tradition
Continues

INTRODUCTION AND RESPONSE

Stories told around fires at the cave's mouth or the riverbank, proverbs to codify conventional wisdom, and myths about real and imaginary happenings—all of these formed the language and the culture that held together a group of intelligent, yet primitive, people. The oral tradition preceded written expression, as it brought a community together by expressing common values and accepted truths through a storyteller's magic and ritual. Our vast heritage of traditional literature, coming to us over time and space, finds new expression through modern multicultural stories based on old truths and modern adaptations.

Hallmarks of traditional literature include

"Once upon a time . . .
a beautiful heroine,
a brave hero,
had a 'problem,'
resolved it, then lived
happily ever after."

What is the first fairy tale that pops into your mind? Identify a story and match its parts to the short plot description above. You may take, for example, *Cinderella, Snow White,* or *Rapunzel,* and determine who the heroine and hero are, what the catalyst for action, or the problem, is, and how it is resolved. Called **story grammar** or **story structure**, this basic narrative flow is a blueprint for traditional literature and, indeed, for most modern stories.

While many myths, legends, folktales, and so on fit into this story structure, some do not. Keep the framework in mind as other tales are discussed, but realize also that traditional literature comes in many forms and motifs, with different characters, elements, settings, and language conventions. This chapter will highlight rich variations in the oral tradition by bringing to your attention folklore from different parts of the world. It will close with some modern adaptations of multicultural traditional literature.

Traditional literature will sometimes be referred to as **folklore,** which has a somewhat broader meaning, but the two terms will be used interchangeably to denote linguistic expressions coming from the oral tradition.

• • • • •
HISTORY OF TRADITIONAL LITERATURE

The compelling nature of **story**, the desire and the need to frame words around events, evolved as our ancestors gained opposable thumbs and brain structures that permitted language to occur. Folklore from prehistoric times, told again and again, never the same way twice, and in every cultural group, entertained and instructed listeners of all ages. Before the printing press and even the scant literacy of medieval times, the common people built a heritage of literary works. Royalty also contributed, and tales, songs, wise sayings, and myths were gradually added as cultures grew and changed.

From early scholars' work we see that folklorists first were captivated by a theory of "monogenesis" to explain these literary phenomena. *Monogenesis* means one *(mono)* beginning *(genesis);* it was thought that all stories came from one place, namely, northern Europe. This has since been refuted with a more logical "polygenesis" theory, which insists that humans in every culture express the same basic needs and desires—to love, to hate, to search for meaning, to laugh, and to learn—and therefore generate similar patterns, characters, situations, and so on.

In the 1800s, while the Brothers Grimm were collecting and publishing household stories, Hans Christian Andersen wrote his original tales in the folkloric style (Haugaard, 1983). Other collections of old stories signaled an ever expanding multicultural base that resulted in significant contributions and influenced the development of modern literature in theme and form. *The Arabian Nights,* translated a century before, in 1704, was just such a collection. Lady Charlotte Guest, translating and adapting *The Mabinogion* (see a recent children's version, Thomas & Crossley-Holland, 1985) from ancient Welsh to English in the mid-1800s, did so in spite of resistance from some scholars who questioned that a woman could accomplish such a feat (Wrenn, 1976)! Russian folktales were collected by Afanas'ev in the mid-1800s, Norwegian tales by Asbjornsen and Moe. Japan, with its rich tradition of story and art, and propelled to some extent by the opening of its borders by Commodore Perry, revealed its flourishing literary and publishing enterprise at that time. *Pinocchio,* an original story written by Carlo Collodi in 1880, popularized Italian folklore; Andrew Lang began his series of adapted fairy tales in the *Blue Fairy Book* (1889) and the *Red Fairy Book* (1890).

In the 1920s, a landmark study, *The Morphology of the Folktale,* gave credibility to the formal exploration of literary structures and paved the way for cross-cultural studies (Propp, 1968). As evidence of this kind of exploration, *Cinderella* has perhaps been studied more than any other tale, and five "types" and over five hundred variants have been identified (Dundes, 1983). Betsy Hearne's study (1989) of *Beauty and the Beast* points out how global versions of this famous story reverberate with similar themes and adapt to changing social and political contexts.

As we become more sensitive to differences and similarities of modern folklore expressed as multicultural literature, it becomes obvious that certain patterns and themes cannot be present in all cultures; nevertheless, striking similarities remain. Modern analyses of folklore tend to take points of view from philosophy, political science, and psychology to explain the origins and functions of these stories and sayings. Thus there are psychoanalytic interpretations, as in Bruno Bettelheim's well-known *The Uses of Enchantment* (Bettelheim, 1976), as well as Marxist interpretations that insist folklore is a metaphor for peasants rising to overthrow the ruling class. When the noted psychologist Carl Jung related modern dreams to primitive myths and rites in an effort to explain how symbols organize and give meaning to life (Jung, 1964), renewed interest and attention focused on folklore and, in particular, on mythology. Studies of myths figured prominently in the work of Joseph Campbell, who revealed hero-myths throughout world cultures (Campbell, 1968). By providing a thorough cross-cultural basis to traditional literature, Campbell advanced the study of folklore and implied that a knowledge of the universality of myth-making could be a step toward cross-cultural understanding.

All these analyses show that folklore has been the continuing study of several academic disciplines and remains so. It merits research and analysis because of the richness and complexity of seemingly simple patterns, verses, and elements. Perhaps this irony—that the most complex of our enduring truths can be expressed in language a child can understand—explains the appeal of traditional literature.

● ● ● ● ●

SUBGENRES OF TRADITIONAL LITERATURE

For purposes of easy classification, traditional forms seem to fall into groups of two that share many characteristics. Each group will be defined in more detail and accompanied by examples following Figure 4.1.

Folk Rhymes and Songs

In the first subgenre, folk rhymes, examples are: Mother Goose rhymes and songs, chants, finger plays, riddles, jump-rope rhymes, proverbs, superstitions, jokes, tongue twisters, and probably more! These verbal phrases demonstrate common

Subgenre	Definition
Folk Rhymes and Folk Songs	Succinct ideas expressed rhythmically, often in rhyme, and sometimes in song. Folk songs are most apt to tell a story through a recurring melodic pattern (many verses).
Parable and Fable	Brief narratives that describe a behavior and then explicitly or implicitly contain a moral. Parables usually have human characters, while fables have animal characters.
Folktales and Fairy Tales	Narratives that include human and/or talking animal characters, and a clean and direct plot with unambiguous right and wrong in the decisive resolution. Folktales are more likely to be about common people, talking animals, and conventional wisdom, while fairy tales are more likely to be associated with magic and royalty.
Myths and Legends	Narratives that explain why natural or cosmic phenomena occur; who our heroes and heroines are; what the relationships of the gods are to humans or to each other. Myths seem to be more otherworldly, or more abstract, while legends begin with a kernel of truth and become exaggerated.

Figure 4.1   Traditional Literature: Subgenres and Definitions

wisdom or just simple nonsense, as in "Red sky at night, a sailor's delight" or "Simple Simon met a pieman. . . ."

"It can be safely stated that the overwhelming majority of nursery rhymes were not in the first place composed for children" (Opie & Opie, 1951, p. 3). Fragments of ballads, folk songs, proverbs, or political statements satirizing the nobility—there are many different explanations as to the origin of what we now call nursery rhymes and their place in traditional literature. The singing game, "Ring O' Roses," has a particularly gruesome origin, some allege.

> Ring-a ring o' roses,
> A pocket full of posies,
> A-tishoo! A-tishoo!
> We all fall down.

The rhyme may date back to the great plague of Europe, spread by rats in the 1300s. A rosy rash was a symptom of the disease, and posies of herbs were carried for protection and to keep the deadly stench from assaulting one's nose. Sneezing was a fatal symptom (marked by the "A-tishoo!"), and the last line mimics death. But another version has a second verse in which "we all get up again" (Opie & Opie, 1951, p. 365).

It is a further testament to the power of these seemingly frivolous and nonsensical rhymes that they survive and indeed, spawn imitations and parodies. Some are truly charming and memorable, giving young children a sense of story, interesting characters, a taste of whimsy, and a shared literary experience. For more discussion of nursery rhymes, see Chapter 5 for picture-book editions and Chapter 2 for a more detailed historical account.

Folk songs use the rhythm and pattern of spoken verses but add elements of music—melody and harmony—to make common wisdom, a story, or simple nonsense more memorable. They include spirituals, ballads, lullabies, work songs, and sea chanteys. Some of these are about heroes and heroines and some describe the cruelty of war, the vagaries of wealth, or the fickleness of love. Here are only a few examples of this subgenre; consult Chapter 10—the Literature unit SINGING SONGS AND STORIES contains many examples. Also, check public libraries or bookstores:

> *Gonna Sing My Head Off,* Kathleen Krull (1992)
>
> *Diane Goode's Book of Silly Stories and Songs,* Diane Goode (1992)
>
> *The Mother Goose Book,* Alice and Martin Provensen (1976)

Parables and Fables

These brief narratives use their short length and terse style to illuminate human foibles. Undesirable human traits such as arrogance and pride are ridiculed, and positive traits are rewarded. There are relatively few traditional parables in children's literature with the exception of biblical stories rewritten for a young audience. Fables are not numerous either, but three great collections have been accessible to children from earliest times: Aesop, of course, from ancient Greece; La Fontaine from France; and the Panchantantra, a collection of fables from India. A second well-known source of Indian fables is the "Jatakas," which are fables depicting Buddha's reincarnations as various animals. Many modern stories are reminiscent of fables in their brevity and pointed moral lessons. Examples of old and new are:

> *Aesop & Company,* Barbara Bader (1991)
>
> *A Chinese Zoo: Fables and Proverbs,* Demi (1987)
>
> *Fables,* Arnold Lobel (1980)
>
> *The Doubleday Illustrated Children's Bible,* Sandal Stoddard (1983)

Folktales and Fairy Tales

These are by far the most numerous in all of folklore and create the body of literature that most people associate with the oral tradition. For the purposes of this discussion the distinction between the two does not matter (if there is any true distinction), and this subgenre will simply be referred to as folktales. Narrative patterns and stylistic language, stock characters and themes, and common folk-loric elements abound in thousands and thousands of stories referred to as fairy tales or folktales.

Narrative Patterns and Stylistic Language

Story structure, introduced at the beginning of this chapter, is a common narrative pattern. Folktales begin with a brief introduction that uses "Once upon a time . . ." or "Long ago and far away . . ." or other stylistic language to alert the listener/reader to the folk quality of the work. In the following example of "The Fisherman and His Wife," **Setting**, denoting time and place, is quickly established with the phrase, "There was once a fisherman who lived with his wife in a pigsty not far from the sea, and every day the fisherman went fishing" (Manheim, 1983, p. 70).

Following this introduction of setting and characters, an event occurs that galvanizes the action; this event is called the **problem**. It can also be a supernatural task undertaken by one of the characters, usually the hero. In "The Fisherman and His Wife," the problem takes shape when the husband catches a talking flounder who promises him anything in return for its life. When his wife hears that her husband let the fish go without wishing for anything, she urges him to go back to the sea and try again. He does, with the refrain "Little man whoever you be,/Flounder, flounder in the sea,/My wife, her name is Ilsebil,/Has sent me here against my will" (Manheim, 1983, pp. 70–71). Very often these tales employ a

From *The Stonecutter* by Gerald McDermott. Copyright © 1975 by Gerald McDermott. Used by permission of Viking Penguin, a division of Penguin Books USA.

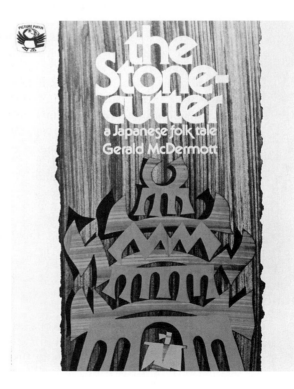

repetitive language pattern that becomes predictable and adds to the escalating tension in the plot as grander and grander events occur. This is called "rising action" or, in the terms of story structure, a series of action/consequence, action/consequence. In this story, the wife wishes first for a cottage, then a stone castle, and next for a palace in which she is king. (Notice the pattern of three events.) Greed grows, and with the flounder's magical help triggered by the magical refrain, she becomes emperor, then pope, and finally she wants to be "like God" (again a series of three). With a storm raging to show that the climax is near, the problem is solved and the fisherman's wife finds herself miraculously back in the pigsty. Similarly, escalating greed is also the subject of a Japanese folktale, *The Stonecutter* (McDermott, 1976), and many more folktales.

This common narrative pattern, or story structure, could be diagrammed as in Figure 4.2.

The structure of folktales has gained attention in recent years because it is believed that children implicitly internalize the structure when listening to many stories. Then when they read, they show better comprehension because they can predict what might happen. Thus, a knowledge of story structure aids reading/listening comprehension and underscores the value of reading aloud to children.

Quite often, the action/consequence sequence is based on a quest undertaken by the hero or heroine. Subplots occur in which a character meets other characters along the journey and has other adventures, leading to the climax, which is that period in the story when tension explodes from all the action and excitement leading up to it. The action/consequence sequence occurs in "The Fisherman and His Wife" when the fisherman entreats the flounder on behalf of his wife each time, and the consequence is a bigger home.

Another narrative pattern in folktales is called the cumulative tale. It is a circular pattern in which events are repeated with one more added each time (see Figure 4.3). *The House That Jack Built* is just such a story (Stevens, 1985). Cumulative aspects are evident in songs and nursery rhymes too.

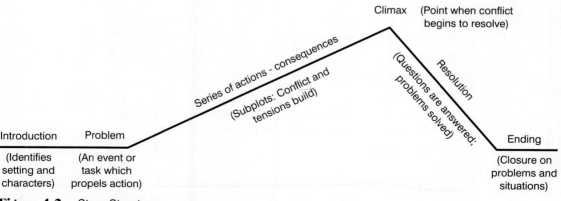

Figure 4.2   Story Structure

Figure 4.3   Cumulative
Structure

Language in folktales tends to reflect some stylized patterns, as the "Once upon . . ." and repeated sayings "Mirror, mirror, on the wall . . ." but generally stories are told in unadorned prose, simple and direct. Modern storytellers use contemporary language so that new listeners can understand. In the spirit of the oral tradition, tales weren't memorized verbatim but grew out of the rapport between storyteller and audience. Thus, modern versions can be a welcome addition to this genre, if the essential nature of folklore is left unchanged.

Stock Characters

Characters are not fully developed in folktales; they are often one-dimensional, or flat. They exist as types to serve the plot. In "The Fisherman," for example, the fisherman is simply a messenger, we know nothing else about him. His wife is only portrayed as greedy. Narrow characterization paradoxically allows the story to have broader appeal because these single, specific traits are recognized by almost everyone!

Characters fall into personality types and roles so that the action can be fast-paced and eventful. Following is a list of typical characters in folktales:

Beautiful maiden

Handsome prince/hero

Eldest son/daughter

Youngest son/daughter

Stepmother

Elderly childless couple

Fool, also known as noodlehead

Trickster

Wise elderly person

Witch/wizard

Fantasy character (leprechaun, elf, fairy, gnome, giant, ogre,
        mermaid/merman, and many more)

Talking animal

Folktales are criticized because characterization is so narrow that characters become stereotypical or a caricature of a type. In other words, the stepmother is always and only evil, and the maiden is always and only passively innocent. Those who make the criticisms sometimes base their accusations on only a few folktales, the very familiar ones. However, these powerful stories are repeated enough to children to question their influence and their likelihood of creating passive females or violent children. Folktales, in spite of their popularity and many virtues, are still problematic to a few concerned adults. However, many have refuted the criticism with reasoned arguments about the cathartic nature of folktales and their importance in the developing intellectual and emotional perspectives of children (Bettelheim, 1976; Chukovsky, 1971). It is vital to present a wide range of folktales so that different character types are evident. There should be many with strong, wise feminine characters (Lurie, 1980) as well as many examples of other kinds of characters both intercultural and intracultural.

Folktale Themes and Elements

Common themes in folklore reflected values, and the values of a pretechnological society dictated that harmony, truth, and goodness be rewarded, while cruelty, deception, and greed be chastised. Fairness and justice ruled eventually. Hard work was honored, wit and intelligence were prized. Sometimes a struggle for power precipitated the outcome, but good always vanquished evil. From folktales our questions of truth, beauty, love, and the deeper philosophical questions concerning the meaning of life can be answered. Lest the themes become too serious, a small body of folklore has humor or nonsense as its theme.

Common folkloric elements include:

Magic objects (wands, staffs, a branch of rowan, everyday
    things invested with magical properties)

Mythical beasts (unicorns, dragons, . . .)

Spells of enchantment (to be turned into an animal, a fool, an
    inanimate object)

A long sleep (as in *Sleeping Beauty* and *Snow White*)

Transformations (from ugly to beautiful, from inanimate to
    real)

Groups of three, seven, twelve, or four (magic numbers proba-
    bly coming from the natural world or symbolic in early
    religious rituals)

Examples of folktales, in addition to those already mentioned in this section, are Joanna Cole's *Best-Loved Folktales of the World* (1982) and Jane Yolen's *Favorite Folktales from Around the World* (1986).

Myths and Legends

When primitive people wanted to explain how the earth began, or why the sun and the moon followed each other in the sky, they created stories. Prescientific explanations of the universe and its workings gave meaning and ritual to the lives of

common people and the powerful alike. When the stories were prompted by questions of an afterlife, or an explanation of what happens after death, otherworlds were created with their own gods and goddesses, heroes, villains, and tricksters. Myths, unlike other stories, developed in relation to each other, so that we have a body of literature based on Greek myths, Roman myths, Scandinavian myths, or other cultural accumulations. (The Greek word for "stories" was *mythos.)*

Mythology is frequently broken into three broad types: creation myths, pourquoi tales, also called nature myths, and hero myths. Sometimes called genesis myths, creation myths depict the struggle to form the earth out of darkness, chaos, or the spirit world. For example, Genesis, the first book in the *Bible,* explains the origin of the Judeo-Christian heritage. Many cultures have an explanation of how the earth began, and this book is an excellent resource: *In the Beginning: Creations Myths from Around the World* (Hamilton, 1988).

Pourquoi stories are myths that explain why natural events occur, such as why thunder rolls in the sky, or *Why Mosquitoes Buzz in People's Ears* (Aardema, 1975). They offer explanations of the seasons, as in the Greek myth of Persephone, goddess of springtime, daughter of the earth goddess Demeter, and her kidnaping by Hades, god of the underworld (D'Aulaire & D'Aulaire, 1962). When Persephone (or Proserpine in Roman myths) does not return to her mother,

Demeter is so heartbroken that she allows winter to overtake the earth, but eventually Persephone's return brings springtime again. It is interesting to think about why and how prescientific societies created stories to rationalize the inexplicable, yet predictable, natural occurrences in the cycle of life.

As myths center on supernatural beings, set in otherworldly places and times, so legends bring mythical qualities to characters who perhaps could have lived in somewhat recognizable places, completing somewhat realistic tasks.

Heroic legends usually describe the exploits of a person who begins life as an orphan or a person of very lowly status, then is elevated to high status through his/her good deeds or quest for greatness. Sometimes a miraculous event occurs to mark the potential hero—an initiation rite, or even a miraculous birth. The young person usually has a wise older mentor to guide him or her. Then the quest is entered with foreboding, because the future hero or heroine is acting against all odds of success. Finally, the climax proves that heroic qualities are within each person, that self-determination and a conscience can allow each of us to succeed.

These hero stories reflect an idealism through a gentle, strong, and innocent character who meets adversity with his or her courage undaunted. Self-doubt is replaced by confidence, and the quest takes on a dimension of self-discovery. The legend of St. George and the dragon (Hodges, 1984), drawn from Edmund Spenser's *Fairie Queen,* is just such a story. In Margaret Hodges' version, George's task, initiated by the queen of the fairies, is to slay a wicked, loathsome dragon. George is young, untested, and accompanied by a beautiful, sorrowful princess, Una, a lamb, and a dwarf. He and his entourage symbolize youthful vulnerability, a

From *Saint George and the Dragon,* illustrated by Trina Schart Hyman. Text copyright © 1984 by Margaret Hodges; illustrations copyright © 1984 by Trina Schart Hyman. By permission of Little, Brown and Company.

dedication to an ideal—ridding the countryside of a terror so magnificent that it has paralyzed the other inhabitants for months. The "Red Cross Knight," as George is known, meets with a hermit who shows him a vision of a heavenly city that will be his reward after a life of good deeds. George, Una, and all then proceed to the valley where the dragon awaits. The battle is horrendous, and only on the *third* day after miraculous healing cures are performed each night can the Red Cross Knight finally slay the monstrous, brassy-scaled beast. As he receives the grateful king's gifts, thanks, and daughter (Una), George recalls his duty to the queen of the fairies. Although he marries, he still continues his brave adventures and attains sainthood, thus fulfilling the hermit's prophecy.

In this English legend, mythological underpinnings, such as innocence and beauty contrasted with evil and ugliness, magical cures, prophetic visions from a wise elder, the straight and narrow path, and the number three, work together. And Trina Schart Hyman's "stained-glass" full-color illustrations of the authentic, Old English countryside, people, and dress convey an emotional, dramatic style.

Legends can elevate a common person into the realm of folklore through the exaggeration and enhancement of character traits. When the exaggeration reaches comic proportions, a tall tale is created. Examples of tall tales in American folklore are stories about Paul Bunyan, the North American logger of tremendous size, Pecos Bill, a Southwestern cowboy, and John Henry, the African-American steel driving man of early railroad-building fame. Perhaps the next millennium will see legends from this century enter folklore.

● ● ● ● ●
EVALUATING TRADITIONAL LITERATURE

Difficulty in evaluating traditional literature may stem from the fact that recently published works are retellings, adaptations, and translations of sometimes very old tales. Questions of authenticity arise, and because the old tales were oral and dynamic, not static artifacts, there is no first version to use as the "correct" or "pure" one. However, by becoming familiar with the classification, definitions, and major characteristics of the subgenres presented in this chapter, you will be able to look for certain aspects unique to this genre: a linear or cumulative story structure; one-dimensional characters with the exception of the hero; clean, spare language with occasional word play and stylistic patterns; and humorous or value-laden themes that speak to the truly important reasons for a society's existence.

What follows is an evaluation scheme based on questions drawn from these salient characteristics of folklore (see Figure 4.4). When selecting a book with audience and purpose in mind, ask questions like those in the chart.

If folklore is presented in a picture-book format, the artwork should be evaluated also in relation to the text. See Chapter 5 for a discussion of evaluating artwork and text.

While there is latitude in accepting renditions of tales, it is wise to be alert to certain inappropriate practices. The most obvious errors occur when stories, movies, video games, or other examples stray from the flavor of the unadorned, sometimes earthy, oral tradition. Walt Disney's versions of the familiar stories,

Subgenre	My Personal Response
Folk Rhymes and Songs	Are they memorable? Compelling? Do they have interesting word plays? Are there tuneful melodies that invite participation?
Fables and Parables	Is there one-dimensional characterization and a succinct plot with an explicit moral lesson?
Folktales and Fairy Tales	Is there stylistic language at appropriate times? Are there recognizable themes, interesting but not complex characters, and authentic cultural elements in the setting?
Myths and Legends	Is the purpose clear (that is, a creation, hero, or pourquoi myth)? Are there authentic settings, characters, and a compelling vision of human interaction in story form?

Figure 4.4   Evaluating Traditional Literature

Cinderella, Beauty and the Beast, and *Sleeping Beauty,* for example, are too pretty, too cute, and too fancy—inappropriate elements have been added. Chattering teacups, simpering heroes and heroines, and comic-book dragons and dwarfs are insulting to the genre. Controversies surrounding these adaptations began with the release of the movie *Snow White* in 1938, and continue today (May, 1984).

●　●　●　●　●
MULTICULTURAL TRADITIONAL LITERATURE

Multicultural literature includes traditional and modern folklore drawn from a distinct cultural group, portraying characters, situations, and a cultural ethos with accuracy and rich detail (Yokota, 1993). Multicultural literature includes literary forms from all enduring centers of civilization: Africa, Asia, Australia and Oceania, Europe, and North and South America. When the term is used in the United States, it frequently refers to literature about people who are outside the sociopolitical mainstream, or people of color—African Americans, Asian Americans, Native Americans, and Hispanics (Bishop, 1992). The use of the term in this way has forced many to consider how language and story perpetuate stereotypes, and also how a dearth of available literature representing a child's own culture can affect development and learning.

Increasing diversity in the number of cultural groups represented in the United States, as seen in the number of school-aged children who do not speak English (Faltis, 1993), necessitates the inclusion of multicultural literature in every aspect of curricula. The value of literature to foster cognitive and affective development is well understood and, particularly for children who are sensitive to their own cultural differences, the comfort and delight that literature brings is a substantial addition to their well-being. This literature should include not just their own cultural literature; a variety that shows similarities and differences can be very important.

What follows is a short description of traditional stories from the diverse cultural groups just mentioned as well as some information about the folklore and several exemplary works. In this section, the emphasis is on retellings of traditional literature; in Chapter 8 modern fiction from several cultural groups will be included. The brevity allows you to search out those titles and authors that most represent what you need. Please note that many of these titles are considered picture books, but this should not lessen the appropriateness of using these multicultural stories with a wide audience. Students of all ages will respond to the tales; often the picture-book format does not detract from their enjoyment by adolescents.

African American

African American folklore comes from many African countries and communities with distinct cultural references: Mali, Ashanti, Senegalese, Yoruba, Swahili, Zulu, and many more. When black slaves were imported to the Americas, remnants of African folklore mixed with Caribbean stories, creating variations and adding new elements. These variations grew and flourished in the American South. Ananse, the trickster-spider from the Ashanti, became "Aunt Nancy" in some tales, and the Brer Rabbit stories, originally collected and retold by Joel Chandler Harris in the late nineteenth century, seem to have come from an African tradition of wily animal characters. As the characters in folklore are so often either good or evil, the ambiguity and enterprise of the trickster's role is especially compelling.

Rich language patterns, plots demonstrating wit and cunning, kindness and generosity, and values such as love of beauty, humor, and perseverance abound in African American literature. *Beat the Story Drum, Pum-Pum* (Bryan, 1980) contains pourquoi tales such as "How Animals Got Their Tails" and "Why Bush Cow and Elephant Are Bad Friends." Artist and storyteller Ashley Bryan's lilting prose echoes the oral flavor of chanted verse.

Set in Zimbabwe, *Mufaro's Beautiful Daughters: An African Tale* (Steptoe, 1987) is a tale of sibling rivalry, with the kind and generous daughter selected to be the king's bride instead of her selfish and greedy sister. A Caldecott honor book, Steptoe's illustrations create a lush, panoramic view of Eastern Africa.

Sundiata, Lion King of Mali (Wisniewski, 1992) is a heroic legend based on the powerful and benevolent Sundiata, who ruled Mali in the fourteenth century. His early life as a crippled and speechless child was transformed by his own bravery and intelligence with the help of an older mentor.

In addition to the books mentioned above and throughout the chapter, these examples of African American folklore could be consulted:

The People Could Fly: American Black Folktales, Virginia
    Hamilton (1985)
The Ballad of Belle Dorcas, William Hooks (1990)

Native American

Native American collections of folklore are relatively recent additions to this genre. Before 1970, few were available (Norton, 1991). Analogous to the many distinct cultural groups in the African American category, Native American cultures are heterogeneous, with features of the plains, the eastern woodlands, the southwestern deserts, and the Native American cultures in Canada all generating cultural differences expressed in ritual and mythology. It should be noted, however, that there are more similarities than differences, and four types, as identified by John Bierhorst (1976), seem to be particularly noticeable in Native American folklore: (1) creation myths that depict an ordered world rising from the chaos of nature; (2) "family drama" or myths resulting from the closeness of persons and families living together in kinship units; (3) hero myths in which the young hero is a trickster until he realizes the importance of social virtue, usually in a quest sequence; and (4) rites of passage, or crossing threshold myths depicting passage in and out of a dream state or a parallel world.

A hero myth, *Anpao: An American Indian Odyssey* (Highwater, 1977), a Newbery honor book, is a collection of these types of myths centering on the boy Anpao and his search for his destiny in the Great Plains and Rocky Mountains. Folklore of the Navajo has been adapted by Shonto Begay (1992) in *Ma'ii and Cousin Horned Toad: A Traditional Navajo Story.* Coyote, a trickster in this and many tales, swallows his cousin in order to get all the corn grown by Horned Toad. His greed backfires, as Horned Toad proves to be an unwelcome stomach guest. Joseph Bruchac and Jonathan London (1992) adapted one of the eastern Native American pourquoi tales in *Thirteen Moons on Turtle's Back* to describe the seasons in poetic language. See also:

> *The Star Maiden: An Ojibway Tale,* Barbara Esbensen (1988)
>
> *Iktomi and the Ducks: A Plains Indian Tale,* Paul Goble (1990)
>
> *Raven: A Trickster Tale from the Pacific Northwest,* Gerald McDermott (1993)

Hispanic American

"Spanish-speaking children are the largest and fastest-growing school-age population of second language learners in the United States" (Faltis, 1993, p. 7). Clearly this dictates a need to become aware of Hispanic folklore and explore possibilities of its enjoyment in classrooms. Given even the best intentions, however, Hispanic traditional literature can be difficult to find. Compounding the difficulty are the many geographical and cultural settings subsumed under the term *Hispanic.* From the island cultures of the Caribbean and Puerto Rico to the southwest deserts, from the tip of South America to the southern United States, one can see vast differences in geography and culture. Also, ancient Mayan, Aztec, and Inca civilizations contrast with the Roman Catholicism of the last five centuries.

These recently published tales contain universal elements of folklore. The first, *How We Came to the Fifth World* (Rohmer, 1992), is an Aztec creation myth describing how the first four worlds were destroyed by the gods of fire, water, air, and earth. *Magic Dogs of the Volcanoes* (Argueta, 1992) explains how magical beasts protected the people of El Salvador from unpredictable eruptions of volcanoes.

Hispanic folklore frequently shows the strong influence of the Catholic faith in stories about holidays and patron saints. *The Lady of Guadalupe* (De Paola, 1980) recounts the Mexican legend of a poor farmer's heavenly vision in 1531, telling him to build a church on a certain site so that the Blessed Virgin could minister to the people.

In a more secular tale, familiar characters—a king, a marriageable daughter, and a suitor—and an impossible task—to guess the kind of leather in a drum—creates a universal story, *The Riddle of the Drum: A Tale from Tizapan, Mexico* (Aardema, 1979). With some help from passersby, the suitor is successful and they live "happily ever after." See also:

Moon Was Tired of Walking on Air, N. Belting (1992)

Where Angels Glide at Dawn: New Stories from Latin America,
     L. Carlson and C. Ventura (1990)

Asian American

Folklore from Japan, Vietnam, China, the Philippines, and other Pacific rim countries constitutes a varied and rich repository from which some authors have based modern retellings and adaptations. Unfortunately, examples are few, and some of the available books contain stereotypes of Asian Americans, presenting characters as devoid of individual characteristics as the five Chinese brothers (Aoki, in Harris, 1992).

Story grammar of traditional Asian folklore seems to have an important difference from the pattern of story grammar that began our discussion of traditional literature. Utako Matsuyama (1983), analyzing Japanese folktales, found that many (80 percent) had no goal structure for the main character; that is, the main character did not identify his/her purpose or goal, and therefore events were more episodic than linear. The structure influenced characters and themes, and Matsuyama attributed this to values derived from Buddhist principles that deny aggression, competition, and individualism.

The Tongue-Cut Sparrow (Ishii, 1987, trans. by Paterson) is just such a story. Because he and his wife have no children, an old man adopts and cares for a little sparrow. His wife grows jealous, and when the sparrow misbehaves, she snips its tongue. Upon her husband's return, she gleefully tells him how she maimed his pet. Horrified, he rushes off to apologize. After helping two workers along the way, he finds the magical castle of the sparrow in the deep bamboo wood, an enchanted place. To repay him for his concern, the sparrow asks the old man to choose between two boxes. He chooses the small box, rather than the large one, because he is old and tires easily. When he arrives home with the box, he and his wife discover gold, silver, and other precious things in the box. She berates him for not choosing the larger box, and goes off to get it. Her journey mimics his, except that she is nasty to everyone. Unable to contain her curiosity, she opens her box before she gets home. Demons and goblins erupt from the box and threaten her, but she runs home as fast as she can. There she repents her greedy ways and becomes a better person.

In this story, the main character, a good person, does not have a goal or desire. He simply reacts to events. The second character, greedy and nasty, pursues her goal and is repaid in kind. This structure indicates a pattern of two episodes, one without a goal and one with a goal. According to Matsuyama's analysis, this story structure is quite prevalent. It would be interesting to see if other Japanese traditional stories exemplified this structure as well.

Folklore from China sparkles in *Yeh-Shen: A Cinderella Story from China* (Louie, 1982) and *The Rainbow People* (Yep, 1989), a collection of folktales from Oakland, California's Chinatown in the 1930s. *Many Lands, Many Stories: Asian Folktales for Children* (Conger, 1987) is a diverse collection of fifteen folktales representing other areas.

● ● ● ● ●
SUMMARY

This chapter presented a story structure to initiate a discussion of traditional literature classified into four subgenres: folk songs and rhymes; fables and parables; folktales; and myths and legends. After a brief history of traditional literature, definitions, characteristics, common themes, characters, elements, and examples were given. Folktales, myths, and legends were especially detailed, as specific stories from collections of the Brothers Grimm, Greek myths, and other sources were summarized. Creation myths, nature myths, and hero myths comprised three basic types of mythology, and legends included stories of heroes and heroines and the exaggeration of tall tales.

Implicit in this chapter was the importance of traditional literature to provide a multicultural dimension to every child's experience. A variety of folklore, from many cultures and representing myriad themes, including humor, should permeate the curriculum, with special attention to the match between the ethnicity of children in a classroom and the multicultural literature presented.

Criteria for evaluation of traditional literature were suggested for all the subgenres.

Examples and some analysis of multicultural traditional literature, as part of the literary heritage of African Americans, Asian Americans, Hispanics, and Native Americans, concluded the chapter. Concerns about stereotypical language and images and inappropriate retellings were raised, as well as about the dearth of books published in this area. However, this decade is seeing a resurgence of interest in publishing multicultural books, and this speaks well for the availability of good books in the coming years. Picture books seem to be prolific, but collections of stories for older readers are scarce.

● ● ● ● ●
IMPLICATIONS FOR INSTRUCTION

In this section, instructional implications of teaching traditional multicultural literature are presented in three phases. The first phase focuses on Reflections, or questions, topics, and so on rising from the chapter that could be articulated, pondered, and discussed. The second phase, Projects, includes ideas for projects for you to do while you pursue this subject. The last part of the section, Activities, offers suggestions that are appropriate for use in primary, intermediate, and middle-level classrooms.

Reflections

1. The term *multicultural literature* incites some people, soothes others. A subject of intense debate, the term has been politicized on all sides. What is your view? How do you define the term?

2. Because characters are often flat, or one-dimensional, traditional literature is easily criticized as stereotypical. Do you think this criticism is justified? Is there a difference between a "type" and a "stereotype?" That is, is one worse than the other? When does a character become a type and when does the type become a derogatory stereotype? Similarly, criticisms of too much violence sometimes accompany translations or retellings. Is this criticism justified? What are your views on these aspects of traditional literature?

3. What do you think about recasting traditional literature into a modern setting with modern characters, such as *Untold Tales* (Brooke, 1992), or rewriting tales from a different point of view, as in *The Stinky Cheese Man and Other Fairly Stupid Tales* (Scieszka, 1992)? Does the retelling detract from the original purpose, or do you think modern children are more likely to appreciate the relevance to their world?

4. Much has been written about Walt Disney's adaptations of familiar fairy tales, such as "Walt Disney Accused" by Frances Clarke Sayers, former writer, critic, and head of the children's division of the New York Public Library (Sayers, 1965). After considering some of the criticisms of Disney movie versions, what do you think? How would you evaluate the movies, and do you think different media affect comprehension and enjoyment of the story?

5. What are the modern myths and legends being created today? Sensitive always to the demands of society's changing icons, what political, economic, sports, or musical heroes and heroines are being invented? What stories, sayings, proverbs, and so on depict modern ironies, modern values, and plots?

Projects

1. Stories in this chapter beg to be told. Become part of the oral tradition and learn to tell a story or polish your storytelling techniques. There are many

resources available to help you, for example, the classic *Storytelling* (Tooze, 1959). Tell your favorite story to a group of children or adults.

2. Research some folklore within an ethnic or cultural group of your choice. You may: (1) collect myths or folktales of that group; (2) collect a particular type, such as pourquoi tales, or concentrate on a certain theme, such as "kindness rewarded," or a character, such as the trickster; (3) find folklore from related groups, such as western and eastern Native American cultures, and look for similarities and differences.

3. A consummate storyteller and author, Isaac Bashevis Singer adapted and created memorable Jewish tales from Eastern Europe, including three Newbery Honor books. For wit, ironic humor, and a unique gift for conveying Yiddish folklore, find out about this Nobel prize winner and master storyteller.

4. The quincentennial of Columbus's 1492 voyage brought forth many points of view in 1992, raising questions of redefining cultural values and judging past historical events through contemporary awareness. In order to grapple with changing values and the effect of past events, compare two accounts of this legendary figure: *Columbus* (D'Aulaire & D'Aulaire, 1955) and *Encounter* (Yolen, 1992). There are many other accounts that offer different points of view as well.

5. Folklore from the subcontinent of India was virtually ignored in this chapter and deserves recognition. Similarly, Australian aboriginal stories are wonderful sources of folk wisdom and practice, as are Eskimo tales. Select a geographical area, find out authors' or adaptors' names that represent traditional literature from that area, read examples, and create your own bibliography.

Activities for the Primary Level

1. In primary grades children can write or tell stories based on pourquoi tales. Think of intriguing topics and have the children generate questions, such as: How did the triceratops get his horns? Why does snow fall from the sky? Who invented the first boat? Let imaginations have free rein.

2. Dramatizing folktales such as "The Three Billy Goats Gruff," "The Three Pigs," or "Goldilocks and the Three Bears" allows children to hear and speak predictable language patterns, to become a character and thus move out of an egocentric perspective and into an empathic one, and to experience the pattern of events that leads to an internalization of story structure. All these activities demonstrate the value of drama and movement, so organize some dramatic experiences for your children to enjoy.

3. For young children, finger plays, nursery rhymes, and chanting and singing games reinforce language and musical development. Find a source you like, such as *Sally Go Round the Sun: Three Hundred Children's Songs, Rhymes and Games* (Fowke, 1970). Although this particular source is out of print, it might be available in your library.

4. Trickster characters, fools or noodleheads, can be found in many folktales, thus providing listening, reading, and discussion possibilities for cross-cultural comparisons. A thematic unit on tricksters, culminating in skits with children dressed appropriately in costume, is entertaining and enlightening. A source for noodlehead stories and songs is *Diane Goode's Book of Silly Stories and Songs* (1992), which contains humorous tales and tunes.

5. If your children watch cartoons on television, have them record the name of a character, the kind of character she or he is (for example, greedy, bad, powerful, helpful, and so on), and a brief summary of the plot. Take the examples, and find some folklore that contains some of the same kinds of characters, actions, and so on. Traditional literature can enhance the experience, provide comparisons, and generally enrich this kind of viewing.

Activities for the Intermediate and Middle Levels

1. Have children bring stories from home, stories about their own heritage, or stories they've adapted from well-known ones. Collect stories from the community, and thus create your own folklore.

2. Children in middle grades enjoy myths, legends, fables, and tall tales, and can be encouraged to create their own, either in written or oral form. After hearing some examples, they will enjoy writing or dramatizing some original stories. Exaggeration, characterization, story structure, and other elements can be taught, using the children's own work and relating it to the examples.

3. When studying folktales from different parts of the world, use a world map on the bulletin board to pinpoint origins of stories. If your curriculum unit distinguishes the types of folktales and myths, you can color-code them, such as blue for pourquoi tales, red for creation myths, and so on.

4. Middle-level children can begin to develop a sensitivity to the depictions of minority cultures in books. It is possible, for example, to discuss how Native Americans have been portrayed as savages and worse. It is not hard to find caricatures, such as *The Indian in the Cupboard* (Banks, 1980), and discuss how that portrayal is racist and harmful. Children can begin to distinguish stereotypes and be alerted to future portrayals.

5. The example describing how Christopher Columbus has been viewed from several different points of view is an activity that middle-level children can learn from, as well. Several books and movies recount Columbus's life and times, his voyage, and his reception in the New World. Discussions of comparisons, dramatic skits, journal-keeping, and research are all activities that middle-level children can enjoy.

• • • • •
REFERENCES

Children's Works Cited

Aardema, V. (1975). *Why mosquitoes buzz in people's ears.* New York: Dial.

Aardema, V. (1979). *The riddle of the drum: A tale from Tizapan, Mexico.* New York: Four Winds.

Argueta, M. (1992). *Magic dogs of the volcanoes.* San Francisco: Children's Book Press.

Asbjornsen, P., & Moe, J. (1953). *East o' the sun and west o' the moon.* New York: Macmillan.

Bader, B. (Ed.). (1991). *Aesop & company.* Boston: Houghton Mifflin.

Banks, L. (1980). *The Indian in the cupboard.* New York: Doubleday.

Begay, S. (1992). *Ma'ii and Cousin Horned Toad: A traditional Navajo story.* New York: Scholastic.

Belting, N. (1992). *Moon was tired of walking on air.* Boston: Houghton Mifflin.

Brooke, W. (1992). *Untold tales.* New York: HarperCollins.

Bruchac, J., & London, J. (1992). *Thirteen moons on turtle's back.* New York: Philomel.

Bryan, A. (1980). *Beat the story drum, pum-pum.* New York: Atheneum.

Carlson, L., & Ventura, C. (Eds.). (1990). *Where angels glide at dawn: New stories from Latin America.* New York: HarperCollins.

Cole, J. (Comp.). (1982). *Best-loved folktales of the world.* New York: Doubleday.

Conger, D. (1987). *Many lands, many stories: Asian folktales for children.* Rutland, VT: Tuttle.

D'Aulaire, I., & D'Aulaire, E. (1955). *Columbus.* New York: Doubleday.

D'Aulaire, I., & D'Aulaire, E. (1962). *Book of Greek myths.* Garden City, NY: Doubleday.

Demi. (1987). *A Chinese zoo: Fables and proverbs.* New York: Harcourt.

De Paola, T. (1980). *The Lady of Guadalupe.* New York: Holiday House.

Esbensen, B. (Ed.). (1988). *The star maiden: An Ojibway tale.* Boston: Little, Brown.

Fowke, E. (1970). *Sally go round the sun: Three hundred children's songs, rhymes and games.* Garden City, NY: Doubleday.

Goble, P. (1990). *Iktomi and the ducks: A Plains Indian tale.* New York: Orchard Books Watts.

Goode, D. (1992). *Diane Goode's book of silly stories and songs.* New York: Dutton.

Hamilton, V. (1985). *The people could fly: American black folktales.* New York: Knopf.

Hamilton, V. (1988). *In the beginning: Creation stories from around the world.* New York: Harcourt Brace Jovanovich.

Highwater, J. (1977). *Anpao: An American Indian odyssey.* New York: Lippincott.

Hodges, M. (1984). *Saint George and the dragon.* Boston: Little, Brown.

Hooks, W. (1990). *The ballad of Belle Dorcas.* New York: Knopf.

Ishii, M. (Retold.) (1987). *The tongue-cut sparrow.* New York: Dutton.

Krull, K. (1992). *Gonna sing my head off.* New York: Knopf.

Lobel, A. (1980). *Fables.* New York: Harper & Row.

Louie, A. (1982). *Yeh-shen: A Cinderella story from China.* New York: Philomel.

Lurie, A. (Retold.) (1980). *Clever Gretchen and other forgotten tales.* New York: Crowell.

McDermott, G. (1976). *The stonecutter.* New York: Viking Penguin.

McDermott, G. (1993). *Raven: A trickster tale from the Pacific northwest.* New York: Harcourt.

Provensen, A., & Provensen, M. (1976). *The Mother Goose book.* New York: Random House.

Rohmer, H. (1992). *How we came to the fifth world.* San Francisco: Children's Book Press.

Scieszka, J. (1992). *The stinky cheese man and other fairly stupid tales.* New York: Viking.

Steptoe, J. (1985). *Mufaro's beautiful daughters: An African tale.* New York: Lothrop, Lee and Shepard.

Stevens, J. (1985). *The house that Jack built.* New York: Holiday House.

Stoddard, S. (1983). *The Doubleday illustrated children's Bible.* New York: Doubleday.

Thomas, G., & Crossley-Holland, K. (1985). *Tales from the maginogion.* Woodstock, NY: Overlook Press.

Wisniewski, D. (1992). *Sundiata, lion king of Mali.* New York: Clarion.

Yep, L. (1989). *The rainbow people.* New York: Harper.

Yolen, J. (Ed.). (1986). *Favorite folktales from around the world.* New York: Random House.

Yolen, J. (1992). *Encounter.* San Diego, CA: Harcourt Brace Jovanovich.

Professional Works Cited

Aoki, E. (1992). Turning the page: Asian Pacific American children's literature. In V. Harris (Ed.), *Teaching multicultural literature in grades K–8* (pp. 109–135). Norwood, MA: Christopher Gordon Pub.

Bettelheim, B. (1976). *The uses of enchantment.* New York: Knopf.

Bierhorst, J. (Ed.). (1976). *The red swan: Myths and tales of the American Indians.* New York: Farrar, Strauss, and Giroux.

Bishop, R. S. (1992). Multicultural literature for children: Making informed choices. In V. Harris (Ed.), *Teaching multicultural literature in grades K–8* (pp. 37–54). Norwood, MA: Christopher Gordon Pub.

Campbell, J. (1968). *Hero with a thousand faces* (2nd ed.). Princeton, NJ: Princeton University Press.

Chukovsky, K. (1971). *From two to five* (rev. ed.). Berkeley, CA: University of California Press.

Dundes, A. (Ed.). (1983). *Cinderella: A casebook.* New York: Wildman.

Faltis, C. (1993). *Joinfostering* (p. 7). New York: Merrill/Macmillan.

Haugaard, E. (1983). *Hans Christian Andersen: The complete fairy tales and stories.* (Trans.). Garden City, NY: Doubleday/Anchor Press.

Hearne, B. (1989). *Beauty and the beast.* Chicago: University of Chicago Press.

Jung, C. (Ed.). (1964). *Man and his symbols.* Garden City, NY: Doubleday.

Manheim, R. (1983). *Grimm's tales for young and old* (pp. 70–71). (Trans.). Garden City, NY: Doubleday/Anchor Press.

Matsuyama, U. (1983). Can story grammar speak Japanese? *The Reading Teacher, 36,* 666–669.

May, J. (1984). Walt Disney and the classics: The critics' opinions. In P. Dooley (Ed.), *The first steps: Best of the early CHLA Quarterly* (pp. 102–104). West Lafayette, IN: Children's Literature Association.

Norton, D. (1991). *Through the eyes of a child.* New York: Merrill/Macmillan.

Opie, I., & Opie, P. (Eds.). (1951). *Oxford dictionary of nursery rhymes* (pp. 3, 365). Oxford: Oxford University Press.

Propp, V. (1968). *Morphology of the folktale* (2nd ed.). Austin, TX: University of Texas Press.

Sayers, F. C. (1965). Walt Disney accused. *Hornbook. 40,* 602–611.

Tooze, R. (1959). *Storytelling.* Englewood Cliffs, NJ: Prentice Hall.

Wrenn, D. (1976). *Welsh history makers.* Yorkshire, England: EP Publishing.

Yokota, J. (1993). Issues in selecting multicultural children's literature. *Language Arts, 70,* 156–167.

Additional Resources

Bierhorst, J. (1988). *The mythology of South America.* New York: Morrow.
Part of the Gods and Heroes of the New World series, Bierhorst identifies geographical regions with common mythologies, analyzes tales, and provides commentary as to motif, characters, and language.

Butler, F. (1989). *Skipping around the world: The ritual nature of folk rhymes.* Hamden, CT: Shoestring Press.

This presents 350 rhymes from many countries, each with background as to local history and how it was acquired. Because the rhymes are grouped thematically, comparisons among countries are possible.

Children's Literature Association Quarterly (15). (1990).

This is a special issue devoted to Australian and Canadian children's literature. Among the articles are "Advocating Multiculturalism . . ." and "In Search of Sedna: Children's Versions of a Major Inuit Myth."

Ellis, S. (1990). News from the north. *Hornbook, 66,* 366–369.

Ellis examines three Canadian fairy tales and gives reasons for their success as literary works. "News from the North" appears frequently in Hornbook, which makes it a good continuing resource for Canadian children's literature; "News from Down Under" highlights Australian children's literature.

MacDonald, M. (1992). *Peace tales: World folktales to talk about.* Hamden, CT: Linnet/Shoestring Press.

A multicultural offering, this presents thirty-four tales with themes of conflict and peace, argument and community. Suggestions for class discussions are included.

Multimedia Catalog of Weston Woods. (1994). Weston, CT. 06880.

Audiovisual adaptations of children's literature are presented for sale, and there are many examples of traditional literature.

Opie, I., & Opie, P. (1974). *The classic fairy tales.* London: Oxford Univ. Press.

Twenty-four fairy tales are presented in their "original" language, with information about their entry into a literary context. This is an invaluable resource for anyone who researches traditional literature.

Swett, J. (1992). "Once there was and was not . . ." folktales: Old, alive, and thriving. In *The Children's Book Bag,* (4th ed.), Boston: Foundation for Children's Books.

Swett discusses and brings to our attention folktales from all over the world. The bibliography is an excellent resource.

Rethinking Columbus. (1991). A special edition of *Rethinking Schools,* a quarterly publication dedicated to informing the public about current educational issues. (Available from 1001 E. Keefe Avenue, Milwaukee, WI 53212).

The special issue was completed with the collaboration of NECA (Network of Educators on the Americas), and contains articles, poems, and lists of resources by Hispanic and Native American educators as well as others.

Tiedt, P., & Tiedt, I. (1990). *Multicultural teaching: A handbook of activities, information and resources* (3rd ed.). New York: Allyn and Bacon.

This clarifies definitions and supports the inclusion of multicultural literature in all phases of the curriculum. Many practical ideas for implementation are included.

Chapter Five

Pictures Tell a Story

• • • • •
INTRODUCTION AND RESPONSE

Color, line, shape, format, texture—all these elements create the artwork in modern children's picture books. Color or the lack of it, bold line or faint, large shapes or small—these are all chosen by illustrators and arranged in a format to bring a text to life on the pages of a book and in the mind of the reader. In this chapter these terms and more will be explored as they are exemplified in children's books.

In order to relate these terms to a picture book, think of Beatrix Potter's *The Tale of Peter Rabbit*, first published in London by Frederick Warne in 1902. Or better yet, get a copy and read it closely as you describe for yourself the elements mentioned above:

Color: What colors predominate? Is there a visual contrast in the colors? Why do you think Potter chose them?

Line: Are the characters outlined? Do the lines show movement? Is there a vertical or a horizontal dimension to the line?

Shape: Are the pictures the same shape or size? Does the shape of the characters change to fit the text?

Format: What effect does the small size have on you? Another feature of format is alternating print and picture. Does it work to tell the story effectively?

From *The Tale of Peter Rabbit,* by Beatrix Potter, by permission of Frederick Warne & Company, copyright © 1902, 1987.

Texture: How do the pictures convey smooth surfaces or
　　　　rough ones? How does Potter achieve these realistic,
　　　　natural woodland scenes? How do the pictures lead
　　　　you into the scene, giving depth to the page?

Two fundamental aspects of artwork remain to be explored: **media** and **style.**
Types of **media** include paints (watercolor and oil-based), chalk, charcoal, woodcuts and linoleum block prints, collage and montage, photographs, and anything
else an artist uses to make the picture. **Style** refers to the combination of everything mentioned to this point. It is the total effect of color, line, media, and every
choice an artist makes as she or he creates the final book. Terms for style can
come from the art world, such as *impressionistic, surreal, expressionistic,* and
cartoon. Style can be described more informally as whimsical, delicate, vigorous,
or decorative.

To conclude our analysis of Beatrix Potter's classic picture book, what medium
is used to capture Peter's hair-raising adventure? And finally, how would you
describe Beatrix Potter's well-known style?

Keep these terms in mind as you read this chapter on children's picture
books. We'll discuss more about them and show examples through notable books.
The goal of the chapter is to show the great variety and charm of picture books,

to increase understanding of some of the more technical aspects of the artwork, and to bring an evaluative criteria forward when we select picture books for schools, home, and libraries. Attention is focused on the artwork first, because it is the art that makes picture books unique in the field of literature for children and adults. By acquiring an "artistic vocabulary," and by understanding how picture books developed, you will be better able to evaluate books and make decisions as to their worth and acceptability.

• • • • •

HISTORY OF THE PICTURE BOOK

Picture books are a fairly recent phenomenon in the literary tradition. Although Bishop Comenius brought out *Orbis Pictus* in 1658, until the late 1800s the illustrated book was the usual kind of book for children. Illustrations in books were either done singularly by hand (each picture or design was laboriously copied in each book) or, when books were printed on the early printing presses, by woodcuts.

Wood block illustrations (as in *Orbis Pictus*) were cheap and easily done. The artist drew a picture on a block of wood and then cut away everything that should not print. "The woodcut enabled many copies to be produced from the same block and . . . was a process particularly suited for combination with printing, since in each case an impression on a sheet of paper was produced from a raised surface" (Whalley, 1975, p. 22).

Another method, which was the opposite of raising the surface, was the **engraved plate**. In this method, the engraver drew the design on a metal plate (copper was used at first) and ink was forced into the design. Printing sheets passed over the plates would retain the inked design. This process was more expensive because of the metal plates, and required more artistry from the engraver. Also, because the surface to be printed was below the sheet of paper instead of above (as in wood block printing) this method took longer and was thus more costly. However, the engraving (or **intaglio** process, as it is sometimes called) allowed for finer details to be included and was popular in the 1800s.

The third and last process that preceded modern printing of pictures was called **lithography**. Actually, this process is still used in modern printing, but with different materials. In this method, based on the antipathy of oil and water, an oil-based chalk or paint was used to draw pictures on a limestone plate, which was then soaked in water. "After ink was passed over the stone, it would only adhere where the chalk had marked the stone, and when a sheet of paper was placed under heavy pressure . . . the original design would print off" (Whalley, 1975, p. 23). Although it was cumbersome, this technique paved the way for future developments in printing and had the most important effect on the illustrations of children's books in the late nineteenth century (Meyer, 1983).

The industrial revolution of the nineteenth century spurred the invention of technology related to printing and reproducing illustrations. A pioneer in this field, Edmund Evans, can be credited with charting the course of modern book illustration because of his work in the late 1800s. He was an illustrator, an engraver, a printer, and a businessman, but his true genius seemed to be the recognition of artistic ability in others. His expertise allowed the artist's vision to remain true in the mass production of book after book. Evans developed a full-color printing process, providing illustrators with the technology to realize images in a more consistent fashion. His artistry graces some early stories, but he was instrumental in encouraging and marketing the work of Walter Crane, Randolph Caldecott, and Kate Greenaway, the triumvirate of the best in early children's book artistry, who set standards for twentieth-century work.

Arguably the most famous of the three is Randolph Caldecott, since the award for the most distinguished picture book published in the United States each year bears his name. The American Library Association awards this medal, and the list of honored books can be found in Appendix A. (The United Kingdom awards the Kate Greenaway medal yearly.)

Caldecott was born in 1846 and died just thirty-nine years later. His art was humorous and whimsical, with rural scenes full of color and robust characters. The medal that bears his name depicts a man on horseback tearing through the countryside, and comes from a story entitled "John Gilpin's Ride" (Caldecott, 1977). Some of his illustrated stories have the distinction of having been continuously in print for over one hundred years. He worked for a bank and sketched, then ill health forced him to retire. He died in the United States and is buried in

From *Randolph Caldecott's Favorite Nursery Rhymes,* copyright © 1980. By permission of F. S. Oppel, Castle Book Sales.

Hey, diddle, diddle,
The Cat and the Fiddle,

23

St. Augustine, Florida. Maurice Sendak, a preeminent figure in children's literature, says of Caldecott's work:

> When I came to picture books, it was Randolph Caldecott who really put me where I wanted to be. Caldecott is an illustrator, he is a songwriter, he is a choreographer, he is a stage manager, he is a decorator, he is a theater person; he's superb, simply. He can take four lines of print that have very little meaning in themselves and stretch them into a book that has tremendous meaning—not overloaded, no sentimentality in it (Billington, 1978, pp. 13–14).

Walter Crane flourished in early picture-book illustration and influenced many later artists. He was born in 1845, a year before Caldecott, and was the son of an artist. Because he thought children liked definite statements in design, his work is characterized by well-defined forms, many profiles, and flat, bright colors (Crane, 1981). There are often elaborate interior settings, with a Greco-Roman look to them.

Kate Greenaway, also born in 1846, usually depicted many children in delicate settings of a rural, idyllic countryside. The children were serious but playful, and dressed in "old-fashioned" costumes. "Hers is a world of childhood where children walk decorously hand in hand, as well as taunt and tease, dance and cry" (Greenaway, 1988, p. 11).

These three artists worked in watercolor, paints, and ink (Caldecott preferred brown), and Evans's engraving and printing allowed the subtle differences of color and brushwork to initiate a new standard of book illustration.

Certainly other outstanding artists of the late 1880s and the 1900s pushed the boundaries of art and language, creating superb picture books. Beatrix Potter comes to mind as a foremost contributor to picture-book artistry. She left her unmistakable print on the children's book world with exquisitely detailed, pastel-tinted woodland animals. Arthur Rackham, Kay Neilson, and, in this century, John Tenniel, N. C. Wyeth, and many others deserve recognition for their unstinting efforts to bring the best to children and youth. Perhaps your favorite has not been mentioned, but in the "Implications for Instruction" you will have the opportunity to find out more about an artist you admire.

By the early 1900s, "Edmund Evans and the great picture book artists—Crane, Caldecott, Greenaway—had accomplished their revolution; and Beatrix Potter had already done all her best work" (Townsend, 1987, p. 140).

England and the European continent continued to produce the best in children's book illustration until the chaos of the First World War devastated industry and art (Bader, 1976). After that time, American assertiveness and expertise as exemplified by the work of Ingri and Edgar D'Aulaire (*Ola,* 1932, and *George Washington,* 1936), Ludwig Bemelmans (*Hansi,* 1934, and *Madeline,* 1939), Marjorie Flack (*Angus and the Ducks,* 1930, and *The Story About Ping,* 1933), and Robert McCloskey (*Make Way for Ducklings,* 1940) shifted preeminence in picture-book artistry to the United States. So many exceptional books continued to be produced that the American Library Association initiated the Caldecott Award in 1938, thus ensuring a legitimate place in literature for the picture book.

From Kate Greenaway's *Old Nursery Rhymes,* unpublished notebook of drawings and watercolors copyright © 1988 by H. Abrams. By permission of the Arents Collections, the New York Library, Astor, Lenox and Tilden Foundations.

In the period between world wars, sometimes called the second golden age of children's literature because of the output of outstanding books and the public's appetite for good reading, American children's book publishing thrived. And, following the cataclysmic upheaval of the forties, the book industry again recovered after the war to lead the world in picture-book production (Bader, 1976). Sadly, there are too many innovative and distinguished books to list here, but it is worthwhile to start with the Caldecott books listed in the Appendix and learn to recognize the many styles those illustrators and authors represent. By becoming acquainted with your favorites, and gradually adding more and more, you will gain an overview of the field to the present time.

One last note before this section on the history of picture books closes, and that is to acknowledge the contribution of Maurice Sendak to contemporary artistry. Winner of perhaps more prestigious awards in children's literature than anyone else, he set the standard by which others judge themselves. For the last three decades, his body of work (over eighty books, set designs for opera, and collaboration on television programs and movies) has explored the meaning of modern childhood. He has become, as he himself said of Caldecott, a songwriter, a choreographer, a stage manager, and simply superb. Always empathetic to the inner child, he is probably best known for his trilogy beginning with *Where the Wild Things Are* (Sendak, 1963), continuing through *In the Night Kitchen* (1970), and culminating with the impressive and enigmatic *Outside Over There* (1981). John Rowe Townsend, critic and writer, says, "He is not merely a master but the one and only grandmaster of the picture book" (Townsend, 1992, p. 306). Continuing in this tradition is his recent book, *We Are All in the Dumps with Jack and Guy* (1993).

DEFINITION AND RATIONALE

Picture books use art and words to tell a story or describe an idea in relatively few pages. Pictures either dominate the text or achieve a balance with it (Sutherland & Hearne, 1984). Sometimes considered the most characteristic form of children's literature, until recently the picture-book format has been almost exclusively associated with young children.

Picture books are frequently a child's first contact with a wider world. Listening and watching an adult read a picture book aloud is the first vicarious journey a young child takes, as the experience introduces abstractions through art and language. Aesthetic values are being formed at this early age (Cianciolo, 1976). This precise combination of art and words is a powerful experience, because it triggers the imagination and introduces concepts for cognitive and language development. Pictures initiate early attempts to acquire visual literacy, so important in a society where some argue that visual transmitters have become the most pervasive bearers of ideas and information (Schwarcz and Schwarcz, 1991). Clearly, the importance of introducing picture books to infants and young children cannot be overstated because of the intellectual and emotional growth they foster.

In this text, the terms *artist* and *illustrator* are synonymous. There is no differentiation between the artwork for a picture book and artwork that sells in the most prestigious gallery. It is unfortunate that illustration is sometimes seen as a smaller expression of artistic talent, when in fact it takes as much, if not more, talent to create the interplay between text and media. The difference between art and illustration is one of philosophy, not of talent or production.

EVALUATION AND METHODOLOGY

It is not easy to evaluate picture books, because evaluation as a process is often subjective and personal. Both art and literature evoke idiosyncratic responses, and when they are combined in one work, the task is doubly hard. It helps to establish criteria, or at least guidelines, as to what is considered "good" or "beautiful." We who are interested in providing the best for children can agree on criteria, even though we may not agree how specific books fit those criteria. Developing the expertise to discriminate comes from practice in applying criteria and from repeated exposure to what has been considered the best (Cianciolo, 1990).

The following evaluation scheme is based on criteria that ask for a personal response, then guide your questioning as to the appropriateness of the text and artwork to your intended audience and purpose (see Figure 5.1).

Perhaps there are other aspects of evaluation rising from your own expertise and purpose. Generate some questions that you think are important and add them to the table, if you wish.

Here is a suggested methodology to follow when determining whether or not you will want to use or purchase a book:

1. Read the book twice, first only looking at the pictures, and then only reading the text. When looking at the pictures, see if the story is "told" well, if the details are accurate, and if the artistic choices are pleasing to you. Then concentrate on the story, on the logical plot and character development, and on the inventiveness of the words and ideas. Does this appeal to you? (When you try this, you may want to read first, and then study the artwork. See which order works best for you.)

2. Think about the effectiveness of the art and the text together. You may want to read the book again, critiquing the integration of text and art. Does each complement the other? The delicate balance between art and language should be achieved with colors, lines, format, texture, shape, media, and style working together in a synchronous whole.

Components	Matching Book to Audience	Matching Book to Purpose
TEXT (What is my personal response?)	Is the theme worthwhile? Is the language suitable (vocabulary, concept density, playful use of words)? Will the plot appeal?	Does this text fulfill my teaching objectives? Does this subject match my curriculum?
ART (What is my personal response)?	Is the artwork original? Unique? Skillful? Are the pictures clear? Does the artwork avoid stereotypes?	Will the artwork please my audience? Does the art convey a story?
COMBINING ART AND TEXT	Are the details in the art matched in the text? Do the language and art complement each other in mood, tone, and style? Does the art balance or extend the text?	Does this book present something unique? Is this a personal gift for a child? Will this book entertain and instruct my children?

Figure 5.1   Evaluating Picture Books

From *Drummer Hoff.* Adapted by Barbara Emberley, illustrated by Ed Emberley © 1967. Used by permission of the publisher, Simon and Schuster Books for Young Readers, New York.

• • • • •
RECOGNIZING MEDIA AND STYLE

A great variety of media (artistic tools or processes used to create pictures) and styles (descriptions of artwork) is found in children's picture books today. Media such as those listed below, with examples drawn from well-known picture books, are used by talented illustrators to create unforgettable scenes.

Type of Media	Example	Illustrator
Woodcuts, block prints	*Drummer Hoff*	Ed Emberley
Collage/montage	*The Snowy Day*	Ezra Jack Keats
Watercolor, gouache, and poster paints	*Miss Rumphius*	Barbara Cooney
Line drawings	*The Silver Pony*	Lynd Ward
Photographs and various combinations of the above.	*Look Up, Look Down*	Tana Hoban

If media is the process, then style is the product. What is the result of all the choices an illustrator makes? The overall effect of the work can be described in artistic styles as mentioned previously: impressionistic, surreal, and so forth (see Glossary for definitions). Following are some examples of noticeable styles; the subgenres described in the next few pages also describe artwork in terms of style.

Style	Example	Illustrator
impressionism	*Lon Po Po*	Ed Young
cubism	*Mother Goose*	Brian Wildsmith
expressionism	*Song and Dance Man*	Stephen Gammell
surrealistic	*Gorilla*	Anthony Browne

In picture books art styles range from the very realistic, even photographic, to abstraction. Usually an artist becomes well known for a certain style, employing similar media, and her/his books are easily recognizable. Tana Hoban photographing in black and white and color, Ezra Jack Keats assembling collages, and Lynd Ward drawing superbly are distinctive in that regard.

Barbara Cooney, on the other hand, experiments with many styles and media. She has used pen and ink, pen and ink with wash, collage, watercolors, acrylics, scratchboard, and lithographs. For *Miss Rumphius* (Cooney, 1982) the art is realistic, yet "naive" in the style of early American art and color, which is in keeping with the subject of the story. Fine line drawings and acrylics cast a nostalgic look at a bygone time.

Because it is a Chinese folktale, Ed Young's impressionistic *Lon Po Po* (Young, 1989), done in full-color pastels and watercolor, uses panels to suggest an Eastern influence. Impressionism plays with light and shadow, and, with the contrast between the black wolf and the colorful children, light is used dramatically to extend the meaning of the story.

Brian Wildsmith's geometric abstract forms show a cubist influence in his *Mother Goose* (Wildsmith, 1964). Patterns of squares and diamonds in rich dark colors permeate every picture. The "modern" look of the cubism contrasts with the traditional Mother Goose rhymes, and we see them in a new way.

In *Song and Dance Man* (Ackerman, 1988) illustrator Stephen Gammell uses a colored pencil to draw stylized, exuberantly expressive characters, particularly the main character, Grandfather. Warm feelings, generated by warm colors, depict an upbeat mood.

Surrealism in *Gorilla* (Browne, 1983), a Kate Greenaway award winner, is evident in the composition of strange objects in the rooms of Hannah's house. The young girl loves gorillas, so a gorilla motif is everywhere—in pictures, in toys, on

From *Miss Rumphius* by Barbara Cooney. Copyright © 1982 by Barbara Cooney Porter. Used by permission of Viking Penguin, a division of Penguin Books USA, Inc.

walls. A disturbing isolationism permeates the story, as Hannah and her father are psychologically distant. Scenes of the "father" gorilla and Hannah dancing, flying through the trees, and enjoying the other gorillas at the zoo underscore the surreal mood of the story.

Black and White (Macaulay, 1990) combines four separate stories, or maybe just one, between its covers. Macaulay's style is different for each of the four quadrants of a double-page spread in this oversize book—one is impressionistic, one representational, one cartoonlike, and the last has a style all its own. Winner of the Caldecott Medal in 1991, this book proved that the picture-book format can be full of surprises!

With so many books available, why were these selected? Many are award winners, and all the artists have a body of work that exemplifies some of the best in children's picture books. Not only do they elicit critical acclaim from adult reviewers, but they also intrigue and delight children who know them. Each book takes children and childhood seriously; there is no patronizing or condescension. Moreover, these books are readily accessible, and most have been reprinted in paperback. No attempt was made to find the newest, most recently published picture books; rather, several decades are represented in the final selection so that a broader scope of commendatory artwork was demonstrated. Some of the books are mentioned again in the following section, allowing for a more in-depth look at them.

● ● ● ● ●
SUBGENRES OF PICTURE BOOKS

For the sake of bringing some order to this genre, certain subgenres can be identified (see discussions of genre classification in Chapter 3). With the identification and delineation of subgenres, evaluative criteria can be more easily applied.

Picture books could be divided simply into fiction and nonfiction, or separated by the artistic media mentioned previously. In the following descriptions, picture books are classified according to content, except for the "wordless" category, which is a format and labeled accordingly (see Figure 5.2). Basically, the picture-book genre is separated into nine subgenres; particular characteristics of each subgenre can be studied. Figure 5.2 shows the nine subgenres and a brief definition and example for each. Then, curricular value and description of artwork for the example are given. These examples should provide models for you to use when classifying a book and determining its usefulness for your purpose.

A B C (Alphabet) Books

Curriculum value: These books teach the concepts of naming, alphabet recognition (visual discrimination), the sound of the initial consonant or vowel, and alphabetical order. These skills form a necessary part of the foundation for reading success.

Subgenre	Definition	Example
ABC (Alphabet Books)	Books that present alphabetical order among objects linked by a unifying theme or idea.	*A Peaceable Kingdom*, by Alice and Martin Provensen
1-2-3 (Counting Books)	Books that present numerical order, sometimes with cardinal and ordinal numbers.	*Anno's Counting Book*, by Mitsumasa Anno
Mother Goose, Nursery Rhymes, and Poetry	Books that present the traditional rhymes as well as modern versions of short, pithy stories that rhyme.	*Mother Goose*, by Brian Wildsmith
Concept Books	Books that define a single thing or idea.	*Light*, by Donald Crews
Traditional or Folk Literature	Although this is an entire genre (see Chapter 4) it is included here because folktales and fairy tales are so often depicted in picture-book form.	*Lon-Po-Po: A Red-Riding Hood Story from China*, by Ed Young
Wordless (Pure) Picture Books	Books that contain little or no print, relying on pictures to tell the story.	*The Silver Pony*, by Lynd Ward
Realistic and fanciful stories (fictional stories, also referred to as picture storybooks)	These are short stories (usually 32 pages) that are about common realistic occurrences or fantasies in children's lives. They may rhyme, but usually do not.	Realistic: *The Snowy Day*, by Ezra Jack Keats Fanciful: *Where the Wild Things Are*, by Maurice Sendak
Nonfiction: Information and Biography	Books that recount facts in an interesting way. This is a genre also (see Chapter 9) but because nonfiction is found in the picture-book format, it is included here.	*Sharks*, by Gail Gibbons
Illustrated Book ("easy reader")	This is a book in which the text becomes more important than the pictures. The artwork accompanies the words, and does not stand by itself.	*Frog and Toad Are Friends*, by Arnold Lobel

Figure 5.2   Subgenres of Picture Books

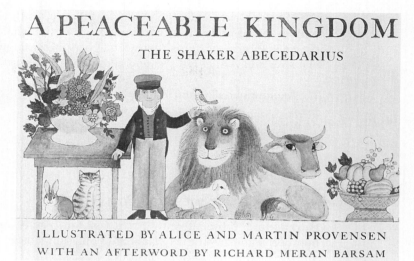

Description of artwork: Done in a naive, simplistic style to fit the text; earth-toned colors are muted and the pages have an antique look in *The Peaceable Kingdom* (Provensen & Provensen, 1978). The Provensens faithfully and accurately capture the whimsy and mood of this folk culture of New England through drawing and painting. The pages are never cluttered, but ordered and busy, like the Shaker life they represent. From alligator to zebra, this illustrated alphabet rhyme comes from a Shaker Manifesto in 1882, and helped to teach children the alphabet with real and imaginary creatures.

Recommended alphabet books

A Northern Alphabet, Ted Harrison (1982)

Chicka Chicka Boom Boom, Bill Martin, Jr., and John Archambault (1989)

Ashanti to Zulu: African Traditions, Margaret Musgrove (1976)

1 2 3 (Counting, or Number) Books

Curriculum value: These books teach and reinforce numeral recognition (often with ordinal and cardinal numbers), the concept of number and quantity, and numerical order.

Description of artwork: Almost wordless, *Anno's Counting Book* (Anno, 1975) uses a **double-page spread** to illustrate numbers from 0 through 12. The landscape changes from a winter white (presumably January) through the succeeding seasons. Each double spread has a numeral on the right and a stack of blocks on the left, with the landscape gradually filling up with the number of things represented by the numeral. Colors range across the whole spectrum, highlighted by the background, which is first white, then increasingly colorful. The curving line of a river adds visual interest and allows the eye to move over the page.

Recommended counting books

Ten, Nine, Eight, Molly Bang (1983)

Numbers of Things, Helen Oxenbury (1968)

Waving, Peter Sis (1988)

Mother Goose, Nursery Rhymes, and Poetry

Curriculum value: Rhyming teaches auditory discrimination (the difference between sounds, such as "Hubbard" and "cupboard"), vocabulary development, and the beginning concept of story.

Description of artwork: Vivid, geometric, sometimes cubist in design. *Brian Wildsmith's Mother Goose* (Wildsmith, 1964) is a riot of familiar rhymes, one to a page. The rather dark jewel-toned pictures contrast with a plain white back-

From *Brian Wildsmith's Mother Goose,* copyright © 1964. Used by permission of the publisher, Franklin Watts, New York.

Ride a cock-horse to Banbury Cross,
To see a fine lady upon a white horse;
With rings on her fingers and bells on her toes,
She shall have music wherever she goes.

8

ground, so that the reader's eye is focused on the essential character and action. An index of first lines helps locate favorites.

Recommended nursery rhymes: (For poetry, see Chapter 6.)

The Mother Goose Treasury, Raymond Briggs (1966)

Mother Goose, Tomie dePaola (1985)

I Saw Esau, Iona and Peter Opie (1992)

Concept Books

Curriculum value: These books are important for very young children because they help to develop concepts. They provide words so that children can label and describe, teaching "what is. . ." and also what is not.

Description of artwork: In *Light,* Crews uses double-page spreads, very few words, dark backgrounds, and landscapes of city and country to illuminate the concept of light (Crews, 1981). Motion is conveyed through **line**—the line of the flood-lights, the line of the lightning zigzagging across the page. A dramatic book, with pleasing symmetry to the pictures, it would be a good bedtime book for a toddler.

Recommended concept books

Of Colors and Things, Tana Hoban (1989)

All Shapes and Sizes, Shirley Hughes (1986)

Boats, Anne Rockwell (1982)

These first four subgenres are appropriate for the youngest child, the infant, to hear and see; books such as those listed are adaptable to the shortest attention span, because there is little story line. Most often a group of separate entities form some pattern—alphabetical, numerical, or topical. The important lesson is that oral language, the language the infant hears, can be represented visually and consistently. Infants and toddlers learn very early what certain books are about; their "reading" begins with the recognition that there is a connection between oral and written language. Pictures help to anchor the more fleeting, ephemeral spoken language.

Traditional, or Folk, Literature

Curriculum value: These stories define literature for young listeners and readers. The beginning of story, with character, plot, setting, and story structure, comes from our foundation of traditional literature. The stories present archetypes, values, lessons, metaphors, and characters to emulate or despise.

Description of artwork: Dark colors for the wolf, contrasted with reds and blues for the girls' clothes, heightens the tensions and lends an impressionistic aura to

Lon Po Po (Young, 1989), the familiar story of cunning and deception. The stark white of the children's wide-eyed innocence catches the reader's eye and provides continuity from page to page. In one double spread, the silhouette literally jumps off the page. Motion is conveyed through the smudged outline of the shadow.

Recommended folk literature: see Chapter 4.

Wordless Picture Books

Curriculum value: While some teachers see these as appropriate for the youngest children, others do not. A reader has to know quite a lot about language in order to articulate the story the pictures represent. Wordless picture books are important for vocabulary development and to reinforce story grammar, or sense of story, that children internalize. Many written and oral language activities can spring from wordless books. Using wordless books with remedial readers is important, because they seem less threatening to troubled readers.

Description of artwork: Black and white, with all the grays in between, the pictures in *The Silver Pony* tell the dream-story of a young boy who wishes desperately for a pony (Ward, 1973). The farm is richly detailed on each page, as is each locale the boy and the magical pony visit. The characters are drawn with elegant

From *The Silver Pony,* by Lynd Ward, copyright © 1973. Used by permission of the publisher, Houghton Mifflin Company.

body language, and show grief, humor, fear, and surprise. The charcoal drawings are magnificent.

Recommended wordless books

School, Emily McCully (1987)

Junglewalk, Nancy Tafuri (1988)

Tuesday, David Wiesner (1991)

Realistic and Fanciful Stories

Curriculum value: Children like to listen to stories about children like themselves, or to have their imaginations charged with fantasies. Talking animals, absurd events, or circumstances just as real as life open up our minds, give us words to cope with emotions, and allow us to see possibilities.

Description of the artwork in the realistic example: *The Snowy Day* (Keats, 1962) is a collage of different colors and prints depicting a young boy's neighborhood outing in the snow. Peter is an African American, one of the first to be pictured prominently in an American picture book. Each page is uncluttered, with colorful cutouts of Peter's form (usually in a snowsuit) and the background only suggested. Pink and blue snowflakes dot the **endpapers**, providing a perfect frame for the story.

Description of artwork in the fantasy: *Where the Wild Things Are* (Sendak, 1963) is a dream fantasy of a little boy, Max, who was sent to his room to cool down after some aggressive play. His "wild suit" foreshadows things to come. As the fantasy takes over, the pictures become larger, until they are double spreads. Sendak uses dark greens and blues with black outline and **cross-hatching** to give texture to the pictures and to create a junglelike setting for the wild things. Although the wild things are fearsome, they are tamed by Max, and the climax of the story is a series of three double-page spreads showing a "wild rumpus." Endpapers are covered with yellow, red, blue, and purple flowers that might have come from a jungle, and they are made darker and more striking with cross-hatching.

Because there are so many recommended realistic and fanciful stories, there is no short list here. You may be guided by the Caldecott list in the Appendix to continue your discovery of this subgenre. You might also consider the work of Leo Lionni, Rosemary Wells, William Steig, Chris Van Allsburg, and other author/illustrators listed in this chapter and in Chapters 4, 7, 8, and 9.

Nonfiction: Information and Biography

Curriculum value: These books allow readers to delve into subjects of special interest, imparting knowledge and encouraging concept and vocabulary development.

Description of artwork: In *Sharks,* Gail Gibbons uses her characteristic format to impart information about shark history, shark anatomy, and the role of sharks in ocean life (Gibbons, 1992). In clear line drawings against shades of blue and green water, sharks are pictured from many angles swimming naturally. Most drawings are labeled, and a line at the bottom of each page has an unpredictable pattern of indentation (a shark's tooth?). Some splashes of warmer colors depicting plants occasionally contrast with the cooler colors of the ocean.

Recommended nonfiction

See Chapter 9, since several of the biographies and informational books listed are picture books.

Illustrated Books (Easy Readers)

Curriculum value: These books provide picture clues for the beginning reader but encourage him or her to concentrate on the words. Thus, decoding skills, such as recognizing sight words, and applying phonic and structural strategies to figure out new words, are practiced.

Description of artwork: In *Frog and Toad Are Friends,* Lobel uses soft greens and browns with a watercolor wash to create stories about these two creatures (Lobel, 1970). The pages are uncluttered, with lots of white space between pictures and words, so that the new reader is not overwhelmed. These talking amphibians share many characteristics with humans in their artistic depictions. (See also Chapter 8.)

Recommended books considered to be easy readers
Leo, Zach, and Emmie, Amy Ehrlich (1981)

A Baby Sister for Frances, Russell Hoban (1964)

• • • • •
THEMES AND CHARACTERS IN PICTURE BOOKS

Certain themes seem to dominate picture books, at least the realistic fiction and fanciful ones. Because the main character is often a small child or an animal, a theme of "small figure becoming powerful or maintaining power over bigger, adult-like characters" is evident. Max, in *Where the Wild Things Are,* is a prime example.

In many modern stories, themes center on emotion—love, sadness, jealousy, fear, friendship, and so on. There are also themes that highlight lessons to learn, such as becoming independent, becoming skillful, building self-esteem, developing empathy, adjusting to change, and meeting new friends. In a trend suggested by Patricia Cianciolo, a noted teacher and critic of children's literature, antiwar themes are becoming more prevalent in picture books for older children (Cianciolo, 1990).

Kinds of characters often depicted in picture books include people disguised as animals, talking animals with human speech and emotions, personified objects, and humans in realistic situations (Norton, 1991).

There are no books mentioned that exemplify themes and characters mentioned above. The omissions are purposeful, so that you test these statements against your developing knowledge of picture books. Select a theme and find a picture book that exemplifies it, or select some picture books and analyze themes and characters to see if the generalizations are accurate.

● ● ● ● ●
CONTEMPORARY TRENDS

Picture books in the nineties continue to be shaped by the forces that have always affected literature and life. Economics of publishing, new technologies, and changing societal values all affect in some way books for children. In this section, recent developments in picture books are mentioned: increasing diversity in subject matter, electronic artistry, internationalism and literacy efforts around the globe, and a marked emphasis in using picture books with older readers.

Trends that began in the 1960s, that decade of turbulent change, continue to evolve and find expression in recent books. Subjects previously considered taboo or inappropriate for young children, such as sexual or physical abuse (*No-No the Little Seal,* Patterson, 1986); homophobia, as in *Daddy's Roommate* (Wilhoite, 1990); AIDS education (*What's a Virus Anyway?* Fassler and McQueen, 1990); and other topics are available. Because of the sensitivity of the topics and the vulnerability of some children, the adult who reviews books and recommends or buys them has a responsibility to think carefully about the match between book and reader.

Writing about the use of computer technology in creating art, former *Horn Book* editor and well-respected critic of children's literature Ethel Heins said that "Book illustrators have been liberated by the sheer wizardry of modern printing technology . . . yet many books . . . were technically brilliant, but empty, vessels" (Kingman, 1986, p. 325). It seems that in too many books, illustrations can now overwhelm the text, rather than achieving the delicate balance with it.

Trends in the publishing industry are driven by economics, and when the economy shrinks, a more conservative approach toward bookmaking occurs. Books go out of print sooner, because publishing houses cannot afford to maintain large inventories. Fewer copies of new books are printed and fewer risks are taken. More traditional tales are redone, and sometimes older classics are reissued, often with new illustrations. For example, in a recent *Children's Books in Print* (1991–1992), nine artists were listed for Beatrix Potter's story of Peter Rabbit.

Ironically, with a conservative market, book sales are enjoying a brisk pace, especially for very young children (infants to age three) and picture books for older children (Cianciolo, 1990). A noticeable increase in "toy" books, including board books, pop-up books, cloth and plastic books, and other activity books, has also occurred.

Internationalism in book publishing creates a wider market for children's books and draws attention to the need for books in third world countries. Accompanying the literacy efforts around the world are demands for stories that reflect diverse, multicultural perspectives. Picture books and easy readers fill a niche for beginning readers and also support social concerns such as stronger families, improved health conditions, and better economic opportunities for people in underdeveloped countries.

Picture Books for Older Readers

Picture books are no longer simply in the domain of young children. Teachers in fifth, sixth, and higher grades are using picture books when subject matter and style are appropriate for their students and curriculum. For educational and aesthetic purposes, picture books provide opportunities to study layout and design techniques, as well as artistic and symbolic language. Visual literacy, certainly a necessary component to intelligent television viewing, may be developed through picture books as well as other media. Clearly an enhancement to all facets of the curriculum, picture books are welcomed increasingly by upper-level teachers. Moreover, the readability levels of some picture books is suitable for middle-school readers (i.e., sixth, seventh, and eighth grades) because the books are not meant to be read *by* young children, but read *to* them.

● ● ● ● ●
SUMMARY

It has been said that picture books are a twentieth-century phenomenon. We have seen how Edmund Evans, Randolph Caldecott, and others set the stage for this rapid burst of expression in the late nineteenth century, and how American creativity has carried the genre forward with great virtuosity since. As we prepare for the twenty-first century, we see an increasing number of picture books available for a wider age range, continually diverse subject matter, and artistic invention through technical wizardry.

This chapter presented picture books in a variety of media and styles, standards for evaluating them, and an artistic vocabulary with which to describe them. Curriculum value related to each subgenre was presented so that a rationale for school use could be readily employed.

Because of the brevity of this chapter, scores of important books, authors, and artists were omitted. The joy and responsibility now lies with you to discover the rich treasury of picture books. You can now display your ability to discriminate between the great and the near-great, the tawdry and the truly rich expressions of visual storying.

● ● ● ● ●
IMPLICATIONS FOR INSTRUCTION

Throughout this chapter, the use of picture books in primary and middle-school classrooms has been encouraged. In this section, implications and suggestions are described more specifically. First, questions under the heading Reflections will allow you to consider the concerns and controversies in the field; next, projects and activities for you and your students are outlined.

Reflections

1. Are children seeing enough representations of their own cultural characteristics and people in picture books today?

2. Controversy is no stranger to picture books. Books such as *Little Black Sambo* (Bannerman, 1899, and see also 1920), *Jake and Honeybunch Go to Heaven* (Zemach, 1982), and *Five Chinese Brothers* (Bishop, 1938) have come under attack for portraying ugly racial stereotypes. What is your response to these books and the controversies they represent?

3. Several educators contend that picture books can and should be used in middle levels and, in fact, in all levels of education. Is there a stigma that keeps picture books relegated to lower levels of education?

4. Is there a relationship between picture books and television? If there is, can you use that connection to promote literacy? How would you do that?

5. How would you describe trends in modern picture book publishing today? What are characteristics of the recent Caldecott award books, for example, and what does that tell us about future directions? Is there too much technical wizardry? Do pictures overpower language?

Projects

1. Describe the artwork and evaluate a number (five, for example) of picture books of your own choosing. Follow the criteria and methodology suggested on page 90, and then prioritize your list from best to worst. For more practice, have a friend evaluate the same five books and compare differences in your final lists.

2. Create some bibliographies appropriate for your own use. Go to libraries or bookstores, or consult *Children's Books in Print* and compile lists of alphabet books, counting books, wordless books, or whatever you need.

3. Select an artist whose work especially appeals to you and create an annotated bibliography of his or her work. Find out what makes the artist's work so appealing to you.

4. Write/make a picture book. Design the format, including cover and endpapers, dustjacket, size of print, pictures, and so forth. Implement your decisions as to color, line, shape, and style, and evaluate the final product.

5. Plan a program for your local library, school, or child-care center for which you select and use picture books. Would you plan something seasonal or celebrate a cultural holiday? What books would you use and why? Who is your audience, and what would you hope to accomplish?

Activities for the Primary Level

1. After reading several alphabet books to a group of children, create with them an alphabet book about their lives and neighborhood. After listing "A" events/things, and "B," and so on, the language will be so inventive and rhythmic it may even rhyme. Children can work independently or in groups to create a class "big" book and design the artwork as well.

2. Eric Carle is a popular artist for young children because of his distinctive formats, color, and texture. After you present several of his books (such as *The Very Hungry Caterpillar,* 1968), encourage children to re-create his style in their own artwork. Plan an "Eric Carle Day" to celebrate his and the children's artistry in picture books. (Another artist could be substituted; you might want to select the children's favorite or your own).

3. Establish "book buddies" by pairing younger children with middle-level children and providing time and selection methods for younger children to read their stories or someone else's to their older buddies. Everyone will benefit. (See also activity number 3 for middle-level children.)

4. There are picture books to dramatize, to sing, and to dance. John Langstaff's *Oh A Hunting We Will Go,* (Langstaff, 1984, illustrated by Nancy Winslow Parker) is a song that children will enjoy and soon begin to create new verses for. Dennis Lee's *Jellybelly* (Lee, 1983), a modern Canadian nursery rhyme collection, will encourage play, chanting, and drama.

5. Providing activities and suggested lists of books for parents who seek help is an important task. Create a bibliography of books that contain gentle bedtime stories so that parents and children can relax from a busy day and enjoy a special time before sleep.

Activities for the Intermediate and Middle Levels

1. Select an illustrator or have the children select one they would like to find out about and reproduce his/her style. The collages of Leo Lionni or Ezra Jack Keats or the impressionistic watercolors of Chihiro Iwasaki or Blair Lent could be starting points. Woodcuts are distinctive and can be attempted at this age as well.

2. Writing activities based on wordless picture books allow middle-level children to use their imaginations and their writing skills. For example, they could describe each page, tell the story, select a character and describe him/her, write a play or poem that evokes a theme or character, re-create the artwork in a puppet or diorama, or select music that relates to the book and write why the music "fits."

3. Reading picture books aloud to younger children is something most middle-level children enjoy. The vocabulary is sometimes surprisingly difficult, so it is appropriate for fifth and sixth graders to practice, then read to their younger "book

buddies." Enjoying literature together is an important way for children of different ages to interact. (See also activity number 3 for primary-level children.)

4. If students are becoming enthusiastic and knowledgeable about picture books, organize a "Mock-Caldecott Committee" that selects a winner from a pile of new picture books. Students' critical thinking skills will be challenged as they analyze the books and defend their choices.

5. Connections with the art program in school are worth exploring. Art and Language Arts teachers could compare their curricula and activities to see if opportunities exist for integration. For example, an art class might investigate or identify artists who illustrate children's books, or find examples in children's books of famous styles of art (such as Impressionism). See also the "Portraits of Women Artists" series mentioned in Chapter 9.

● ● ● ● ●
REFERENCES

Children's Works Cited

Ackerman, S. (1988). *Song and dance man.* Illustrations by Stephen Gammell. New York: Knopf.

Anno, M. (1975). *Anno's counting book.* New York: Crowell.

Bang, M. (1983). *Ten, nine, eight.* New York: Greenwillow.

Bannerman, H. (1920). *Little black Sambo.* South Yarmouth, MA: A. D. Bragdon.

Bishop, C. (1938). *Five Chinese brothers.* New York: Putnam.

Briggs, R. (1966). *The Mother Goose treasury.* New York: Coward-McCann.

Browne, A. (1983). *Gorilla.* New York: Knopf.

Caldecott, R. (1977). *John Gilpin and other stories.* New York: Warne.

Carle, E. (1968). *The very hungry caterpillar.* New York: World.

Cooney, B. (1982). *Miss Rumphius.* New York: Viking Penguin.

Crane, W. (1981). *An alphabet of old friends and the absurd ABC.* New York: Metropolitan Museum of Art.

Crews, D. (1981). *Light.* New York: Greenwillow.

dePaola, T. (1985). *Mother Goose.* New York: Putnam.

Ehrlich, A. (1981). *Leo, Zach, and Emmie.* New York: Dial.

Emberley, B. (1967). *Drummer Hoff.* Englewood Cliffs, NJ: Prentice Hall.

Fassler, D., & McQueen, K. (1990). *What's a virus anyway? The kids' book about AIDS.* Burlington, VT: Waterfront Books.

Gibbons, G. (1992). *Sharks.* New York: Holiday House.

Greenaway, K. (1988). *Kate Greenaway's Mother Goose* (p. 11). New York: Harry N. Abrams.

Harrison, T. (1982). *A northern alphabet.* Plattsburgh, NY: Tundra.

Hoban, R. (1964). *A baby sister for Frances.* New York: Harper.

Hoban, T. (1989). *Of colors and things.* New York: Greenwillow.

Hoban, T. (1992). *Look up, look down.* New York: Greenwillow.

Hughes, S. (1986). *All shapes and sizes.* New York: Lothrop.

Keats, E. J. (1962). *The snowy day.* New York: Viking.

Langstaff, J. (1984). *Oh a hunting we will go.* New York: Atheneum.

Lee, D. (1983). *Jellybelly.* Toronto: Macmillan of Canada.

Lobel, A. (1970). *Frog and toad are friends.* New York: Harper & Row.

Macaulay, D. (1990). *Black and white.* Boston: Houghton Mifflin.

Martin, B., Jr., & Archambault, J. (1989). *Chicka chicka boom boom.* Ill. by Lois Ehlert. New York: Simon & Schuster.

McCully, E. (1987). *School.* New York: Harper.

Musgrove, M. (1976). *Ashanti to Zulu: African traditions.* Ill. by Leo and Diane Dillon. New York: Dial.

Opie, I., & Opie, P. (1992). *I saw Esau.* Cambridge, MA: Candlewick.

Oxenbury, H. (1968). *Numbers of things.* New York: Watts.

Patterson, D. (1986). *No-No the Little Seal.* New York: Random House.

Potter, B. (1987). *The tale of Peter Rabbit.* New York: Frederick Warne.

Provensen, A., & Provensen, M. (1978). *A peaceable kingdom.* New York: Viking Penguin.

Rockwell, A. (1982). *Boats.* New York: Dutton.

Sendak, M. (1963). *Where the wild things are.* New York: Harper & Row.

Sendak, M. (1970). *In the night kitchen.* New York: HarperCollins.

Sendak, M. (1981). *Outside over there.* New York: HarperCollins.

Sendak, M. (1993). *We are all in the dumps with Jack and Guy.* New York: Michael di Capua.

Sis, P. (1988). *Waving.* New York: Greenwillow.

Tafuri, N. (1988). *Junglewalk.* New York: Greenwillow.

Ward, L. (1973). *The silver pony.* Boston: Houghton Mifflin.

Wiesner, D. (1991). *Tuesday.* New York: Clarion.

Wildsmith, B. (1964). *Brian Wildsmith's Mother Goose.* New York: Franklin Watts.

Wilhoite, M. (1990). *Daddy's roommate.* Boston: Alyson Pub.

Young, E. (1989). *Lon Po Po.* New York: Philomel.

Zemach, M. (1982). *Jake and Honeybunch go to heaven.* New York: Farrar, Strauss and Giroux.

Professional Works Cited

Bader, B. (1976). *American picture books from Noah's ark to the beast within.* New York: Macmillan.

Billington, E. (Ed.). (1978). *The Randolph Caldecott treasury* (pp. 13–14). New York: Frederick Warne.

Children's books in print. (1991–1992). New York: R. R. Bowker.

Cianciolo, P. (1976). *Illustrations in children's books.* Dubuque, IA: Wm. C. Brown.

Cianciolo, P. (1990). *Picture books for children.* Chicago: American Library Association.

Kingman, L. (1986). (Ed.). *Newbery and Caldecott medal books 1976–1985* (p. 325). Boston: Horn Book.

Meyer, S. (1983). *A treasury of the great children's book illustrators.* New York: Harry N. Abrams.

Schwarcz, J., & Schwarcz, C. (1991). *The picture book comes of age.* Chicago: American Library Association.

Sutherland, Z., & Hearne, B. (1984). In search of the perfect picture book definition. In P. Barron & J. Burley (Eds.), *Jump over the moon: Selected professional readings* (pp. 12–14). New York: Holt, Rinehart & Winston.

Townsend, J. R. (1987). *Written for children* (3rd ed.). New York: Lippincott.

Townsend, J. R. (1992). *Written for children* (4th ed.). New York: HarperCollins.

Whalley, J. I. (1975). *Cobwebs to catch flies: Illustrated books for the nursery and schoolroom, 1700–1900* (pp. 22, 23). Berkeley, CA: University of California Press.

Additional Resources

Abraham Lincoln. (1982). [Sound Filmstrip]. New Rochelle, NY: Spoken Arts.
This filmstrip shows the lithography created for Ingri and Edgar D'Aulaire's biography of Lincoln, which was published in 1939 by Doubleday.

Annual illustrations of children's books. (Yearly). Picture Book Studio, distributed by Simon & Schuster, New York.
  The official catalog of the annual Bologna International Children's Book Fair Illustrators' Exhibition includes many international illustrators' work.
Evolution of a graphic concept: The stonecutter. (1977). [Sound Filmstrip]. Weston, CT: Weston Woods Studios.
  A filmstrip demonstrates Gerald McDermott's artistic process as his Japanese folktale evolved from film to collage for a picture book.
Kingman, L. (Ed.). (1978). *The illustrator's notebook.* Boston: Horn Book.
  In this series of articles about notable illustration taken from the Horn Book magazine, many Caldecott artists discuss their work.
Lanes, S. (1984). *The art of Maurice Sendak.* New York: Abrams.
  This fine book includes Sendak's biography and notes about all of his work. It is a personal and affectionate look at this major artist.
Marantz, S. (1992). *Picture books for looking and learning.* Phoenix: Oryx.
  After a brief introduction to the anatomy of a picture book, media, and techniques, Marantz presents a page-by-page analysis of forty-three books.
Nodelman, P. (1988). *Words about pictures.* Athens, GA: University of Georgia Press.
  Nodelman's thesis is that pictures tell stories through design, styles, codes, tension, action, irony, and rhythm.
Sendak, M. (1988). *Caldecott and company.* New York: Noonday Press, di Capua Books, Farrar, Strauss & Giroux.
  The first part includes essays about Caldecott and other illustrators, including Walt Disney and Edward Ardizzone. The second half concentrates on Sendak's own work.
Shulevitz, U. (1985). *Writing with pictures.* New York: Watson-Guptill.
  Uri Shulevitz explains clearly the many technical aspects of creating a picture book. Color, line, shape, format, media, and style are all exemplified through his own and others' work.

Chapter Six

Poetry as Sound, Story, and Symbol

● ● ● ● ●

INTRODUCTION AND RESPONSE

"I," Says the Poem

> "I," says the poem arrogantly,
> "I am a cloud,
> I am a tree.
>
> I am a city,
> I am the sea,
> I am a golden mystery."
>
> How can it be?
>
> A poem is written
> by some someone,
> someone like you,
> or someone like me
> . . .
>
> *Eve Merriam*

A poet chooses each word in a poem with care and precision for its sound and meaning. As the excerpt from the poem above demonstrates, every word is purposeful, creating repetition and rhythm that bring the reader to a new insight, a thought aptly expressed in poetic form. As Eve Merriam says, poems aren't "golden mysteries," but are written by people to express a thought, a feeling, or, sometimes, just nonsense. And each reader brings his or her own response to the poem, creating a meaning that is unique to him or her.

Since poems are written by "someone like you or someone like me," try writing your own poem now. To get started, it might help to look again at the kind of poem Eve Merriam wrote, and use it as a model. She personified a poem by giving it a voice, an "arrogant" and "matter of fact" voice. Think of something inanimate and give it a voice or other human characteristics such as vision (what does it see?) or audition (what does it hear?). Bring an object to life through your own unique choice of words, using repetition, rhythm, or other qualities of poetry drawn from your experience with this genre.

In this chapter we will discuss what poetry is—and what it isn't. Several forms, or subgenres, of poems are described with examples, and an evaluation scheme for children's poetry is presented. Classic and contemporary poets' work shows how poetry uses its power to delight, to instruct, and to release our imaginations.

• • • • •
DEFINING POETRY

Poetry is a succinct expression that captures the essence of an idea or an object. The **sounds** of poetry come from the pulsating beat of rhythm, repetition, and sometimes rhyme of the words. Poetry is meant to be spoken or read aloud. Often poetry tells a **story**, and when the words are set to music, the story becomes even more memorable. Because it suggests and hints at meanings, poetry seems more abstract, more **symbolic** than other writings. It is personal, concise, "imaginatively intense language, usually in verse" (Frye, Baker, & Perkins, 1985, p. 356).

Poets must be the most insightful users of language because they distill human emotions and thought into words. They help us see familiar things in a unique way (Worth, 1992) and communicate what is sometimes impossible to explain. How do you describe the scent of a rose? The love for a child? The horror of famine and starvation? Putting words around ideas or crystallizing emotions through symbols demands the most imaginative, yet practical, explanations of human and natural events.

Like other literary genres, poetry is difficult to define precisely. However, its qualities, or characteristics, have been described by many and a consensus emerges. When compared to prose, poetry is brief, intense, and patterned. Poetry has more intensity than prose, it uses more figurative language, and it follows sometimes rather strict structures. Structure refers to formulaic patterns that have evolved over time, such as sonnets, limericks, and haiku.

Defining poetry for children is no different than defining poetry for everyone. Simply put, there is no demarcation between "adult" poetry and "child" poetry (Clark, 1983). As in all literature, a sense of audience is intuited by the reader, so children's poetry is that which children read and enjoy.

As one of the premier poets of the twentieth century, Robert Frost, said, a poem "begins in delight and ends in wisdom." Emily Dickinson, a notable poet of the preceding century, recognized and defined poetry through a physical sensation as she read a text. She said, "If I read a book and it makes my whole body so cold no fire can ever warm me, I know that it is poetry. If I feel physically as if the top of my head were taken off, I know that it is poetry." Poetry speaks to us, grabbing our attention immediately with an emotional and cognitive hook, or it just is not poetry.

HISTORY OF POETRY FOR CHILDREN

Even before William Blake wrote his poetry collection entitled *Songs of Innocence* (1789), children's poetry was evident in nursery rhymes and Sunday-school hymns. However, Blake's poems celebrated childhood rather than admonishing children, and for this reason his work changed perceptions of what poetry could and should be. The first line in this collection of twenty-three poems (also illustrated by Blake himself), "Piping Down the Valleys Wild," became a phrase associated with the joy and innocence of childhood. Much more than nursery rhymes or rhymed moral lessons, these poems captured a lyrical quality attuned to a child's understanding and expression (Carpenter and Prichard, 1984).

A harbinger of "nonsense" poetry was Edward Lear (1812–1888). With his whimsical limericks and celebrated poems (such as "The Owl and the Pussycat") and the drawings and illustrations with which he accompanied them, Lear strove to amuse and entertain children with no condescension or sentimentality. His *Book of Nonsense* (1846) was immediately popular and although he did not invent the limerick, it has come to be associated with his name (Meyer, 1983). As Lewis Carroll pushed boundaries in children's fantasy, so Edward Lear gave free rein to imaginary beasts and situations in verse, creating a foundation for broad humor and wit.

One of the first story poems captivating adults and children alike, "The Pied Piper of Hamelin," was written by Robert Browning in 1842. This popularized a form of poetry called **narrative** poetry, and found its audience quickly and surely.

The Victorian and Edwardian periods in England, sometimes called the golden age of children's literature, produced notable poetry for children in addition to novels mentioned earlier (see Chapter 2). Christina Rossetti, Robert Louis Stevenson, Walter de la Mare, and A. A. Milne set standards for children's poetry in the late 1800s and early 1900s.

In the United States, poetry for children began to flourish in the 1920s (Hopkins, 1993). This century has seen increasing diversity in poetic forms and subject matter (e.g., the work of poets such as Langston Hughes, who was first to portray an African American experience in poetry for children). The 1950s brought collections by John Ciardi and David McCord; the 1960s and 1970s saw efforts to bring a new realism to poetry. Humor from Shel Silverstein proved to be popular; his *Where the Sidewalk Ends* (1974) was on the *New York Times* best-seller list for three years. In the last decade, Jack Prelutsky's poems, as in *The New Kid On the Block* (1984), have captured the attention and interest of many elementary-school children.

Recent years have signaled a continuing and abiding interest in contemporary poets and their work. Awards now recognize significant contributions to this genre and content is varied, reflecting the multiculturalism and realism in the lives of today's children.

Following is a list of milestones in children's poetry. Perhaps you know some, most, or just a few of the works. Which ones would you keep in the canon of children's poetry, and which ones would you delete? Note that the decades between Langston Hughes and Nancy Willard have been left blank so that you can select your own poets and their collections.

1789	*Songs of Innocence,*	William Blake
1822	*A Visit from St. Nicholas,*	Clement Moore
1842	*The Pied Piper of Hamelin,*	Robert Browning
1872	*Sing-Song,*	Christina Rossetti
1885	*A Child's Garden of Verses,*	Robert Louis Stevenson
1913	*Peacock Pie,*	Walter de la Mare
1926	*When We Were Very Young,*	A. A. Milne
1932	*The Dream Keeper and Other Poems,*	Langston Hughes
1981	*A Visit to William Blake's Inn,*	Nancy Willard
1988	*Joyful Noise,*	Paul Fleischman

● ● ● ● ●
EVALUATING POETRY

Given the characteristics of poetry that speak to its emotional intensity, rhythmic and figurative language, and compactness, it stands to reason that poetry is evaluated by the presence or absence of those characteristics. Or, as is more often the case, the degree of compactness, emotional intensity, or rhythmic language determines a poem's success or failure. A poem is as compact as it needs to be and, similarly, as intense and as rhythmically appealing.

We judge poems by our emotional reaction and our intellectual standards based on what we have learned about poetry. We select poetry for our own personal enjoyment, or for use in a classroom, or for other purposes in our writing and speaking.

Choosing between "good" poems is difficult, but having a purpose helps us make the right choice. However, there are qualities that are common in mediocre poems that are never acceptable in poetry for children—the negative qualities of sentimentality, didacticism, condescension, and nostalgia. Sentimentality is a shallow or false emotion that masks or tries to manipulate a heartfelt response. Poetry of the nineteenth century is sometimes seen as sentimental, like the verses on greeting cards that are often overstatements of love or romance.

When the message of a poem or prose tends to educate or instruct the reader in a heavy-handed way, we call the poem didactic. Much of children's literature over the years has been considered didactic. Condescension is a matter of tone; it creates a patronizing air of treating the child/reader/listener as someone of little knowledge or experience. There is no dignity afforded to the audience. Nostalgia is also a matter of tone, and appears when the poet writes with a backward view toward childhood, creating a childhood that should have been instead of recognizing realism. Simply stated, sentimentality, didacticism, condescension, and nostalgia have no place in poetry.

Evaluation leads some critics to distinguish between poetry and verse (Lukens, 1990). Poetry is seen as the better of the two, as it represents a loftier, rarer, and finer expression of distilled thought and emotion. Verse, on the other hand, can be pleasant and entertaining, but is occasionally contrived and awkwardly written. Greeting cards, commercial slogans, rap and other song lyrics, and the rhymed couplets in some picture books (Dr. Seuss, for example) are viewed as verse, but not true poetry. This distinction, if we find truth in it, colors our evaluation of a written work.

Whether or not we differentiate poetry from verse, our task is still to determine a poem's (or verse's) worth, its quality, and its effectiveness. We are still evaluating intensity, precise and imaginative word choices, and meaning, regardless of what the work is labeled when our judgment is made.

In the evaluation scheme in Figure 6.1, criteria in the form of questions are posed so that you can evaluate a poem or a group of poems for your own use. Read the poem aloud, read it silently, and study what the poet does to achieve a certain tone and effect.

Figure 6.1   Evaluating Poetry

Criteria	My Personal Response	Matching Poem to Purpose, Audience
Emotional intensity	Does the poem capture my attention immediately? Do I feel wonder? delight? excitement? sadness? Is the poem sentimental, nostalgic, or condescending?	Does it stretch my audience's imagination and empathy? Will my audience understand the humor? Is the subject appropriate?
Rhythmic and figurative language	Are images vivid? Are there appropriate word choices? Is the rhyme forced? or natural?	Will the images provoke recognition? Will the poem support "teachable moments" for alliteration, onomatopoeia, rhyme scheme and other poetic elements?
Brevity	Is a unique view expressed in an economy of words? Does the form or shape contribute to its meaning?	Does it fit into the time limits of my curriculum? Will the poem sustain attention?

● ● ● ● ● ●

SUBGENRES (FORMS) OF POETRY

There are many forms of poems and, indeed, poets are continually experimenting with new forms. In this section we explore prevalent forms of children's poetry, realizing that others are possible. As in other genres, it is impossible to categorize everything neatly into forms. In an effort to standardize terminology to compare with other chapters, these forms are analogous to subgenres. They represent the ways the poetry genre can be categorized. However, because they are commonly named forms in most other studies, they will be called forms here. Next, **ballads, narrative poetry, lyrical poetry, free verse, haiku, limerick, concrete poetry,** and prescriptive forms such as **cinquain** and **diamante** are defined and exemplified.

Ballads

Originally ballads were narrative poems in short stanzas that were composed for singing. Troubadours in medieval times sang of heroes and happenings, unrequited love, and revenge, and the rhyming probably helped in memorizing such songs. Frequently there were refrains that repeated between stanzas, or verses. Ballads tell stories in stanzas, usually four lines, as in the following first four stanzas of "Jackaroe," a traditional ballad of English origin (Siegmeister, 1964). A jackaroe is a girl who disguises herself as a soldier or sailor in order to be with her lover.

JACKAROE

There was a wealthy merchant,
In London he did dwell,
He had a lovely daughter,
The truth to you I'll tell.
(Oh, the truth to you I'll tell.)

She had sweethearts aplenty
and men of high degree,
There was none but Jack the sailor
her true love e'er could be.
(Oh, her true love e'er could be.)

Now Jackie's gone a-sailing
with trouble on his mind,
To leave his native country
and his darling girl behind.
(Oh, his darling girl behind.)

She went into a tailor shop
and dressed in men's array,
And stepped on board a vessel

to convey herself away.
(Oh, convey herself away.)
. . .

Narrative Poetry

Like ballads, narrative poems tell a story but the verses are longer and there is typically no refrain. Well-known classics such as *'Twas the Night Before Christmas* (Moore, also titled *A Visit from St. Nicholas*, 1822), *The Pied Piper of Hamelin* by Robert Browning, and *The Highwayman* by Alfred Noyes exemplify narrative poetry at its best.

Lyrical Poetry

Lyrical poetry is personal and descriptive with no prescribed length or structure. It typically captures an imaginary moment or reveals a feeling. Lyrical poetry lends itself well to music, as the poem's lyrics could be the words to a song.

Who Has Seen the Wind?

Who has seen the wind?
    Neither I nor you:
But when the leaves hang trembling,
    The wind is passing through.

From *The Highwayman* by Alfred Noyes. Illustrations copyright © 1990 by Neil Waldman. Reproduced by permission of Harcourt, Brace and Company.

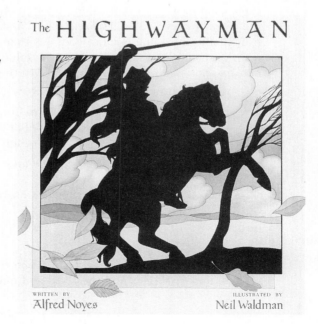

The HIGHWAYMAN

WRITTEN BY
Alfred Noyes

ILLUSTRATED BY
Neil Waldman

> Who has seen the wind?
>   Neither you nor I:
> But when the trees bow down their heads,
>   The wind is passing by.
>
>   *Christina Rossetti*

Free Verse

Poetry that has no discernible pattern of form is called **free verse**. It depends on the natural rhythm of language to provide a structure. Quite often free verse does not rhyme, but the words portray images, feelings, and thought in a unique way.

Poem

> I loved my friend.
> He went away from me.
> There's nothing more to say.
> The poem ends,
> Soft as it began—
> I loved my friend.
>
>   *Langston Hughes*

Haiku

Haiku is an ancient Japanese form of three-line poetry. It is a sophisticated expression in which the meaning is often elusive. Haiku seems simple because of the poem's brevity, but its five-syllable first line, seven-syllable second line, and five-syllable third line is more complex than it seems because of the reduction of text. Also, haiku focuses on an immediate occurrence—often something in nature—not something that happened in the past (Esbensen, 1975).

> Small bird, forgive me.
> I'll hear the end of your song
> in some other world.
>
>   —*Anonymous (translated by Harry Behn)*

A **tanka** is a poetic form in which two seven-syllable lines are added to a haiku.

Limericks

Limericks are five-line poems in which the **rhyme scheme** is a, a, b, b, a (the first, second, and fifth lines and the third and fourth lines rhyme). There is a definite, rollicking rhythm in the flow of the lines. Limericks are often funny when they describe or compare something out of the ordinary.

There Was a Young Lady Whose Nose

There was a Young Lady, whose Nose
Continually prospers and grows;
When it grew out of sight,
She exclaimed in a fright,
"Oh! Farewell to the end of my Nose!"

Edward Lear

Concrete Poetry

A poem written in the shape of a tree, an ice-cream cone, an animal, or something that visually reinforces the meaning of the whole is called a concrete poem. By arranging the words, and even the punctuation marks, in a picture, the poet creates a new form that is unique to a specific poem. The following poem, *Forsythia,* uses words and letters to illustrate the sprawl of forsythia branches as the plant announces spring.

Cinquain, Diamante, and Other Forms

A cinquain is a five-line poem that follows this pattern:

first line	=	two syllables
second line	=	four syllables
third line	=	six syllables

The poem "Forsythia" by Mary E. Solt from *Concrete Poetry: A World View* compiled by Mary E. Solt. Copyright © 1968 Hispanic Arts and 1970 Indiana University. Used by permission of Indiana University.

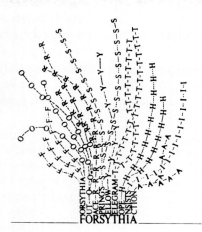

fourth line   =   eight syllables
fifth line   =   two syllables

Influenced by Japanese haiku and tanka (Esbensen, 1975), a cinquain magnifies the importance of finding the perfect match between word and meaning. A derivative form of cinquain doesn't count syllables but uses words instead.

first line   =   one word (giving the title)
second line   =   two words (describing the title)
third line   =   three words (expressing an action of the title)
fourth line   =   four words (expressing a feeling of the title)
fifth line   =   one word (a synonym of the title).

The following example of a cinquain was written by a fourth grader.

Ice Cream

Ice Cream
yummy, delicious,
scooping, eating, licking,
a very nice taste.
Dessert.

A diamante is a seven-line poem that forms a diamond shape.

first line   =   one word (subject, a noun)
second line   =   two words (adjectives)
third line   =   three words (verbs or verb forms)
fourth line   =   four words (a phrase related to subject)
fifth line   =   three words (verbs or verb forms)
sixth line   =   two words (adjectives)
seventh line   =   one word (an antonym of the subject).

Diamantes are interesting because they can begin with one topic and end with its opposite. The shift occurs in the fourth line, which should be pertinent to both. This example, written by a sixth grader, demonstrates the shift.

Diamond
brilliant, expensive,
sparkling, glittering, polishing,
Mined under the earth's soil
digging, chipping, working
cheap, dark
Coal.

Cinquains and diamantes represent poetic forms that do not depend on rhyme but still rely on crucial knowledge of word choice to convey a thought. Because of their "rules," children treat these forms as word puzzles and find them challenging but satisfying—as both readers and writers.

Other forms of poetry are created as adult and child poets explore ways to express thoughts and feelings. In his novel experiment in teaching urban children to write poetry, the noted poet Kenneth Koch (1970) used these words in the beginning of a three-line verse to encourage children to write

> I wish . . .
> I wish . . .
> Sometimes I wish . . .

Children, finishing the lines, wrote about their wishes and dreams, and they used language imaginatively. Some critics concluded that what the children produced was not poetry, but the process encouraged them to play with words and begin to learn the "bare bones of poetical structure" (Barrett, 1981, p. 101).

● ● ● ● ●
ELEMENTS OF POETRY

As the "tools of the trade," poets, teachers, and critics use language to talk about poetry and prose. As mentioned in Chapter 3, aspects of analysis give all who study literature a vocabulary to discuss and evaluate it. Many of the terms included there, especially in the figurative language section, are pertinent to poetry. Terms like *alliteration, metaphor, simile, symbol, personification,* and *allusion* bring an understanding to the richness of a poem's meanings. Other elements in that section can be applied to poetry to allow us to appreciate the complexity of a poet's work.

This section then extends literary elements by adding three more terms necessary to poetic analysis: *onomatopoeia, internal rhyme,* and *rhyme scheme.* These three seem to be essential to understand poetry in the beginning of an analysis. Because poetry is complex, especially when rhythm and stress are studied, you are encouraged to continue beyond what this text provides. A good resource is Laurence Perrine's *Sound and Sense: An Introduction to Poetry* (1982).

Onomatopoeia, that wonderful word that looks like a mouthful of vowels with an occasional consonant thrown in, refers to words that sound like their meanings. The "meow" of a cat, the "sizzle" of a hamburger frying in a pan, the "oomph" of someone sitting on a soft sofa—all these words sound like the action itself. Of course poetry, with its emphasis on just the right word for the precise movement, uses onomatopoeia. Sometimes onomatopoeic words are coined for just the right phrase, as in Lewis Carroll's famous nonsense poem, "Jabberwocky." A verse of Eve Merriam's "What in the World?" also demonstrates onomatopoeia.

What in the World?

What in the world
    goes whiskery friskery
        meowling and prowling
           napping and lapping
               at silky milk?
Psst,
What is it?

What in the world
    goes leaping and beeping
        onto a lily pad onto a log
           onto a tree stump or down to the bog?
Splash, blurp,
Kerchurp!

Eve Merriam

This excerpt from Eve Merriam's poem also shows internal rhyming. *Leaping* and *beeping* are chosen to give the line rhythm; because the words sound alike, the line picks up speed as well. Thus movement is conveyed through internal rhymes.

Rhyme scheme has been described in the section about limericks, and it refers to a pattern created at the end of lines by the rhyming words. For example, the limerick is a, a, b, b, a. A couplet, or two lines that rhyme, is a, a. What is the rhyme scheme of "Jackaroe," the ballad mentioned previously?

• • • • •

CONTEMPORARY POETS AND ANTHOLOGIES

There are many outstanding twentieth-century poets who weave word magic in their contributions to literature for children. Identifying outstanding poets is no easy task, so we will be guided by selection committees who bestow awards on worthy recipients. In 1977 the National Council of Teachers of English (NCTE) initiated an Award for Excellence in Poetry for Children, which is given for the body of a poet's work. Those who have received this honor are David McCord, Aileen Fisher, Karla Kuskin, Myra Cohn Livingston, Eve Merriam, John Ciardi, Lilian Moore, Arnold Adoff, and Valerie Worth. All these poets are prolific; their poems appear in many anthologies and in their own collections.

The American Library Association has awarded the Newbery Medal to two poetry books: *A Visit to William Blake's Inn* (Willard, 1981) and *Joyful Noise: Poems for Two Voices* (Fleischman, 1988). These honors prompted a renewed interest in poetry.

In addition to the significant poets and their collections mentioned in this chapter, here are some recent multicultural and general collections that will help you discover contemporary works for children. There are many new, exciting collections related to topics, as well. Consult reviewing sources such as *Horn Book Magazine* or the *Bulletin of the Center for Children's Books* for outstanding poetry written for children and adolescents and, in some cases, by children and adolescents.

General Anthologies

Sunflakes: Poems for Children, Lilian Moore (comp.), (1992)

This Same Sky: A Collection of Poems from Around the World, Naomi Nye (1992)

The Dragons Are Singing Tonight, Jack Prelutsky (1993)

Sing a Song of Popcorn: Every Child's Book of Poems, Beatrice Schenk de Regniers, Eva Moore, Mary Michaels White, & Jan Carr (selectors), (1988)

And the Green Grass Grew All Around: Folk Poetry from Everyone, Alvin Schwartz (selector), (1992)

African American Poetry

In for Winter, Out for Spring, Arnold Adoff (1991)

Nathaniel Talking, Eloise Greenfield (1989)

Pass It On: African-American Poetry for Children, Wade Hudson (comp.), (1993)

Asian American Poetry

In the Eyes of the Cat: Japanese Poetry for All Seasons, Demi (1992)

The Animals: Selected Poems, Michio Mado (1992)

Hispanic and Caribbean Poetry

Sing to the Sun, Ashley Bryan (1992)

Coconut Kind of Day: Island Poems, Lynn Joseph (1990)

Caribbean Canvas, Frane Lessac (comp.), (1989)

A Fire in My Hands: A Book of Poems, Gary Soto (1991)

Neighborhood Odes, Gary Soto (1992)

Native American Poetry

Rising Voices: Writings of Young Native Americans, A. Hirshfelder and B. Singer (selectors), (1992)

Dancing Teepees: Poems of American Indian Youth, Virginia Driving Hawk Sneve (1989)

SUMMARY

Poetry, at the heart of literature for children, beats strongly in our contemporary lives. A great variety of subject matter for all ages, from the youngest listeners to the most sophisticated readers, can be found in many excellent collections and anthologies. The writings of modern poets, coming from urban and rural multi-cultural perspectives, are easily accessed in libraries, schools, and bookstores.

This chapter presented a wide range of children's poetry and identified notable poets and some of their well-known works. A brief look at the beginnings of modern poetry began this discussion, followed by an attempt to define poetry, or at least, because a precise definition proved to be elusive, a recounting of characteristics of poetry.

Poetry is characterized by qualities of brevity, emotional intensity, rhythmic and figurative language, and a structure that marks its difference from prose. An analogy might be: Poetry is to language as ballet is to dance. That is, poetry is language at its most precise, at its most controlled, sophisticated, symbolic, and intense. Ballet, of all the dance forms, seems to be also very controlled, precise, sophisticated, and intense. Both demand a willingness to soar beyond the usual and the easy, with great rewards possible at the end.

Subgenres of poetry described and exemplified in this chapter were: ballads, narrative poetry, lyrical poetry, free verse, haiku and tanka, limericks, concrete poetry, and other forms (cinquain, diamante, and formulaic patterns). Many of the examples were drawn from notable contemporary poets' work, and these poets, many of whom have won awards, were listed so that their contributions can be studied and appreciated.

IMPLICATIONS FOR INSTRUCTION

In this section you will have a chance to reflect on the ideas, definitions, and examples presented in this chapter. in addition, projects and activities with children are described and you are encouraged to try them.

Reflections

1. Reflect on your own experiences with poetry. Have you written poems? What childhood memories of poetry can you recall? Who are your favorite poets?

2. Many children do not seem to enjoy poetry, and probably some adults would profess a distaste for poetry too. Why do you think poetry is not appreciated by everyone?

3. How would you characterize the differences between adult and children's poetry? How do you define poetry?

4. Why do many young children think that poetry must rhyme? Do young children need rhyme? Does poetry have to rhyme for young children?

5. We associate poetry with sound, meter, rhythm, and all auditory aspects of language, but is there a visual dimension as well? What is visual about poetry, and when do we learn the visual structure?

6. Is Dr. Seuss a poet?

7. Poetry is sometimes used effectively with disabled readers who are overwhelmed by the demands of prose. What are circumstances in which you might use poetry with poor readers, and what are some poems that might work?

Projects

1. Begin your own personal poetry file. Collect poems that appeal to you, and categorize them into topics that are relevant to your use. You may want to collect "weather" poems, "animal" poems, "peace" poems, or "Vermont" poems. Whatever you choose, an important criterion for selection is your own satisfaction with a poem for your own needs.

2. Choose a favorite poet of your own or a favorite of children. Research his or her life and work and, if possible, plan a program for children or adults based on the poet. Create a bibliography of his or her work. For example, Eve Merriam has a rich store of poetry for children, and Nancy Larrick is an anthologist whose books range over rural, urban, young, old, classical, and contemporary poems, by children and for children.

3. Organize a poetry-reading session with colleagues or friends. Rehearse, then read orally some of your favorite poems, or write some of your own. Add a musical background or combine your talents with another performance artist.

4. Find out if your state Arts Council, Humanities Council, or another group will help sponsor a poet in the school or classroom. Many states offer opportunities for "artists in residence" at elementary schools, middle schools, or community centers, while many poets, artists, dancers, and musicians are eager to share their talent with children.

5. Experiment by writing a sonnet, a haiku, a limerick, and other poetic forms. Which ones are most difficult? Is it easy to see why word choice is so crucial for precision and beauty?

6. What kind of poems do children prefer? Conduct an experiment with a group of children by selecting some poems and judging their response to them. For information about research in this area, consult studies in children's poetry preferences (Terry, 1974; Fisher & Natarella, 1982).

Activities for the Primary Level

1. Do some "word gathering" poetry. Elicit from a group of young children words that are "snow" words, or "green" words, or pick another topic. You may be surprised at the variety. When many words have been gathered and listed, you and the children can categorize them. The natural rhythm of language will be

apparent when the categories are read aloud. The topic word becomes the title of the poem, and the last line can be anything to summarize the activity. Here is a word-gathering poem completed in a kindergarten classroom.

Snow

Slushy, icy, white and brown,
falling from the sky,
tasting on my tongue,
Snowballs, forts, igloos,
Snowpants, mittens, boots, skis, suspenders,
No School! Yeah!

Williston Kindergartners

2. Read a poem aloud every day to young children. Don't isolate poetry into a certain time period or subject area, but instead draw from your poetry file poems that fit into every subject or celebration.

3. Find poems that can be illustrated, or set some to music or movement. Nancy Larrick, a noted anthologist, combines poetry and song for young children in *Songs from Mother Goose* (Larrick, 1989) and *Let's Do a Poem* (Larrick, 1991).

4. Encourage your children to write cinquains, diamantes, or "I wish . . ." poems. Young children often believe that poetry must rhyme, so the structure of these forms allows them to see poetry in a new way. Playing with word poems can begin with (read down)

P	play	please	peek
O	one	open	out
E	extra	everything	eensy
M	measure	Michael	man

or find words (adjectives) that use the letters of a person's first name to describe that person

E	xcellent
M	illion-dollar smile
I	lluminating
L	ovely
Y	outhful

and combine with Emily's self-portrait.

5. Combine poetry and prose. For example, if you are reading aloud *Crow Boy* (Yashima, 1955), also present a poem that expresses what the main character might feel. "Crows," by David McCord (Dunning, *et al.,* 1966) is a poem that Chibi would like. For character development in a novel, consider with children which poem might describe a character, or have been written by a character,

From *Knock at a Star,* by X. J. and Dorothy M. Kennedy; illustrated by Karen Ann Weinhaus. Illustrations copyright © 1982 by Karen Ann Weinhaus. By permission of Little, Brown and Company.

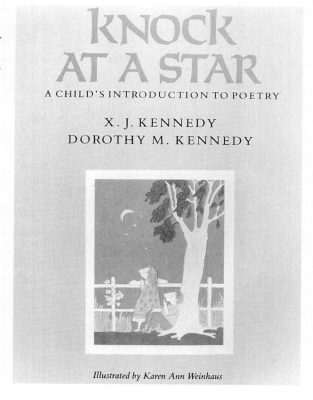

Illustrated by Karen Ann Weinhaus

or might express what the main character is feeling. This activity works well in the middle grades too. Can you think of some examples?

Activities for the Intermediate and Middle Levels

1. Middle-level children too can write poetry. In addition to forms presented in this chapter, you can try rap, concrete poetry, or description poems. Examples and suggestions can be found in the Kennedys' *Knock At a Star* (1982). Here is an example of a class poem in which children described a raindrop.

Poetry Splash

What is a raindrop?
A raindrop is. . .
  wet water,
  cold, maybe warm,
  a signal to put on your raincoat,
  a drink to a butterfly.

The beginning of a flood,
a cool day,
a farmer's friend,
fun for kids.

A lifesaver to a flower,
a sign to hurry and get home,
a sign to get your umbrella,
a warning to go inside.

A liquid,
a blurry window,
a song,
An orchestra tuning up.

Summit Street School

2. Alfred Noyes's dramatic poem, *The Highwayman,* inspired artwork in three very different styles. With your students, compare the artistic versions of Mikolaycak (Noyes, 1983), Keeping (Noyes, 1980), and Waldman (Noyes, 1990) as you match words to a visual rendition. Which do you prefer? Which do your students prefer?

3. Combining poetry and artwork, music, movement, and drama sometimes yields great satisfaction. Imagine the pictorial possibilities with

The Falling Star

I saw a star slide down the sky,
Blinding the north as it went by,
Too burning and too quick to hold,
Too lovely to be bought or sold,
Good only to make wishes on
And then forever to be gone.

Sara Teasdale

What music would you choose to accompany one of the poems found in this chapter, such as "Who Has Seen the Wind?" or "Jackaroe" or one of your choice? Performance possibilities abound with a poem like "Forty Performing Bananas," from *The New Kid on the Block* (Prelutsky, 1984, p. 147).

4. Develop a class poetry book, *Reading and Writing Poetry.* Include the children's favorite poems, ones they have chosen to read orally and ones they have proudly written. This will be the anthology they turn to again and again.

5. Choral reading is another way to enjoy poetry with a class. Two-by-two oral reading is another. For choral reading, assign lines or couplets to students one at a time, then listen to the poem as the lines are spoken by different voices.

Sometimes high voices can read a part of a line, and low voices the next. Evaluate the total effect with your students. Was the enunciation clear enough? Loud enough? Was appropriate expression used for the meaning of the line? Was the oral rendition dramatic enough? Choral reading brings many poems to life in a class that enjoys sound and story.

Joyful Noise (Fleishman, 1988) provides a great introduction to two-by-two oral reading if your students are new to it. Two students reading orally together, in question/answer or in parts of phrases, make this kind of poem an interesting oral-reading project for a pair.

● ● ● ● ●
REFERENCES

Poetry and Children's Works Cited

Adoff, A. (1991). *In for winter, out for spring.* New York: Harcourt.

Bryan, A. (1992). *Sing to the sun.* New York: HarperCollins.

de la Mare, W. (1989). *Peacock pie.* New York: Holt.

Demi. (1992). *In the eyes of the cat: Japanese poetry for all seasons.* New York: Holt.

de Regniers, B. S., Moore, E., White, M. M., & Carr, J. (Eds.). (1988). *Sing a song of popcorn.* New York: Scholastic.

Dunning, S., Lueders, E., & Smith, H. (Eds.). (1966). *Reflections on a gift of watermelon pickle.* Glenview, IL: Scott, Foresman.

Fleischman, P. (1988). *Joyful noise: Poems for two voices.* New York: Harper.

Greenfield, E. (1989). *Nathaniel talking.* New York: Writers and Readers.

Hirshfelder, A., & Singer, B. (Sel.). (1992). *Rising voices: Writings of young Native Americans.* New York: Scribners.

Hudson, W. (Comp.). (1993). *Pass it on: African-American poetry for children.* New York: Scholastic.

Joseph, L. (1990). *Coconut kind of day: Island poems.* New York: Lothrop, Lee, & Shepard.

Kennedy, X. J., & Kennedy, D. (1982). *Knock at a star.* Boston: Little, Brown.

Larrick, N. (Ed.). (1989). *Songs from Mother Goose.* New York: Harper.

Larrick, N. (1991). *Let's do a poem.* New York: Delacorte.

Lessac, F. (Ill.). (1989). *Caribbean canvas.* New York: Lippincott.

Mado, M. (1992). *The animals: Selected poems.* New York: McElderry.

Moore, L. (Comp.), (1992). *Sunflakes: Poems for children.* New York: Clarion.

Noyes, A. (1981). *The highwayman.* (Ill. by Charles Keeping). London: Oxford.

Noyes, A. (1983). *The highwayman.* (Ill. by Charles Mikolaycak). New York: Lothrop, Lee, & Shepard.

Noyes, A. (1990). *The highwayman.* (Ill. by Neil Waldman). New York: Harcourt Brace Jovanovich.

Nye, N. S. (1992). *This same sky.* New York: Four Winds.

Prelutsky, J. (1984). *The new kid on the block.* New York: Greenwillow.

Prelutsky, J. (1993). *The dragons are singing tonight.* New York: Greenwillow.

Schwartz, A. (Sel.). (1992). *And the green grass grew all around: Folk poetry from everyone.* New York: HarperCollins.

Silverstein, S. (1974). *Where the sidewalk ends.* New York: Harper & Row.

Sneve, V. D. H. (1989). *Dancing teepees: Poems of American Indian youth.* New York: Holiday.

Soto, G. (1991). *A fire in my hands: A book of poems.* New York: Scholastic.

Soto, G. (1992). *Neighborhood odes.* New York: Harcourt.

Willard, N. (1981). *A visit to William Blake's inn.* New York: Harcourt Brace Jovanovich.

Yashima, T. (1955). *Crow boy.* New York: Viking.

Professional Works Cited

Anderson, W., & Groff, P. (1972). *A new look at children's literature.* Belmont, CA: Wadsworth.

Barrett, E. (1981). Intent and practice in Kenneth Koch's 'wishes, lies, and dreams' and 'rose where did you get that red?' *The lion and the unicorn, 4,* 93–104.

Carpenter, H., & Prichard, M. (1984). *The Oxford companion to children's literature.* New York: Oxford University Press.

Clark, L. (1983). Poetry unfettered. In J. May (Ed.). *Children and their literature: A readings book* (pp. 133–137). West Lafayette, IN: Children's Literature Association.

Esbensen, B. (1975). *A celebration of bees.* Minneapolis, MN: Winston.

Fisher, C., & Natarella, M. A. (1982). Young children's preferences in poetry: A national survey of first, second, and third graders. *Research in the Teaching of English, 16,* 339–353.

Frye, N., Baker, S., & Perkins, G. (1985). *The Harper handbook to literature* (p. 356). New York: Harper & Row.

Hopkins, L. B. (1993). American poetry for children—the twentieth century. *Fanfare, 1,* 75–82.

Koch, K. (1970). *Wishes, lies, and dreams.* New York: Chelsea.

Lukens, R. (1990). *A critical handbook of children's literature* (4th ed.). Glenview, IL: Scott, Foresman/Little, Brown.

Meyer, S. (1983). *A treasury of the great children's book illustrators.* New York: Harry N. Abrams.

Perrine, L. (1982). *Sound and sense: An introduction to poetry* (6th ed.). New York: Harcourt Brace Jovanovich.

Siegmeister, E. (1964). *The Joan Baez songbook* (p. 80). New York: Ryerson Music.

Terry, A. (1974). *Children's poetry preferences.* Urbana, IL: National Council of Teachers of English.

Worth, V. (1992). Capturing objects in words. *The Horn Book, LXVIII,* 568–569.

Additional Resources

Golodetz, V. (1990). Poetry is alive-o. *The children's book bag* (unpaged). Watertown, MA: Foundation for Children's Books.
The Children's Book Bag is published quarterly by the Foundation for Children's Books; this issue is devoted to poetry. Recommended collections and anthologies are described and listed for the youngest listeners, new readers, intermediate readers, and older readers.

Hearne, B., & Elleman, B. (1984). Poetry for children. *Booklist,* June 15, 1984.
This Booklist reprint of a bibliography of poetry collections of high quality is available from the American Library Association, 50 E. Huron St., Chicago, IL 60611.

O'Neill, M. (1961). *Hailstones and halibut bones.* New York: Dell (Trumpet Club special edition, 1989). Ill. by John Wallner.
These poems of color create lovely images and motivate poetry writing and art in many children's classrooms.

The Poet's Pen. Cambridge Development Laboratory, Inc., 86 West St., Waltham, MA 02154.
A computer program that teaches children in grades two through seven to write three poetic forms—diamante, cinquain, and haiku.

Prelude Series 7. The Children's Book Council, 67 Irving Place, New York, NY 10003.
The Prelude series consists of audiotapes of notable authors, poets, illustrators, and critics, such as "Reading Black American Poetry and African Folktales" by Ashley Bryan and "Sharing Poetry with Children" by Eve Merriam, sharing their wealth of information about children's books and timely topics. The Children's Book Council calls these tapes "mini-seminars on using books creatively."

Chapter Seven

Imaginary Worlds of Fantasy

INTRODUCTION AND RESPONSE

In fantasy, authors draw their inspiration and creative impulses from the real world, referred to as the **primary world**, or they imagine a **secondary world** in which fantastic characters or events occur. Lloyd Alexander, a well-known author of children's fantasy, says, "Fantasy deals with the impossible, not the illogical. Creating a secondary world where the impossible becomes ordinary does not carry with it a license to do as one pleases. In its conception and in its deep substructures, the fantasy world must, if anything, be more carefully rationalized than the real world" (Alexander, 1987, p. 196). Alexander remarks on a key element in fantasy, that the secondary world must be logical, with an inner consistency to its natural laws.

A writer's work is considered to be within the fantasy genre if at least one element is outside the realm of possibility (Cameron, 1962). Fantasy is a careful blend of realism and impossibility, with fantasy elements closely related to natural occurrences, but with a unique aspect of their own. In animal fantasies such as *Watership Down* (Adams, 1974) the fantastic element is the humanized animals. Hazel, Fiver, Bigwig, Woundwort, and other animals speak, share their feelings, plan for the future, and solve problems like humans. However, they retain most of the characteristics of their species—size, shape, instinct, and habitat in the primary world.

This chapter presents subgenres of fantasy, and all have in common an element of impossibility that separates them from realism—not the same element, to be sure, but something that causes a reader to suspend disbelief and enter an imaginary secondary world or to accept an impossible fact in the primary world.

Figure 7.1   Identifying Elements of Fantasy

Title	Fantasy Element
Tuck Everlasting	
The High King	
A Wrinkle in Time	
Pippi Longstocking	
The Velveteen Rabbit	

As you begin thinking about fantastic elements that lead to a categorization of fantasy, study the following list of well-known fantasies that will be used in this chapter to exemplify several subgenres. If you are familiar with them, write what fantastic element is present in each that allows the work to fit into the genre of modern fantasy (see Figure 7.1). In other words, why are these works considered to be fantasies?

Understanding and anticipating unique aspects of fantasy will help readers to comprehend and enjoy this sometimes abstract genre. By definition, fantasy is more abstract than realistic fiction. All fiction requires a suspension of disbelief to enter the time, place, and circumstances that an author creates. However, fantasy pushes the boundaries of realism, as it invents and constructs metaphors for the real world. Fantasy demands more from readers—more attention, more suspension of disbelief, and more imagination.

This chapter describes modern fantasy as it has evolved from traditional literature. Its characters, themes, plots, and settings enrich children's literature and delight children, showing them the combined power of imagination and story. An evaluation scheme for modern fantasy based on the particular differences of subgenres is presented after a brief look at the development of modern fantasy in the last century. The chapter continues with a closer look at each of the subgenres, some outstanding contemporary writers, and a summary. Then, Implications for Instruction offers ideas for personal development and professional involvement with children.

● ● ● ● ●
HISTORY OF MODERN FANTASY

Fantasy for children has its roots in traditional literature. From the talking animals of fables to spells of magic and incantation, traditional literature provided imaginary settings and events that are recalled in modern fantasy. Likewise, characters from traditional literature, such as fairies, ogres, mermaids, and giants, appear in modern fantasy. Folktales, anonymous and deeply rooted in a folk culture, preceded and gave impetus to modern fantasy.

In the nineteenth century, a transition between the shorter fairy tale and modern novels of fantasy can be seen in two major contributions to children's literature. First, *The Three Bears* by Robert Southey (published in 1837) was so similar to folktales that its origin continues to be in doubt. However, in Southey's version, which immediately popularized the story, an old woman trespasses into the bears' house, but later versions substituted a young girl named Silver-Hair, who finally became Goldilocks by the turn of the century (Opie & Opie, 1974).

Second, the fairy tales of Hans Christian Andersen paved the way to modern fantasy. His poetic, ephemeral stories blended successfully the two strains of modern fantasy and traditional folklore. Translated to English and published in 1846 under the title *Wonderful Stories for Children,* these modern fairy tales evoked contemporary issues as well as timeless ones.

The true beginning of modern fantasy in children's literature, according to critic John Rowe Townsend (1987), coincided with the publication in the early 1860s of Lewis Carroll's *Alice's Adventures in Wonderland* and Charles Kingsley's *Water Babies.* Their appearance ushered in a remarkable period in which children's books began to achieve a certain status in the literary world and grew more plentiful to serve a rising middle class. As the better known of the two, *Alice,* with its absurdist logic, created a compelling secondary world, a "wonderland" in which the succession of fantastic creatures provided a counterpoint to the always practical and forthright Alice. Reverend Charles Dodgson, better known as Lewis Carroll, a shy unmarried professor of mathematics at Oxford University, wrote *Alice* and its sequel, *Through the Looking Glass* (1871), for the daughter of a dean at the college.

Another minister, George MacDonald, was to have a profound effect on modern fantasy. In his allegorical quest-romances, which included *At the Back of the North Wind* (1871) and *The Princess and the Goblin* (1872), MacDonald helped to establish the modern tradition known as sacred or ethical fantasy (Moss & Stott, 1986) in which themes of eternal goodness and truth prevail. The high fantasies of C. S. Lewis and J. R. R. Tolkien, with their strong themes of goodness overpowering evil, owe a debt to MacDonald's fantastic stories of quest-romance.

"By the end of the nineteenth century fantasy as a literary genre had gained full acceptance" (Levin, 1987, p. 167). E. Nesbit's richly textured fantasies, such as *The Enchanted Castle* (first published in 1907 and reissued in 1992), and Rudyard Kipling's animal fantasies were immensely popular on both sides of the Atlantic. Carlo Collodi created *Pinocchio* (1889), an animated toy fantasy, while folklore from Russia, Eastern Europe, Scandinavia, the British Isles, Asia, and other parts of the world was collected and retold in updated publications. (See Chapter 4.)

Considered to be the first modern fantasy in the United States, *The Wonderful Wizard of Oz* (Baum, 1900) achieved popularity but no critical acclaim. When compared to other famous fantasies of the time, such as *The Wind in the Willows* (Grahame, 1908) and *Peter Pan* (Barrie, 1904), Baum's work was thought to lack coherence, but subsequent years have softened that judgment.

Highlights of modern fantasy in the twentieth century are listed on the next page. Perhaps your favorite fantasy is listed; if it is not, add it to the chronological order. As you look at the list, think about what makes these books memorable. Would you agree that these selections represent the most notable contributions to modern fantasy? (Picture books have been excluded. See Chapter 5 for fantasy in picture books.)

1900	*The Wonderful Wizard of Oz*, L. Frank Baum
1904	*Peter Pan*, James Barrie
1908	*The Wind in the Willows*, Kenneth Grahame
1922	**Dr. Dolittle*, Hugh Lofting
1926	*Winnie-the-Pooh*, A. A. Milne
1934	*Mary Poppins*, P. L. Travers
1937	*The Hobbit*, J. R. R. Tolkien
1945	*Pippi Longstocking*, Astrid Lindgren
1950	*The Lion, The Witch and the Wardrobe*, C. S. Lewis
1952	*Charlotte's Web*, E. B. White
1953	*The Borrowers*, Mary Norton
1962	**A Wrinkle in Time*, Madeleine L'Engle
1964	*The Book of Three*, Lloyd Alexander
1968	*A Wizard of Earthsea*, Ursula LeGuin
1975	**The Grey King*, Susan Cooper
1989	*Eva*, Peter Dickinson

*Denotes a Newbery Award winner

● ● ● ● ●

SUBGENRES OF MODERN FANTASY

Modern fantasy consists of a great variety of stories, a variety that begs for some kind of classification. Subgenres form naturally around common characteristics in this diverse genre. High fantasy, time fantasy, and science-fiction fantasy seem to be clear-cut, with common aspects, usually relating to a secondary world, uniting each of them. Animal fantasies have as their common aspect and fantasy element the **personification**, or anthropomorphizing, of animals. Extraordinary characters and inventions is a subgenre that includes people who can perform impossible feats, inventions that are imbued with magical power, animated toys, tiny people (leprechauns, sprites, and others), large people (giants), and other people whose appearance marks them as mystics. Extraordinary characters could also include ghosts, vampires, ghouls, mermaids, the "faery folk," and other terrible and wonderful beings (McHarque, 1972).

Each of the subgenres (see Figure 7.2) is described in more detail in the following section and a few examples of contemporary works are listed. Continue to add your own examples as you visit libraries and bookstores and read reviews in children's literature journals. And remember, although categories will help in classifying literature, some stories defy clear-cut definitions and boundaries.

Figure 7.2   Subgenres of
Modern Fantasy

Subgenres of Modern Fantasy
Animal Fantasy
High Fantasy
Time Fantasy
Science-fiction Fantasy
Extraordinary Characters and Inventions

Some may overlap into two subgenres, and some into no subgenre at all. Categorization should not become the purpose of studying literature, but a means to studying, comparing, and enjoying.

Animal Fantasies

Animal fantasies come from one of the oldest forms of literature, the beast tales (Swinfen, 1984). Fables, folktales, and other forms of traditional literature showed human affinity to animals in the many depictions of anthropomorphism. In traditional literature, animals were often seen as guardians of a secret wisdom, the wisdom of the earth in its natural state.

In modern fantasy, the best examples of children's literature show a careful blend of human characteristics with animal qualities. It has been said that E. B. White studied spiders for three years before he wrote *Charlotte's Web,* which could account for his finding the perfect balance of Charlotte's ruthlessness in some things and compassion in others.

Reprinted with permission of Atheneum Publishers, an imprint of Macmillan Publishing Company from *Mrs. Frisby and the Rats of NIMH* by Robert C. O'Brien. Pictures by Zena Bernstein. Copyright © 1971 Robert C. O'Brien.

Modern animal fantasies are most often set in the primary world and show animals in a quest for a better life. Sometimes the quest entails a band of small animals seeking to overpower larger, evil adversaries and restore, or create, a more just society. Thus animal fantasies satirize modern predicaments today, such as our political struggles to reach an ideal state. *Mrs. Frisby and the Rats of NIMH* (O'Brien, 1971), the most recent animal fantasy awarded the Newbery Medal, is just such a story.

A more recent tetralogy by Brian Jacques, beginning with *Redwall* (Jacques, 1987), also centers on the quest for an egalitarian, peaceful society. In the third book of the series, *Mattimeo* (Jacques, 1990), the plot focuses on the adolescent Mattimeo mouse, son of Matthias (hero of the first book) and grandson of Martin (hero of the second book). The story begins with the kidnapping of the Redwall Abbey children, among whom is Mattimeo, by Slazar the Cruel, a vile fox, and his band of stoats, rats, and weasels who will sell the children into slavery in Malkariss. Matthias and other Abbey warriors follow in hot pursuit, aided by the badger Orlando, who is looking for his kidnapped daughter as well. In the meantime the Abbey falls prey to General Ironbeak, his lieutenant Mangiz, and their band of evil birds. Finally, deep in the forbidding and treacherous underground city, Mattimeo's band of children and his father's warriors join forces to topple the horrendous power of Slazar and the ruler, also named Malkariss. Through guile and cunning, the elderly animals outwit General Ironbeak back at the Abbey, and peace is restored for a time. This complex fantasy, with three major subplots and hundreds of characters shifting continually, has coherence because of the compelling story line and skillfully drawn animal characters. It is a story of great heroism, with a reluctant adolescent mouse finding that he has courage and stamina, and that he can live up to his family's proud tradition. Happy endings are vital in these struggles of good and evil.

In addition to the all-animal fantasy, there are stories in which humans and animals interact. *The Mouse and the Motorcycle* (Cleary, 1965) and two subsequent books about Ralph, the articulate, daring mouse, illustrate humorous and positive relationships between animals and humans.

Animal fantasies, whether they are set in the real world or in a secondary world, allow us to regard history or contemporary life through the eyes of a being similar to us, yet distinctively different. This perspective, from an animal's point of view, challenges our prejudices and causes us to reexamine our relationships with the animal kingdom. After knowing Wilbur, from *Charlotte's Web,* do we not regard pigs as smarter, more caring, and more interesting? Whimsical, realistic, or allegorical, the best animal fantasies combine humanitarian ideals with a good story.

Recommended animal fantasies

The Song of Pentecost, W. J. Corbett (1983)

The Mouse and His Child, Russell Hoban (1967)

Ace, the Very Important Pig, Dick King-Smith (1990)

Catwings, Ursula LeGuin (1988)

The Cricket in Times Square, George Selden (1960)

The Book of the Dun Cow, Walter Wangerin, Jr. (1978)

High Fantasy

The term *high fantasy* is a fairly recent one. Although we don't know who first used the word *high,* we know that this subgenre evolved from an old form of literature, the medieval romance of the eleventh and twelfth centuries. In this form, legendary exploits of King Arthur and his knights heroically questing for the holy grail are given shape in a literary world. *High* has come to signify a fantasy that resides in a secondary world marked by a medieval ethos of chivalry, honor, and codes of behavior. Perhaps it also refers to the seriousness of purpose and lofty idealism of the hero's quest, which is essentially to restore the world to its innocent, Garden-of-Eden state. This secondary world, magical and at risk, propels theme, characters' actions, and outcomes. It is sometimes called a **perilous realm** because of the danger and suspense. Unicorns, dragons, potions, runes, and magical swords are common in this realm.

Secondary worlds are crucial aspects of high fantasy; indeed most of the great fantasies are named after their worlds—Narnia, Middle-Earth, Earthsea, and Prydain, to mention a few. They are the central symbol of the fantasy, and in order to encourage a reader to step into the world, these secondary worlds must have a logic and an inner consistency that permits belief. They are close enough to the primary world to allow identification, yet far enough away to allow the creation of fantastic creatures and unlikely occurrences.

Because modern high fantasy relates to an older form, the romance, certain characteristics prevail:

- the hero or heroine is an orphan, or of lowly status;
- a destiny is placed on the hero or heroine by a wise, older mentor or an enigmatic character;
- the destiny takes the form of a quest in which the hero/heroine must find something or do something involving danger and hardship, and usually great cost and personal sacrifice as well;
- the destiny, after it is accepted by the hero/heroine, is imbued with great moral fervor, because a clear distinction exists between right and wrong, good and evil;
- the secondary world in which this happens is a medieval world, marked by medieval dress and weaponry, castles, a "simple" way of life, and no technology;
- the climax of the quest is an apocalyptic battle between a small number of "good" forces led by the hero/heroine and a huge army of evil forces;
- characters are flat (except for the hero/heroine); personalities are not developed because action and theme are most important.

Characteristics of high fantasy are summarized in Figure 7.3.

High fantasy is by its nature philosophical, allowing an author to define and separate goodness and evil. Moral dimensions of high fantasy build on ethical and sacred foundations. The main character is a common person who is called upon

Figure 7.3   Characteristics of High Fantasy

Hero or Heroine	Usually an orphan or a person of lowly status
Destiny	A wise, older mentor assigns a task; the task involves great cost and personal sacrifice; the task clearly distinguishes right and wrong
Secondary World	A medieval world, with castles, magic, and no technology
Quest	The journey taken by hero/heroine to accomplish the task; at the end of the journey there is an apocalyptic battle between good and evil
Characters	Characters are generally flat or one-dimensional, with little or no development

to perform beyond his or her capabilities, but somehow summons the strength to do it. Invited by a herald to do a task that is seemingly impossible, the main character often is persuaded by a bit of magic. High fantasy gives us all hope that we, too, can rise beyond our capabilities to achieve our hopes and expectations.

The works of MacDonald, Lewis, and Tolkien defined and heavily influenced this subgenre. As a medieval scholar and a Christian, C. S. Lewis drew especially evocative imagery from biblical and literary sources for his Narnian Chronicles, of which *The Lion, the Witch and the Wardrobe* is first in the series of seven.

Lloyd Alexander's *The High King* (1968) mirrors characteristics of high fantasy. Drawn from *The Mabinogion,* an ancient Welsh collection of four branches of Celtic mythology, the perilous realm is called Prydain, and the hero, Taran, grows from assistant pig keeper to high king when he at last vanquishes evil and discovers his true parentage. The fifth in a series called the Prydain Chronicles, *The High King* combines ancient folklore with a modern story of friendship and a search for self-discovery.

In the four preceding Prydain Chronicles, Taran grows from a young boy to a young man through many adventures that test his soul. His relationship with Eilonwy, an intelligent and articulate princess, grows from their bickering adolescence to a lasting love. In this last chronicle, all Prydain is in jeopardy because Arawn, death-lord of Annuvin, has captured Gwydion's magical sword, Dyrnwyn, and a prophecy of doom spreads across the land. Taran must accept the challenge to rally the cantrevs to fight the death-lord, who grows stronger each day. Familiar characters from previous books are called upon to help—Princess Eilonwy, Fflewddur Fflam, whose harp strings break when he exaggerates, Gurgi, half-person, half-animal, Doli of the Fair Folk, and many others. Taran's responsibility grows, and when Math, high king of Prydain, Coll, a father figure, and other patriots are killed, Taran can barely continue his quest. Irrevocably drawn to the last battle, Taran defeats three cauldron-born (evil soldiers who never die) on the summit of Mt. Dragon, descends into Annuvin, and with the flashing sword kills the serpent that the transformed Arawn had become. Taran then ascends the throne, with

Eilonwy as his queen. Eilonwy gives up her magical power and immortality to become the Queen.

This series has maintained its popularity and its magic through the years (Tunnell & Jacobs, 1988). As high fantasy, it tackles themes such as the use and abuse of power, the meaning of life and death, and justice for all under the law. Lloyd Alexander, of course, continues to add to his impressive bibliography of fantasy, as evidenced by his recent *The Remarkable Journey of Prince Jen* (1991). (See Chapter 10 for its inclusion in a literature unit.)

Other contemporary authors use the structure and elements of high fantasy to create compelling and action-packed fantasies. *The Grey King* (Cooper, 1975), winner of the Newbery award, weaves King Arthur legends into a modern retelling. Will, as a modern boy and an "old one," is destined to keep the power of light alive in our world. As the seventh son of a seventh son, his destiny is mystical indeed.

High fantasy includes other stories set in secondary worlds, with heroes and heroines, journeys, battles between good and evil, and magic as key ingredients. Ursula LeGuin's four books in the *Earthsea* series, beginning with *A Wizard of Earthsea* (1968), marks the youth, middle age, and old age of Ged, archmage of Earthsea, as he discovers his power, uses it to further his own ends, and pays a heavy price. After repenting, Ged finally develops into the master wizard who truly understands balance in all things—Earth and Sea, light and dark, birth and death, real and ideal. (To use *A Wizard of Earthsea* with adolescents, see activity 7 at the end of this chapter.)

In this series, as well as in many others, the knowledge of one's true name plays an important part in the fantasy. Folklore engenders the notion that inherent in each person and object is a true, secret name. Knowing that true name either gives one control over a person or object, or makes one responsible for that person or object.

Closely resembling folktales, some high fantasies seem to be modern retellings of ancient stories, when in fact they are newly created. The secondary, medieval world provides a powerful setting and thus justifies their inclusion into high fantasy. A recent example is *The Fields and the Hills* (Bakken, 1992).

Recommended high fantasies

The Island and the Ring, Laura Stevenson (1991)

The Dragon's Boy, Jane Yolen (1990)

The Shadow Warrior, Patricia Zettner (1990)

Time Fantasy

The notion that time runs in several directions has long fascinated authors, scientists, and philosophers. Is time cyclical, or is it linear? Are there other worlds in different time schemes? In time fantasies, authors construct **parallel worlds** that touch our primary world in magical places, allowing time travel back and forth.

Another world running simultaneously to ours presents all sorts of possibilities in literary invention. In addition, there are historical time fantasies, or time-warp fantasies, in which a character from the present can go back in time, or a character from long ago can come to the present. The author of such a fantasy must create an accurate historical period as well as a logical method of transportation.

Natalie Babbitt plays with the notion of time in *Tuck Everlasting* (1975), in which members of the Tuck family gain immortality by drinking water from a spring in the woods by Winnie Foster's house. The story is told from Winnie's point of view and presents her feeling—that the absence of time in one's life is a burden too heavy to bear. At the end she chooses to forego an immortal life. Was her choice the better one?

Arguably one of the best time fantasies and the one against which others are invariably judged is *Tom's Midnight Garden* (Pearce, 1958). When his brother contracts measles, Tom is sent to live with a boring aunt and uncle. One sleepless night a clock in the hall strikes thirteen, and Tom slips out into the backyard, which has become a garden. He meets a little girl, Hatty, and in subsequent meetings she is different ages in a changing garden. Puzzled, he finally solves the mystery with the help of an elderly woman who lives upstairs. Winner of the Carnegie Medal, this book will cause a reader to regard time differently ever after. As time shifts, its fluidity suggests to us thoughts of actions and consequences, growing older and younger, the way we use time in our lives, and time's relativity.

Recommended time fantasies

A String in the Harp, Nancy Bond (1976)

Stonewords, Pam Conrad (1990)

The Secret World of Polly Flint, Helen Cresswell (1984)

A Dig in Time, Peni Griffin (1991)

Sing for a Gentle Rain, J. Alison James (1990)

The Root Cellar, Janet Lunn (1983)

Science-Fiction Fantasy

Science-fiction fantasy's secondary world is always the future. More speculative and more fantastic than other subgenres, it has evolved from science fiction, itself a fairly recent subgenre in literature.

Science fiction, as a literary form, began with the publication of Mary Shelley's *Frankenstein* in 1817 (Carpenter & Prichard, 1984). By introducing medical technology with the transplanting of a human brain, Mary Shelley explored futuristic social ramifications of such science. Jules Verne launched this subgenre firmly in the last century with his fantastic and stunning predictions of future technology in *Voyage to the Center of the Earth* (1864) and other books.

Science fiction, a blend of rational technological explanations and a literary form called story, seems a paradox. Can an author mix cold hard facts and futuristic machinery into a compelling narrative with interesting characters? If there is too much science, the story suffers; on the other hand, story must accommodate scientific information unobtrusively. The best science fiction not only balances science and fiction, but also provides a vision of the future. It can cause us to rethink gender roles, to plan for a just society, and to reshape institutions—and it can warn us what might happen if we do not change our habits.

The distinction between science fiction and science-fiction fantasy is none too clear, but the latter is a more accessible, less hard-core version of science fiction. In science-fiction fantasy less attention is paid to the accurate scientific explanation of phenomena and more attention is paid to the literary balance of story and phenomena. Whether or not a story is considered science fiction or science-fiction fantasy depends on the degree to which scientific data are based on fact or fiction. When the story is much more important than the science, it is appropriately called science-fiction fantasy. In most examples of this subgenre for children, the term *science-fiction fantasy* or simply *science fantasy* is used.

Technological invention attracts children who have grown up with Nintendo and computers, who understand almost intuitively how to program a VCR. Recent books of science-fiction fantasy capitalize on interests of children and encourage them to think about solutions to today's problems, using technology as well as human creativity and intelligence.

Just such a story, *Away Is a Strange Place to Be* (Hoover, 1989), begins in a futuristic A.D. 2349. Abby Tabor is kidnapped from her home and taken to Vita-Con, a habitat created in outer space to alleviate population crowding on earth. Her insufferable companion is Bryan, a rich kid whose parents have actually arranged to have him taken to VitaCon and its "young pioneers" colony, where behavioral misfits are controlled by stun-guns and harsh overseers. Using her intelligence and self-reliance, Abby escapes. Upon her return to earth, she arranges care and education for other young pioneers. In this story, Hoover shows what earth might become in 350 years. It is a dystopian (rather than utopian) view of an overcrowded, uncaring world. In an action-packed narrative, the characters of Abby and her foil, Bryan, are well developed, each balancing the other. VitaCon becomes the antagonist to Abby's role as protagonist; the habitat is an antiseptic, mind-controlling, heavily monitored, and impersonal force. As science-fiction fantasy, the mesmerizing story balances well with futuristic technology.

Another science-fiction fantasy for older readers is *Eva* (Dickinson, 1989). When the brain of a young girl is transplanted into the body of a chimpanzee, she becomes the person of the future, combining human traits with an animal's prowess and strength. Ethical questions pertaining to organ transplants, the use of this hybrid creation for good or evil purposes, and the advantages and/or disadvantages of procreation are addressed. Eva has to learn to balance her human memories of self with the animal she has become. Her appearance frightens and intrigues parents, friends, and those who want to exploit her. In this provocative novel, Dickinson urges us to think about the repercussions of new biological sciences.

Recommended science-fiction fantasies

When the Tripods Came, John Christopher (1988)

From *Eva* by Peter Dickinson, copyright © 1988. Used by permission of Delacorte Press Permissions Department.

Enchantress from the Stars, Sylvia Engdahl (1970)
Letters from Atlantis, Robert Silverberg (1990)
Strange Attractors, William Sleator (1990)

Extraordinary Characters and Inventions

Children's literature is replete with extraordinary characters drawn from the experiences of childhood. Nannies who turn common outings into adventures, toys who come to life, tiny people who live in familiar nooks and crannies—all these are easily imagined by most children. Characters like Mary Poppins and Pippi Longstocking have long delighted children with their superhuman feats. Many modern fantasies contain make-believe characters who act in realistic situations. Superman and other comic-book heroes and heroines come from a tradition of magical characters in folklore and myth. Special powers of all these characters lift the stories into the fantasy realm. Lloyd Alexander writes eloquently about populating an imaginary world with all manner of imaginary characters when he says "They must have real weight, solidity, dimension. Their fantastic condition must speak to our real one" (Alexander, 1987, p. 196).

A contemporary story with mythlike dimensions is *Maniac Magee* (Spinelli, 1990). Maniac is truly an extraordinary character with superhuman attributes, but the story is so realistic that some might argue that it is not a fantasy at all. However, his extraordinary ability to run, the depth of his compassion, and his other unique qualities—even his heroic separation from other characters—cast him into the fantasy genre. Jerry Spinelli, the author, calls him a legendary hero drawn from common childhood memories and myths (Spinelli, 1991).

Since *Gulliver's Travels* delighted readers, miniature worlds and tiny people have held a special fascination for those who appreciate fantasy. A gentle, microcosmic world of a dollhouse contrasts with the harsh reality of Lucie Babbidge's existence in *Lucie Babbidge's House* (Cassedy, 1989). Tiny dollhouse figures come to life and offer happiness and acceptance to Lucie, who is ridiculed by adults and

From *Maniac Magee* by Jerry Spinelli. Copyright © 1990 by Jerry Spinelli. By permission of Little, Brown and Company.

other children. As a retreat from despair and confusion, the dollhouse and its family help Lucie to overcome her insecurity. This is a book that demonstrates the power of fantasy to change the life of an unhappy little girl, although sometimes it is not too clear about the line between realism and fantasy. The dollhouse works as a way into the fantasy world, which is in Lucie's mind.

Personified dolls and toys represent an obvious magical element in children's books. Who among us has not dreamed of a talking, comforting teddy bear? Memorable toys, like those in *Winnie-the-Pooh* (Milne, 1926) and in the sentimental *The Velveteen Rabbit* (Williams, 1922), become real as they move and act in the primary world.

Supernatural characters create wonderment and sometimes lift the curtain to another world of suspense, terror, or laughter. *The Wish Giver* (Brittain, 1983) comes to Coven Tree and its inhabitants find out that wishes can be dangerous. A Newbery Honor Book, it is one of four about the quirky mythical town.

For older readers, Brother Rush in *Sweet Whispers, Brother Rush* (Hamilton, 1982) is a ghost who comes to his niece and helps her to understand her brother's illness. The story focuses on family relationships in the desperate circumstances of loss and illness much more than the fantasy element. However, Tree's experiences confronting the ghost and reaching through the mirror to journey with him are powerful and imaginative.

Two fantasies that are of questionable value are *The Indian in the Cupboard* (Banks, 1980) and *Charlie and the Chocolate Factory* (Dahl, 1972). Because of the stereotypical nature of the characters, these fantasies perpetuate ideas of racial inferiority. Little Bear, the small Indian in the cupboard, is savage and naive, speaking in the most unlikely guttural syntax (Slapin and Seale, 1988). The Oompa-Loompas in the chocolate factory, coming from darkest Africa, are primitive, rhythmic, exactly alike, and devoid of humanizing characteristics. Although they are popular with children, fantasies with demeaning extraordinary characters should not be tolerated.

Recommended fantasies with extraordinary characters

The BFG, Roald Dahl (1982)

Gregory, Maw, and the Mean One, David Gifaldi (1992)

Shoebag, Mary James (1990)

The Dark Thirty: Southern Tales of the Supernatural, Patricia
    McKissack (1992)

EVALUATING FANTASY

Good fantasy has to be compelling and well written, with action and some well-developed characters, hallmarks of all literature. Because of the particularly fanciful nature of this genre, attention must be paid to fantasy elements and how they are used. Fantasy elements could be a secondary or parallel world as the setting, a bit of magic, a personified animal or toy, or an extraordinary character who is good or evil. These elements must be a convincing part of the plot, rising

Figure 7.4   Evaluating Modern Fantasy

Subgenre	My Personal Response
Animal Fantasy	How believable are the anthropomorphic animals? Which animal characteristics do they retain while adding human ones?
High Fantasy	Is the main character heroic enough? How believable is the secondary world? Is the quest dramatic and purposeful? What philosophical truths underlie the heroic quest?
Time Fantasy	Is the passage between times convincing? If two time periods are shown (e.g., historical and modern), are they both authentic? Are characters compelling and the plot well paced?
Science-fiction Fantasy	Does the technology seem contrived? What does the human dimension add? In what way does the story raise questions about the future?
Extraordinary Characters and Inventions	Are characters stereotypical? How plausible is the relationship between extraordinary and ordinary?

from an inner coherence of the entire story. Logic and consistency have an important part in fantasy, as they help a reader cross the threshold into a secondary world; we must believe in the fantasy, understanding and enjoying the transformation of truth in another dimension.

In evaluating a work of fantasy, pay attention to

- how fantasy elements are used;
- how the balance between fantastic imagery and what we perceive realism to be is achieved; and
- how inevitable and moving the plot is.

In addition to these general elements, some particular questions related to each of the subgenres are listed in Figure 7.4. Of course, as you select books, your purpose and audience must also be considered.

●　●　●　●　●
NOTABLE AUTHORS OF FANTASY

Although several authors and notable books have been mentioned within each subgenre, there are of course many more significant works of fantasy. In addition to the recommended list following each subgenre, the following names of reputable authors are offered to allow you to explore libraries and bookstores and search for fantasies that appeal to you. It seems that more often in fantasy than in other genres, authors write several books based on a series of characters centered in one place, such as the Chronicles of Narnia (seven books), or Susan Cooper's The Dark Is Rising, a series of five books. For that reason, authors are listed rather than single titles. A suggested project in the Implications for Instruction section in this chapter will outline a strategy to get to know these authors. The subgenre following an author's name gives some indication of his or her specialty.

Lucy Boston (time fantasy)

Eleanor Cameron (time fantasy)

John Christopher (science-fiction fantasy)

Alan Garner (high fantasy)

Diana Wynne Jones (extraordinary characters)

Penelope Lively (time fantasy)

Anne McCaffrey (science-fiction fantasy)

Robin McKinley (high fantasy)

Andre Norton (science-fiction fantasy)

Patricia Wrightson (extraordinary characters)

● ● ● ● ●
SUMMARY

In the mid-1800s, modern fantasy developed from fairy tales, myths, legends, fables, and other narratives of traditional literature. By the end of the century, a recognized genre had been established. Extraordinary characters, secondary worlds, a touch of the impossible—all of these fantasy elements and more found their way into remarkable and compelling books for children.

More abstract than other genres, fantasy requires a willing suspension of disbelief. Like poetry, fantasy explains universal truths through metaphor. Fantasy is serious, with profound issues of good and evil, mortality and immortality, compassion and revenge inherent in stories. Fantasy is humorous, poking fun at our eccentricities and revealing human nature from a different point of view.

The importance of reading fantasy was implicit in each section. As stated, fantasy liberates the imagination as it suggests alternatives in a secondary (or a primary) world and encourages divergent thinking. Oftentimes it depicts moral and ethical dimensions in characters and actions. Fantasy challenges the status quo in ways that realistic fiction cannot.

This genre was defined by the caveat that at least one impossible element makes the work a fantasy. Subgenres arise from the grouping of common elements inherent in a set of fantasies, and the elements most often relate to the setting or characters created by an author. Examples of subgenres were given, including animal fantasy, high fantasy, time fantasy, science-fiction fantasy, and extraordinary characters and inventions. Each of the subgenres was further described and at least one contemporary work within it analyzed. To summarize, here are subgenres with the impossible element that provides a foundation for the fantasy.

Subgenre	Impossible Element
Animal fantasy	Anthropomorphized animals
High fantasy	Secondary world
Time fantasy	Parallel or historical world
Science-fiction fantasy	Future world
Extraordinary characters and Inventions	Anthropomorphized characters or objects

Because of the wealth of offerings in modern fantasy, a section on notable authors filled out the general discussion and suggested a search for interesting books.

• • • • •

IMPLICATIONS FOR INSTRUCTION

This section is divided into three parts. *Reflections* will give you a chance to reflect on some of the ideas, issues, and controversies presented in the chapter. Many of the Reflections are multifaceted, so that groups of people can react to different parts of the main idea inherent in each question. *Projects* will encourage your direct involvement with the material. *Activities* are suggested so that you can bring fantasy and children together in a classroom or similar setting. Activities for the primary level focus primarily on animal fantasies because other subgenres for younger readers are relatively rare, except as read-aloud books. Activities for intermediate and middle grade readers are more diverse.

Reflections

1. Are you drawn to a particular subgenre of fantasy? Does the romantic quest appeal to you? Or animal fantasies? Or the supernatural? What are your feelings toward fantasy as a whole? What are your childhood memories of reading fantasies?

2. Consistency, logic, and rationality in a fantasy are often overlooked because fantasy elements are more spectacular and thought-provoking. Think about the realism of a particular fantasy, however, such as *A Wrinkle in Time* (L'Engle, 1962) or *The Wonderful Wizard of Oz* (Baum, 1900). Reflect on the balance of realism and fantasy and how the author worked to achieve it.

3. If you were creating a fantasy world, what would it be like? What kinds of creatures would populate the world? Who (or what) would run the world? What laws or principles, scientific and political, would govern your world?

4. Is modern fantasy a popular genre today with children? Do some children seem to prefer it? When and what kind of children do you think are drawn to fantasy? Test your predictions against some research on children's preferences.

5. How does the hero/heroine in fantasy differ from heroes and heroines in realistic stories? (You can quickly preview the next chapter to recall some main characters in realism, if you want.) Compare two similar characters (in age and sex), one from fantasy and one from realistic fiction, such as *Maniac Magee* and *Bingo Brown*, for example.

6. You'll notice there is no multicultural bibliography in this chapter. Do you think children of color are adequately represented in this genre? Can you find some examples of characters from different cultural groups in modern fantasy?

7. Are you concerned about the stereotypical characters in *The Indian in the Cupboard* and *Charlie and the Chocolate Factory*? Do you agree with the criticism? Are there other fantasies that are questionable in this sense?

Projects

1. Select one of the authors in the "Notable Authors of Fantasy" section and develop an annotated bibliography of his/her work. You may want to choose your author by previewing some of his/her books in a library, by reading about the author in a reference such as *Twentieth Century Children's Writers*, (Kirkpatrick, 1985), or by asking around for preferences from friends.

2. Try some classifying by subgenre to see if the categories work for you. For example, take the five titles found in Figure 7.1, at the beginning of this chapter, and categorize them according to the subgenres given. Since most are mentioned in the remaining sections, you can test your hypotheses.

3. What are the origins of some folkloric elements in fantasy? For example, why are the numbers 3 and 7 often significant? Are there other significant numbers? What colors are associated with magic? What are some plants, animals, and symbols that are often associated with magic and fantasy? How do these bits of common wisdom affect our lives today?

4. Write a short story related to one of the subgenres. What if you wanted to create a character who traveled back in time to another period—the Revolutionary War, for example? Why would a character want to do that, and how could she/he? Explore some of the intricacies of writing fantasy.

5. How much fantasy is published each year, compared to realistic fiction or nonfiction? Gather some market research on fantasy's current place in children's literature. What percentage of books for children published each year is considered to be fantasy?

Activities for the Primary Level

1. Read an animal fantasy with children, then encourage them to bring an animal or bird to life in a story. Personified mice, rabbits, donkeys, crows, and eagles have roles in many animal fantasies, and can motivate the writing process in young writers. Encourage children to tell about what the animal

sees, hears, smells, touches, and tastes in a story with a beginning, a middle, and an end.

2. Children will enjoy bringing a toy or a stuffed animal to school and writing stories about it. Personifying beloved toys will lead to further animal fantasies. As described in the first activity, starting with the senses is a good way to develop an animal's or a toy's personification. An example of this happened in a second-grade classroom recently. A teacher and her students together kept a daily journal accompanied by a toy bear. Each child took the journal and the toy bear home on a rotating basis and parents were encouraged to help their child write about the day from the bear's point of view. The parents were drawn into school activities from another perspective, and the children enjoyed being with the toy bear.

3. Young children can create a secondary world based on their predictions about the future. After reading aloud books like *The Magic School Bus Lost in the Solar System* (Cole, 1990) or *The Green Book* (Walsh, 1982) and brainstorming future communities, children can draw or build a fantasy world that incorporates their own ideas.

4. Time travel in the easy reader *Dinosaurs Before Dark* (Osborne, 1992) takes two children back in time to when dinosaurs lived. Their travel is generated by a wish as they hold a book with a scene pictured on the book's jacket. Many primary children can read this fantasy, make a wish, and then describe their imaginary visits. (Have some colorful book jackets around depicting interesting places that would encourage children to write or speak of imaginary adventures.)

5. Films, videotapes, and audiotapes provide fantasy experiences for children, and often can be related to books or characters already known. Explore resources—in video stores, the Weston Woods catalog, or libraries—for connections to books, and compare versions of fantasies.

6. Children enjoy dressing up as their favorite fantasy characters, at Halloween or other times. Dressing as a book character can also include realistic characters as well.

Activities for the Intermediate and Middle Levels

1. Before Halloween, present some literary ghosts to motivate children into language arts activities—writing stories, poems, or plays; creating bulletin boards and puppets; or simply choosing stories for reading groups. (Ghouls, vampires, giants, or other suitable extraordinary characters could be substituted.) If Halloween is not a holiday you celebrate, perhaps there are other times and reasons to enjoy fantastic characters, from dragons to dinosaurs.

2. Work with children to organize a scavenger hunt through several high fantasies to find: swords, chalices, runes, potions, medieval customs and food, real animals, imaginary animals, real people, imaginary people, symbols of evil, symbols of good, and so on.

3. Create a secondary world with dioramas or other three-dimensional displays. For example, children could build a scene from Narnia or from Norton Juster's *The Phantom Tollbooth* in a shoe-box or on a table. Land forms, characters in costume, and flora and fauna require careful reading and problem-solving in the accurate construction of such a scene.

4. After reading high fantasy, make a list of the characteristics of a hero or heroine with your children. Coming from lowly status and rising to a position of power and authority, accepting a difficult task, and overthrowing evil incarnate, should make a hero or heroine interesting and motivating to many students. (You might want to discuss if there are differences between heroes and heroines, and compare some well-known ones.)

5. Story structure in high fantasy is predictable, with events usually following the order on page 135. With class participation, build a story staircase using a work of high fantasy such as *The Shadow Warrior* (Zettner, 1990), beginning with the introduction, continuing through the quest, and ending with the great battle.

6. If you salute an "author of the month" in your literature program, make sure fantasy authors are included.

7. Two activities excerpted from a study guide on *A Wizard of Earthsea*, a young-adult book, follow. Use them as models for similar activities when you create study guides based on literature that you want to explore with children.

Common elements in the story (categorizing and labeling)

In the lists of three phrases or words below, see what they have in common, then find another phrase or word that fits and write it on the fourth line. On the fifth line below each group, write how they are related (the first is done for you):

"Wicked as woman's magic"	Skiorh
"Rules change in the Reaches"	Jasper
"Infinite are the arguments of the Mages"	Pechvary
"Third time is the charm"	4. _____
Common sayings (proverbs) of Earthsea	5. _____

Roke	Herbal
Re Albi	Chanter
Gont	Hand
4. _____	4. _____
5. _____	5. _____

Raven	Finding
Falcon	Binding
Otak	Weatherworking
4. _____	4. _____
5. _____	5. _____

Figure 7.5   Balance of
Earthsea

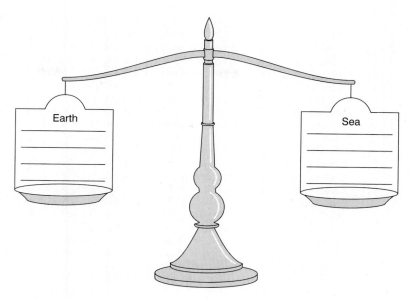

The concept of equilibrium (determining theme)
The world of Earthsea existed through a reconciliation of opposing forces. What
are some of those forces? Add them to the balance pictured in Figure 7.5.

● ● ● ● ●

REFERENCES

Children's Works Cited

Adams, R. (1974). *Watership down.* New York: Macmillan.
Alexander, L. (1964). *The book of three.* New York: Holt.
Alexander, L. (1968). *The high king.* New York: Holt.
Alexander, L. (1991). *The remarkable journey of Prince Jen.* New York: Dutton.
Babbitt, N. (1975). *Tuck everlasting.* New York: Farrar.
Bakken, H. (1992). *The fields and the hills.* New York: Clarion.
Banks, L. (1980). *The Indian in the cupboard.* New York: Doubleday.
Barrie, J. (1991). *Peter Pan.* New York: Viking. (1904).
Baum, L. F. (1900). *The wonderful wizard of Oz.* New York: Morrow.
Bond, N. (1976). *A string in the harp.* New York: Atheneum.
Brittain, B. (1983). *The wish giver.* New York: Harper.
Cassedy, S. (1989). *Lucie Babbidge's house.* New York: Crowell.
Christopher, J. (1988). *When the tripods came.* New York: Dutton.
Cleary, B. (1965). *The mouse and the motorcycle.* New York: Morrow.
Cole, J. (1990). *The magic school bus lost in the solar system.* New York: Scholastic.
Conrad, P. (1990). *Stonewords.* New York: Harper.
Cooper, S. (1975). *The grey king.* New York: Atheneum.
Corbett, W. J. (1983). *The song of Pentecost.* New York: Dutton.
Cresswell, H. (1984). *The secret world of Polly Flint.* New York: Macmillan.
Dahl, R. (1972). *Charlie and the chocolate factory.* New York: Knopf.

Dahl, R. (1982). *The BFG*. New York: Farrar, Strauss & Giroux.
Dickinson, P. (1988). *Eva*. New York: Delacorte.
Engdahl, S. (1970). *Enchantress from the stars*. New York: Atheneum.
Gifaldi, D. (1992). *Gregory, Maw, and the mean one*. New York: Clarion.
Grahame, K. (1984). *The wind in the willows*. New York: Penguin. (1908).
Griffin, P. (1991). *A dig in time*. New York: Macmillan.
Hamilton, V. (1982). *Sweet whispers, Brother Rush*. New York: Philomel.
Hoban, R. (1967). *The mouse and his child*. New York: Harper & Row.
Hoover, H. (1989). *Away is a strange place to be*. New York: Dutton.
Jacques, B. (1987). *Redwall*. New York: Philomel.
Jacques, B. (1990). *Mattimeo*. New York: Philomel.
James, J. A. (1990). *Sing for a gentle rain*. New York: Atheneum.
James, M. (1990). *Shoebag*. New York: Scholastic.
Juster, N. (1961). *The phantom tollbooth*. New York: Random House.
King-Smith, D. (1990). *Ace, the very important pig*. New York: Crown.
LeGuin, U. (1968). *A wizard of Earthsea*. New York: Parnassus.
LeGuin, U. (1988). *Catwings*. New York: Orchard.
L'Engle, M. (1962). *A wrinkle in time*. New York: Farrar.
Lewis, C. S. (1988). *The lion, the witch and the wardrobe*. New York: Macmillan. (1950).
Lindgren, A. (1950). *Pippi Longstocking*. New York: Viking Penguin.
Lofting, H. (1988). *The voyages of Dr. Dolittle*. New York: Delacorte. (1922).
Lunn, J. (1983). *The root cellar*. New York: Scribner's.
McKissack, P. (1992). *The dark thirty: Southern tales of the supernatural*. New York: Knopf.
Milne, A. A. (1988). *Winnie-the-Pooh*. New York: Dutton. (1926).
Nesbit, E. (1907). *The enchanted castle*. (Reprinted in 1992). New York: Morrow Books of Wonder.
Norton, M. (1953). *The borrowers*. New York: Harcourt.
O'Brien, R. (1971). *Mrs. Frisby and the rats of NIMH*. New York: Atheneum.
Osborne, M. P. (1992). *Dinosaurs before dark*. New York: Random.
Pearce, P. (1958). *Tom's midnight garden*. Philadelphia: Lippincott.
Selden, G. (1960). *The cricket in Times Square*. New York: Farrar.
Silverberg, R. (1990). *Letters from Atlantis*. New York: Atheneum.
Sleator, W. (1990). *Strange attractors*. New York: Dutton.
Spinelli, J. (1990). *Maniac Magee*. Boston: Little, Brown.
Stevenson, L. (1991). *The island and the ring*. Boston: Houghton.
Tolkien, J. R. R. (1938). *The hobbit*. Boston: Houghton Mifflin. (1937).
Travers, P. L. ((1934). *Mary Poppins*. New York: Harcourt.
Walsh, J. P. (1982). *The green book*. New York: Farrar, Straus.
Wangerin, W., Jr. (1978). *The book of the dun cow*. New York: Harper.
White, E. B. (1952). *Charlotte's web*. New York: Harper & Row.
Williams, M. (1991). *The velveteen rabbit*. New York: Doubleday. (1922).
Yolen, J. (1990). *The dragon's boy*. New York: Harper & Row.
Zettner, P. (1990). *The shadow warrior*. New York: Atheneum.

Professional Works Cited

Alexander, L. (1987). Opening statement to 'The perilous realms: A colloquy.' In B. Harrison & G. Maguire (Eds.), *Innocence and experience* (p. 196). New York: Lothrop, Lee & Shepard.
Cameron, E. (1962). *The green and burning tree*. Boston: Little, Brown.
Carpenter, H., & Prichard, M. (1984). *The Oxford companion to children's literature*. New York: Oxford University Press.
Kirkpatrick, D. (Ed.). (1985). *Twentieth century children's writers* (2nd ed.). Chicago: St. James Press.

Levin, B. (1987). Introduction to fantasy: the perilous realms. In B. Harrison & G. Maguire (Eds.), *Innocence and experience* (p. 167). New York: Lothrop, Lee & Shepard.

McHarque, G. (1972). *The impossible people.* New York: Dell.

Moss, A., & Stott, J. (1986). *The family of stories.* New York: Holt, Rinehart & Winston.

Opie, I., & Opie, P. (1974). *The classic fairy tales.* London: Oxford University Press.

Slapin, B., & Seale, D. (Eds.). (1988). *Books without bias: Through Indian eyes.* Berkeley, CA: Oyate.

Spinelli, J. (1991). Maniac Magee: Homer on George Street. *Horn Book, LXVII,* 1, 40–41.

Swinfen, A. (1984). *In defence of fantasy.* London: Routledge & Kegan Paul.

Townsend, J.R. (1987). *Written for children* (3rd rev. ed.). Philadelphia: Lippincott.

Tunnell, M., & Jacobs, J. (1988). Alexander's chronicles of Prydain: Twenty years later. *School Library Journal,* April 1988.

Additional Resources

Arrowsmith, N. (1977). *A field guide to the little people.* New York: Hill and Wang.
This study describes the realm of faery, with seventy-nine entries explaining the lineage, habitat, appearance, and general characteristics of all in the elf world. Will-o'-the-wisps, pixies, seal people, moss people, leprechauns, and many others are included. See also Faeries (1978), described and illustrated by Brian Froud and Alan Lee. New York: Harry N. Abrams.

Blount, M. (1974). *Animal land: The creatures of children's fiction.* New York: Avon.
From Toad in Wind in the Willows to Jack London's White Fang, animals in fantasy and realistic fiction are studied in a social and literary context.

Boyer, R., & Zahorski, K. (Eds.). (1977). *The fantastic imagination.* New York: Avon.
An anthology of notable high fantasy, this volume also includes brief biographies of the writers. George MacDonald, J. R. R. Tolkien, C. S. Lewis, Ursula LeGuin, and others are represented.

Butler, F., & Rotert, R. (Eds.). (1986). *Triumphs of the spirit in children's literature.* Hamden, CT: Shoe String Press.
Twenty-five essays about well-known fantasies and realistic fiction by critics are included, with an introduction by Madeleine L'Engle and foreword by Marcia Brown.

Flender, M., & Landes, S. (1987). *A Book Wise curriculum guide to the Magician's Nephew.* Cambridge, MA: Book Wise, Inc.
This curriculum guide to literature, as well as many others published by Book Wise, contains many activities suitable for middle school students. Quite thorough, numbering 57 pages, the guide focuses on this C. S. Lewis classic and one of the Narnian Chronicles.

Townsend, J. R. (1971). *A sense of story: Essays on contemporary writers for children.* Boston: Horn Book.
Nineteen eminent children's authors are profiled and their works analyzed in this volume. British, American, and Australian writers such as Lucy Boston, Andre Norton, Ivan Southall, and others are included.

Travelers in time. (1990). Cambridge, England: Green Bay Publications (72 Water Lane, Histon, CB4 4LR).
This volume contains proceedings of the 1989 Summer Institute held at Cambridge University by Children's Literature New England. Speakers whose talks are presented include: Virginia Hamilton, Penelope Lively, Peter Dickinson, Susan Cooper, and others.

Chapter Eight

Realism in Present and Past

• • • • •
INTRODUCTION AND RESPONSE

Elderly stepparents May and Ob have taken care of Summer since she was orphaned at six years old. Now twelve and grieving because of May's recent death, Summer must carry on even though Ob is withdrawing from daily activities and communication. Worried, Summer tries to find a way to ease the pain of loss for both of them. So begins Cynthia Rylant's touching realistic novel, *Missing May* (1992), winner of the 1993 Newbery Award. As contemporary realistic fiction, this story is set in the real world of a West Virginia town, with credible characters and a believable plot. So compelling is the writing that we immediately relate to the circumstances and the characters. We enter Summer's world vicariously, knowing that this situation could really happen. Events, emotions, setting, and characters mirror life as we understand it to be.

Realistic fiction is the most popular genre of children's fiction. Many children want to read about characters just like themselves in situations that they recognize. Common experiences, from the joy of achieving a goal to the pain of losing a friend, are described in fiction. Within the bounds of story, we see ourselves, our families, and our neighborhoods.

Because this is a popular genre, with many different kinds of stories, this chapter will no doubt trigger reading experiences remembered from your childhood. To begin thinking about these stories, recall now some realistic books from your memories of early reading. If you were asked to name a work of realistic fiction that had a profound effect on you as a child or adolescent, what would it be?

Spend a moment searching for a "best" book, and write its title or something about it here.

_____

Why do you think it was an important book for you at the time?

Perhaps your book will be mentioned in the discussion of realistic fiction that follows. The discussion is actually divided into two parts, but both parts deal with realistic prose fiction. First, realistic fiction is defined. Then the terms *contemporary* and *historical* are related to time periods, followed by the value of each for children. As this genre has been controversial in its realistic portrayal of problems children and adults face, several books have been hallmarks of change. These books will be highlighted in a brief history of realistic fiction.

Next, subgenres of contemporary fiction will be presented, with examples of recent mainstream and multicultural stories. An evaluation scheme for realistic fiction follows the subgenres, and a list of notable authors concludes the first half of the chapter.

Historical realistic fiction is the subject of the second part. A definition, themes, and subgenres based on historical eras are offered, along with guidelines for the evaluation of historical fiction.

A special bibliography of international realism, with contemporary and historical examples, lists books of recent copyright not previously mentioned in subgenres. Controversies inherent in a graphic depiction of realism are highlighted in the summary. How "real" can literature for children be? Controversies frequently center on elements of violence, profanity, sexuality, and other aspects of reality that are found in children's books. These aspects often invite censorship; if censorship is applied, what is an intelligent response? The summary suggests a mechanism for dealing with this sometimes explosive situation. Finally, Implications for Instruction elaborates on the importance of this genre by providing strategies and projects for classroom use.

Because there are so many examples of realistic fiction mentioned in this chapter, someone new to children's literature may feel overwhelmed. If so, it is important to preview the chapter for titles and then construct a reading list with one or two examples for each subgenre. As previously expressed in this text, it is crucial that children's books be read alongside the descriptive and evaluative material so that opinions can be formed and validated.

● ● ● ● ●
DEFINING REALISTIC FICTION

Fiction is the organization of a series of patterns we call story (Nodelman, 1992). Fiction, or story, is the most characteristic mode of children's literature; it is what we generally think of first when we define literature for children. Realistic fiction, then, is the "real" story; it is what we perceive reality to be, filtered through the literary devices of story. What we perceive reality to be, or the "real world," is slightly different for each of us, as our perceptions are individualistic and come from a composite of psychological and physical attributes. When our unique perceptions as readers and authors are fastened onto the fictional world of literature with its demands of plot, theme, setting, character, and so forth, realism is subjective and abstract. Thus it becomes fiction, which is a metaphor for truth. Jill Paton Walsh, a writer and critic, points out the dual nature of *real* and *imaginary* when she says, "Realistic fiction is about imaginary people, living in imagined contexts, doing what was never done, saying what was never said" (Walsh, 1981, pp. 35–36).

As authors draw a story from the real world, they fictionalize as they create scenarios and characters, and invent plots and points of view. This is the art of telling a story. Nevertheless, the story is grounded in common perceptions of what life is like. Realistic fiction must be believable when tested against our perceptions of reality, and good writers can help readers see common and familiar things in a new way. Conversely, good writers also help us see uncommon and unfamiliar things in situations that seem real, helping us learn from vicarious experience just as we learn from actual experience.

Realistic fiction requires the balance between make-believe and reality, as does fantasy. However, fantasy interjects another element, a magical element, that realistic fiction does not (see Chapter 7). Children are sometimes confused between the realism and the fiction of a contemporary or historical story. If it seems real, how can it be fiction? By reading and writing stories about familiar experiences and by describing characters, children can develop a sense of what is fiction and what is not. Comparing fiction and nonfiction (see Chapter 9) will also help to internalize differences.

Contemporary and Historical Realistic Fiction

The terms *contemporary* and *historical* refer to setting. Contemporary is present time; historical is past. The dividing line between present and past is sometimes vague, however. Moreover, what is contemporary for an adult may not necessarily be contemporary for a child, the primary audience for a book. A story set in the late 1960s, for example, is likely to be in the distant past for a child. In this chapter, an arbitrary line about the middle of the century will be used to separate historical from contemporary. That is, books with stories about ancient times continuing until World War II and its aftermath will be considered historical fiction; books dealing with the 1960s and beyond will be considered contemporary.

Value of Contemporary Realism

Children and adolescents learn about themselves, their peers, and a wider span of relationships, problems, and ideas through literature that reflects reality. A friendship between a child and his pet is realistically portrayed in *Henry and Mudge and the Wild Wind* (Rylant, 1993). When books such as this one depict situations and events that are easily within a child's understanding, the realism aids involvement and empathy. Even when stories are far removed from a child's point

He whistled "Jingle Bells."

He whistled "Happy Birthday."

He even whistled "The Star-Spangled

Banner" (not very well).

11

of reference, realism is the bridge that often carries readers into the unknown. Thus literature extends the range of life experiences, as it allows a safe exploration of human relations and geography through the imagination of the reading process. Through imagination, readers can live vicariously in a Somali village or an urban apartment. Characters who are solving problems, building self-esteem, and learning to cope with disabilities, for example, serve as models for living in our contemporary world.

Value of Historical Realism

Children relive the past through historical realism. They can gain an understanding of their own heritage or someone else's in books that portray the human condition with dignity. By looking at the past through a compelling story, readers see interrelationships of past and present—how the past influences the present and predicts the future. Historical realism helps children see and judge the mistakes of the past. Because **change** is a constant condition of life, historical fiction helps readers realize that change is essential—that growth and development depend on change.

• • • • •
HISTORY OF REALISTIC FICTION

Realistic fiction began with Daniel Defoe's novel, *Robinson Crusoe,* which was published in 1719. Although not written principally for children, it proved to be popular with a wide audience and encouraged many other writers to experiment with a realistic, though fictionalized, story. A few years later, in 1744, John Newbery began publishing realistic and didactic stories such as *A Little Pretty Pocket Book* for children.

Outstanding realism of the nineteenth century and the early twentieth is captured in the following list. (Note how many of the books have been made into movies. Realism makes for easier adaptation than other genres.)

1826　*The Last of the Mohicans,* James Fenimore Cooper

1865　*Hans Brinker, or the Silver Skates: A Story of Life in Holland,* Mary Mapes Dodge

1868　*Little Women,* Louisa May Alcott

1876　*The Adventures of Tom Sawyer,* Mark Twain

1883　*Treasure Island,* Robert Louis Stevenson

1884　*Heidi,* Johanna Spyri

1888　*Otto of the Silver Hand,* Howard Pyle

1911　*The Secret Garden,* Frances Hodgson Burnett

1932　*Little House in the Big Woods,* Laura Ingalls Wilder

1938　*The Yearling,* Marjorie Kinnan Rawlings

What would you add to the list? Have some outstanding books been omitted?

Great adventures, as in *Tom Sawyer,* unforgettable characters *(Heidi),* and the depth of emotional intensity *(The Secret Garden)* have rendered these stories classics. Other books portraying families in crisis, children coping with adversity, adventure, and mystery have been written by such authors as Juliana Horatia Ewing, Charlotte Yonge, Charles Dickens, O. Henry, Sir Arthur Conan Doyle, and Kate Douglas Wiggin, to name just a few.

From the Victorian era through the early twentieth century, authors produced many stories of sentimental and idealized family life in which children were unrealistically portrayed. As a counterpoint to the sweetness and light, Robert Louis Stevenson's *Treasure Island* brought a new ingredient of swashbuckling high adventure to literature for children. Similarly, Howard Pyle popularized historical realism with his tale of medieval German robber barons in *Otto of the Silver Hand.*

One has only to look at the list of early Newbery winners, beginning in 1922, as well as awards in other countries to note the prevalence of realistic fiction, both contemporary and historical. Many outstanding books enabled children to read stories about their own communities and the wider world. In fact, the period from 1925 through 1940 was called a golden age of children's literature in the United States (Smith, 1963) because of the high quality of many books. Laura

Ingalls Wilder's seven Little House books typified this productive period, as did the poignant realistic animal story *The Yearling*.

After World War II, realistic fiction in the United States began to show more diversity in character and conflict. An early coming-of-age novel that set the stage for a new realism was *Catcher in the Rye* (Salinger, 1951). Teenaged Holden Caulfield's language, behavior, and alienation is still controversial.

Family stories continued to be the norm, but a new kind of family story, *Harriet the Spy* (Fitzhugh, 1964), proved to be prophetic in its more realistic depiction of children. Harriet was a strong-willed, intelligent, somewhat disobedient, humorous, and curious girl, and the novel revealed a psychological and philosophical depth new to children's realistic fiction (Wolf, 1975).

As society moved through the turbulent 1960s, children's literature also felt the clash of different values. What had been considered inappropriate in reading material for children was questioned, as authors wrote books that actually reflected the lives children were leading. The young author S. E. Hinton wrote about violence between socioeconomic classes and an unconventional family headed by an older brother in *The Outsiders* (1967). Other groundbreaking books in the 1960s broke taboos in children's literature when they dealt with controversial topics such as sexuality, death, dysfunctional families, alcoholism, drugs, eating disorders, and abuse. Paul Zindel, M. E. Kerr, Norma Klein, and other authors wrote to a young adult audience, embracing issues that were new. *Are You There, God? It's Me, Margaret* (Blume, 1970) was one of the tamer ones, speaking frankly about menstruation. By the 1980s, there seemed to be no topic that was not tackled within the context of fiction for young people. Book after book cast a juvenile protagonist into lifelike circumstances. Some were well written, but more often than not they were didactic, shallow, and narrow stories, usually written in first person to convey personal alienation and hostility (Egoff, 1980). When the shock value of some of the more lurid stories, such as the anonymous *Go Ask Alice* (1971), had run its course, a more evenhanded, balanced story resulted.

In the last decade and a half, writers seem to have moved from a restrictive focus on a problem to a more inclusive view, balancing all elements of story. No longer is a novel defined by its problem; the condition is part of characters' lives. Examples bringing about this change to a fuller treatment of realism were Newbery award winners *Bridge to Terabithia* (Paterson, 1977), *Jacob Have I Loved* (Paterson, 1980), and *Dear Mr. Henshaw* (Cleary, 1983).

In addition to the new realism, contemporary realistic fiction broke barriers of other kinds. African American characters slowly became more obvious in important roles, though until the 1970s, they were not necessarily more frequently portrayed (Carlson, 1970). *Zeely* (Hamilton, 1967) was one of the first books that was not self-consciously about the tensions of racism or integration; it simply told a riveting story about a young girl in the South.

Each first in making children's fiction more realistic could no doubt be documented, and the resulting list would illustrate parallels between literature and society's changing attitudes that are mirrored in fiction. Because there are more elderly people in society today, books with intergenerational stories are more numerous. An emphasis on multiculturalism and internationalism pays heed to the many schoolchildren who come from Europe, Asia, and other parts of the world. Stories of homeless families and children proliferate as economic conditions force that reality on many. Books reflect changing gender role identities, and families are defined in many ways—single parent, double parent, grandparent, foster parent, stepparent, and any combination. Although there is much to be done to make minority cultures more significant in children's literature, some progress is evident (Sims, 1987).

SUBGENRES OF CONTEMPORARY REALISTIC FICTION

Because life is complex and multifaceted, realistic fiction, which mirrors life, has myriad subjects and themes. And writers of realistic fiction use the whole scope of conflicts—person against self, person against other, person against nature, and person against society—sometimes in the same book. Writers use flashbacks, different points of view, and stylistic devices such as dialects in conversation to a greater extent in realistic fiction than in other genres. Instead of the predictable happy ending, realistic fiction experiments with open-ended stories. Due to wide-ranging subjects and forms in realistic fiction, subgenres are not as clear-cut as they are in fantasy, for example, or in poetry.

Typically, realistic fiction has been categorized as animal realism, survival stories, family and school stories, mystery and adventure, sports, humor, series books, and problem novels. All these categories seem a bit cumbersome because rarely is a book just a "horse story" or just a "sports story." Relationships between characters, interactions among literary elements, and fully developed characters ensure books that are not easily pigeonholed. Therefore, a more sensible method might be to look for another way of dividing the genre into manageable parts. For purposes of discussion, the typical subgenres mentioned above will be grouped into two super-categories: **Focus on Character** and **Focus on Plot.** In the character focus, stories that are considered survival, animal realism, and family and school stories (including what were formerly problem novels) are grouped together because the main character or characters assume primary importance in the novel. His or her actions, relationships, and introspections take precedence over other story elements. Character development drives the action instead of simply being a part of it.

In the latter category, Focus on Plot, action and events seem more prominent and characters are not so individualistic. Sometimes they exist merely to serve the plot and push it forward. Focus on plot includes sports, mystery and adventure, humor, and series books (see Figure 8.1).

Figure 8.1 Subgenres of Contemporary Realism

Focus	Subgenre
Character	Survival, family and school stories, and animal realism.
Plot	Sports, mystery and adventure, humor, and series books.

Focus on Character

In these books, the protagonist makes self-discoveries and develops as a more knowledgeable and compassionate person, whether alone or as part of a family group. In these coming-of-age novels, themes are often articulated as

- Forming one's own identity
- Reconciling personal goals with broader family, societal, and peer goals
- Proving competence and building self-esteem
- Learning to take care of others
- Overcoming prejudice
- Gaining independence

The following three subgenres illustrate these themes as each focuses on persons growing into greater responsibility and awareness of themselves and the world around them.

Survival Stories

Usually survival stories pit protagonist against nature, with nature becoming a symbolic antagonist. However, urban survival stories show protagonists battling against an uncaring environment as well. Two well-known survival stories have been mentioned previously: *Island of the Blue Dolphins* (O'Dell, 1960) and *Hatchet* (Paulsen, 1987). Survival stories depend on a careful description of the rural or urban setting to challenge the main character and dramatize the danger. Proving competence in physical and psychological terms is always at the heart of these stories.

Recommended survival stories

Julie of the Wolves, Jean Craighead George (1972)

Toughboy and Sister, Kirkpatrick Hill (1990)

Slake's Limbo, Felice Holman (1974)

Family and School Stories (including problem novels)

Whether overcoming problems at school or at home, child and adolescent characters are depicted with a wide range of experiences that reflect reality in the present time. Because there are many thousands of books in this subgenre, an annotated list of recommended books follows. Some reading choices must be made if these books are all unfamiliar to you, so be guided by the brief annotation and begin to make a list of future reading if you have not done so already.

Recommended family and school novels with contemporary problems

Nothing But the Truth, Avi (1991). When Philip is suspended for humming the national anthem during English class, issues of free speech become embroiled in media coverage. Teachers, administrators, friends, and family play unpredictable roles.

What Hearts, Bruce Brooks (1992). Four short stories reveal the complexities of Asa's life as he copes with a vindictive stepfather, frequent moves, and, finally, first love.

The Chocolate War, Robert Cormier (1974). Jerry Renault at first refuses to sell chocolates for a fund-raising drive at school, following orders from a powerful secret organization, the Vigils. When he disregards further orders, the Vigils and the school authorities imperil his life.

Wolf, Gilian Cross (1991). In England, Cassy is sent to live with her mother so that her grandmother can protect her from her father, a suspected I.R.A. terrorist.

Memory, Margaret Mahy (1987). Jonny leaves home with the memory of his sister's death haunting him and finds Sophie, an elderly woman suffering from memory loss associated with Alzheimer's disease.

Somewhere in the Darkness, Walter Dean Myers (1992). Jimmy Little's father, a dying escapee from prison, takes him on an odyssey back to the rural south.

Dicey's Song, Cynthia Voigt (1982). In this continuation of *Homecoming* (1981), Dicey Tillerman and her three siblings learn to trust, accept, and love their grandmother in Maryland. The Tillerman saga continues in other books, as well.

Animal Realism

Contrasted with animal fantasy, in which animals are personified, these stories treat them realistically. Horses, dogs, mountain lions, and coyotes are characters through which the balance between the natural world and humans is shown. Relating to animals reveals character development, as animals frequently seem to affect a special bond of friendship with children. The growing relationship between a child and an animal unfolds as each learns to trust the other. The recent Newbery winner, *Shiloh* (Naylor, 1991), which is set in West Virginia, exemplifies the unique love between a boy and his dog. Marty loves and feeds a scared, starved animal and protects it from its abusive owner.

Recommended realistic animal stories

The Incredible Journey, Sheila Burnford (1961)

King of the Wind, Marguerite Henry (1948)

The Deer Stand, Anne Monson (1992)

Marsh Cat, Peter Parnall (1991)

Focus on Plot

Many stories of contemporary realistic fiction focus on an action-packed plot that propels characters through a series of exciting events. In contrast to books mentioned in the previous section, character development is minimal in these stories, and setting is simply described. Emphasis is on the topic that defines these subgenres: sports, mystery and adventure, humor, and a large category called series books. Series books actually cover many topics and will be defined later.

Books in these subgenres sometimes constitute light reading, as they tend to be less profound, less challenging, and more entertaining. Accessible to many readers, these books can often lure an unmotivated reader into the pages of the most current popular fiction. This is not to say that thoughtful, even provocative books are not found in these subgenres, because they are. But the vast majority of these stories are amusing, fast-paced, and undemanding. In the following descriptions of subgenres, the recommended books are compelling and well written and have more substance than the usual. But, as in all genres of children's literature, a wide range of quality exists and it is the reader's responsibility (adult and child) to search for the best.

Sports Stories

Sports stories use the vehicle of fiction to explain the rules of the sport and to initiate the beginner into its demands and rewards. Sports stories are sometimes seen as metaphors for fostering an American way of life—urging competition, winning, and achieving a tangible goal. In the best sports stories, competitors view the outcome with grace, realizing that "winning isn't everything" or learning the hard lessons of loss. Baseball, basketball, hockey, soccer, skiing—contemporary realistic fiction includes stories about these sports and many more. Male and female characters are found in title roles, although males dominate the field.

Robert Lipsyte's *The Brave* (1991) tells a gripping story of a young boxer, Sonny Bear. Son of a white father and a Native American mother, Sonny's only positive childhood memories are training with his Uncle Joe on the Onondaga Reservation. When he goes to New York City, Sonny gets into trouble immediately with hustlers and a drug run. While Sonny is in police custody, the Sergeant, a fighter from Lipsyte's earlier book *The Contender* (1967), recognizes his potential. He sends Sonny back to Uncle Joe for more training and then helps him enter the Gotham Gloves series of title fights. Sonny battles his internal rage throughout the story, trying to turn it into productive competition instead of self-defeating annihilation. Scenes from New York drug dens, violent prisons, and the boxing ring are vivid in their realism.

Recommended sports stories

Moves Make the Man, Bruce Brooks (1984) (basketball)

Tackle without a Team, Matt Christopher (1989) (football)

When the Mountain Sings, John Maclean (1992) (skiing)

Finding Buck McHenry, Alfred Slote (1991) (baseball)

Taking Sides, Gary Soto (1991) (baseball)

Mystery and Adventure

Suspense, danger, and drama permeate stories that keep readers turning pages. We read with a flashlight under the covers when we were young; now some of us have "graduated" to Agatha Cristie, Tony Hillerman, and Tom Clancy, ensuring that mysteries will always be a part of our reading repertoire. For children today, good contemporary mysteries and adventures are exciting and full of interesting plot twists and vicarious thrills.

In Isabelle Holland's *The Unfrightened Dark* (1990), Jocelyn, a blind high school student, must confront the danger that threatens her beloved guide dog and other animals as they disappear in her town. With the help of two friends and aided by her keen hearing, Jocelyn tracks down the animal kidnappers and brings them to justice.

For younger readers, the Encyclopedia Brown books, such as *Encyclopedia Brown Sets the Pace* (Sobol, 1982), include ten short mysteries that are complete in a few pages. Encyclopedia, a fifth-grade student in Idaville, is so named because of his quick thinking and the logic he brings to bear on the cases his father, the chief of police, brings home.

Recommended mysteries and adventures

A Kind of Thief, Vivien Alcock (1992)

Don't Look Behind You, Lois Duncan (1989)

From the Mixed-Up Files of Mrs. Basil E. Frankweiler, E. L. Konigsberg (1967)

Humor

Writing humorous books, really funny books, takes a great sense of humor, a command of the language, and knowledge of children. A special gift, humor can easily slip into sarcasm or satire and cease to be funny. Events that may be funny to one person are not necessarily funny to another. Thank goodness there are writers who bring a comedic touch to fiction and entertain while causing us to regard the world with more insight.

From *Anastasia at This Address* by Lois Lowry copyright © 1991. By permission of the publisher, Houghton Mifflin Co.

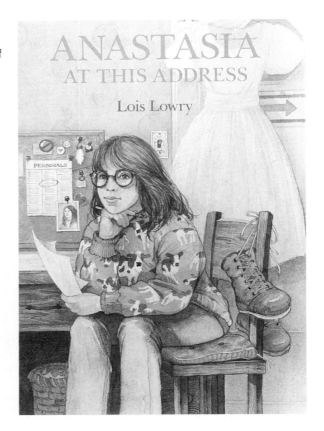

Lois Lowry is well known for her funny books about Anastasia Krupnik, one of which is *Anastasia at This Address* (1991). Living in Boston with a father-professor, mother-artist, and little brother Sam, Anastasia is a worthy successor to Harriet the Spy. Family life and good friends help Anastasia meet and conquer the mountains and molehills of adolescence. In this particular story, Anastasia answers an ad from an SWM in the personal column of the newspaper. Their correspondence continues as Anastasia gets more and more creative in her responses to his questions and comments. When the mystery man arranges a trip to Boston to meet her (nicknamed "Swifty" in the letters), she has to decide whether or not to live up to her own fraudulent descriptions.

Recommended humorous books

Bingo Brown, Gypsy Lover, Betsy Byars (1990)

The Bagthorpes Liberated, Helen Cresswell (1989)

Electing J.J., James Vanoosting (1990)

Series Books

The term *series books* denotes a group of cheaply produced mass-marketed books centering on the adventures of upwardly mobile American youths dating from the early 1900s. Action-packed series—The Rover Boys, The Bobbsey Twins, The Hardy Boys, Tom Swift, and the most popular of all, Nancy Drew, actually were written by a "literary machine" called the Stratemeyer Syndicate. At the turn of the century Edward Stratemeyer was a successful author of dime novels, or popular fiction aimed toward adolescents. He concocted a plan that would make money, produce a handsome product, employ writers, and provide fiction for this segment of the population, who now had some leisure time to read. Stratemeyer fashioned story ideas into three-page outlines, and then sent these sketches to aspiring writers who had answered classified ads in New York newspapers (Watson, 1991). Books were churned out monthly under fictitious names according to a formula devised by Stratemeyer. He controlled the editing, publishing, and distribution. When he died in 1930, his daughter, Harriet Stratemeyer Adams, took over the empire and continued the formulaic tradition while writing some of the Nancy Drews herself.

Series books were criticized as vulgar, tawdry, and even "subliterature," and many libraries refused to buy them (Soderburgh, 1980). However, as attitudes changed toward appropriateness and suitability in children's books, and the sustained popularity of these series continued to drive this phenomenon in the publishing industry, controversy faded.

Even though series books are no longer seen as harbingers of moral decay, the dilemma of popularity versus quality remains. Teachers want children to self-select books that are entertaining and enlightening, and often series books only entertain. Susceptible to the latest fad, they have a short demand-period in libraries and schools that must always spend wisely for lasting value. Examples of contemporary series books are: Babysitters Club (Scholastic), Sweet Valley Twins (Bantam), Sweet Valley High (Bantam), Fear Street (Archway), and many others.

EVALUATION OF CONTEMPORARY REALISTIC FICTION

Contemporary fiction must resonate with realistic situations, problems, and characters. Realism mirrors life as we believe it to be, and in fiction, sometimes the mirror turns into a window, a telescope, or a magnifying glass. Nevertheless, the reflection of the image is faithful to our perception of reality.

In evaluating realistic fiction for your personal reading, or for school, home, or library, certain criteria are applied to all literature. A good story, well told, that enlightens as well as entertains is key to our enjoyment. We want to be cognitively and emotionally engaged. We care about characters and are curious about what will happen to them. (Sometimes we're sad when the story is over.)

Figure 8.2   Evaluating Realistic Fiction

Subgenres	My Personal Response
Focus on Character (stories of survival, family and school, and animal realism)	How do characters grow and learn about the world and themselves? Is character development consistent with the theme? What kind of role models do characters provide?
Focus on Plot (stories of sports, mystery and adventure, humor, and series)	Is the plot fresh and new? (Not contrived or predictable?) How has the author used language effectively? Is the theme worthwhile?

Other criteria especially pertinent to realism stem from personal values and play against the purposes and audience for whom we select books. These criteria relate to questions implicit in realism:

- How graphically can writers describe violence or sexuality?
- What kind of language is appropriate? Or inappropriate?
- Are there topics or themes that are not suitable?

With these three questions and your personal responses in mind, consider the additional questions in Figure 8.2, which are related to character development and plot.

● ● ● ● ●
NOTABLE AUTHORS OF CONTEMPORARY AND HISTORICAL REALISM

In addition to the authors of the recommended books following each subgenre, the authors who are listed below are prolific and have been recognized as exemplary. Many have also received recognition through lists of books published by organizations such as the International Reading Association (see "Children's Choices" in each October issue of *The Reading Teacher*, for example), and the American Library Association "Notable Books."

Authors for Older Readers (ages 11 and up)

Patricia Beatty	Patricia Clapp	Paula Fox
Frank Bonham	Vera & Bill Cleaver	M. E. Kerr
Eve Bunting	Amy Ehrlich	Harry Mazer

From *Lyddie* by Katherine Paterson, jacket illustration by Debbi Chabrian. Copyright © 1991 by Katherine Paterson. Used by permission of Lodestar Books, an affiliate of Dutton's Children's Books, a division of Penguin USA Inc.

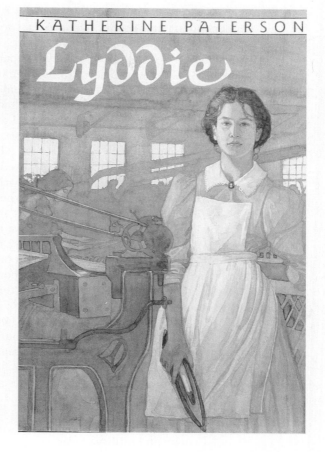

| Norma Fox Mazer | Kit Pearson | Ivan Southall |
| Farley Mowat | Robert Newton Peck | John Rowe Townsend |

Authors for Intermediate Readers (ages 8–11)

Julia Cunningham	Patricia Reilly Giff	Jean Little
Paula Danziger	Jamie Gilson	Patricia Maclachlan
Paul Fleischman	Johanna Hurwitz	Zilpha Keatley Snyder
Sid Fleischman	Lois Lenski	Jerry Spinelli

● ● ● ● ●

HISTORICAL REALISTIC FICTION

As she was stirring a pot of oatmeal over the fire, Lyddie saw the massive bear's head poke through the open door of the cabin. She urged Mama, Charles, and the babies up into the loft before the bear ransacked their pitiful belongings. That snowy Vermont night in 1843 saw the beginning of Lyddie's journey to become independent and productive as a factory worker in the textile mills of Lowell, Massachusetts. The bear proved to be a catalyst for each move Lyddie made, becoming a symbol for the many obstacles she had to overcome. *Lyddie* (Paterson, 1991), a powerful story of courage, conviction, and tenacity, represents one of the best examples of historical realism in children's fiction. Meticulously researched, the economic and social changes of the New England industrial revolution are searingly portrayed through Lyddie's triumphs and setbacks.

Historical realism re-creates the past with attention to an accurate representation of what we know to be factual. Although the story is fiction, made up of characters who may or may not have lived, the important element is the historical context of time and place interacting with personal and societal attitudes. Historical fiction dramatizes and humanizes the sterile facts of history.

Themes in historical realism echo themes in contemporary works: gaining independence, becoming more sensitive to the needs of others, broadening one's world view, coping with life's problems, and proving competence. What seems to be different in historical realism as compared to contemporary stories is the emphasis on *change* that frequently permeates the work. Very often the main character is a catalyst for change, and tension arises in the story when "old" attitudes clash with "new."

Other themes specific to historical fiction are listed below. As you think about these themes, generate examples in your own mind of actual stories, or ask others for examples from their childhood reading.

- Clash between indigenous peoples and invaders
- Love of the land
- Upholding loyalty and honor
- Cruelty and futility of war

● ● ● ● ●
SUBGENRES OF HISTORICAL FICTION

In five chronological categories, beginning with ancient times and continuing through the first half of the twentieth century, historical fiction for children demonstrates powerful themes in a realistic world. Broad historical eras outlining the categories, or subgenres, have been arbitrarily chosen; they are the Ancient World, the Medieval World, Exploration and Colonization, Westward Expansion and Industrialization, and the Early Twentieth Century (see Figure 8.3). In the subgenres that follow, a very brief explanation hits the high points of each era. As usual, descriptions of some novels are followed by a recommended list. In most cases, each author has several noteworthy books to his or her credit, so if a particular book is unavailable in your search for these, try another. You are encouraged to add your preferred historical realism, and to continue to look in libraries, schools, and bookstores for additional worthy books. For example, the Scott O'Dell award is given every year by the Bulletin of the Center for Children's Books to an outstanding book of historical fiction.

Figure 8.3 Subgenres
of Historical Realism

Approximate Dates	Subgenre
Beginning of recorded time to A.D. 400	The Ancient World
A.D. 400 – A.D. 1500	The Medieval World
A.D. 1500 – A.D. 1800	Exploration and Colonization
A.D. 1800 – A.D. 1900	Western Expansion and Industrialization
A.D. 1900 – A.D. 1950	The Early Twentieth Century

The Ancient World

Stories set in this period, from earliest recorded time to the fall of the Roman Empire (about A.D. 400) seem almost mythlike in their antiquity. However, using careful research to uncover the few facts available, gifted authors re-create life and times in ancient cultures.

Rosemary Sutcliff is unsurpassed for her ability to bring contemporary relevancy to stories of ancient times in Britain. Her *Song for a Dark Queen* (1978) describes a female warrior, Queen Boudicca, as she leads her people in eastern England against Roman invaders about A.D. 50. It is a sad story because the Dark Queen is doomed to fail; nevertheless, her personal courage and intelligence light this shadowed period.

Mollie Hunter, a Scots storyteller, writes of an earlier period in *The Stronghold* (1974), a Carnegie award winner. Hunter explains the origin of **brochs**, mysterious circular fortresses on the Orkney Islands of Scotland, as she invents a story of a young man, Coll, who builds these structures to repel attacks from foreign invaders. Conflicts between tribal life and religious practices of the Druids are dramatized as Coll tries to save his love from sacrifice.

Recommended books of the ancient world

Shiva: An Adventure of the Ice Age, J. H. Brennan (1989) (Europe)

The Bronze Bow, Elizabeth George Speare (1961) (Israel)

The Magic Amulet, William Steele (1979) (North America)

Children of the Fox, Jill Paton Walsh (1978) (Europe)

The Medieval World

Beginning with the Dark Ages and continuing into the Renaissance, this period covers more than one thousand years, from A.D. 400 to about A.D. 1500. In Europe, as well as in Asia, Africa, and the Americas, certain cultures ruled through conquest and subjugation. Roman Catholicism permeated much of Europe, providing a political structure for future nation-states to emerge. In Asia, the Byzantine Empire flourished.

Other great civilizations in the Americas (the Aztecs and the Mayas, for example), Africa (the Mali), and Asia (dynasties in China and Japan) rose and fell in cycles of historical importance.

Human drama set on these historical stages portrays tales of chivalrous knights, feudal wars, and the bravery of individual men and women. Marguerite DeAngeli's *A Door in the Wall* (1949), a Newbery award winner, was set in the fourteenth century and told of a young crippled boy who wanted to be a knight's page. Robin learned that reading and patience were "doors in the wall" of ignorance and prejudice, as he finally accepted the challenges of his disability.

The Striped Ships (McGraw, 1991) carried William the Conqueror to England's shore in 1066. A young Saxon, Juliana, saw the ships in the distance and then lived through the turmoil that followed the Norman victory at the Battle of Hastings. Juliana's persistence and love for her family proved key to her survival.

Recommended books of the medieval world

Hakon of Rogen's Saga, Erik Christian Haugaard (1963)
     (Scandinavia)

The Trumpeter of Krakow, Eric Kelly (1966) (Poland)

The Shining Company, Rosemary Sutcliff (1990) (England)

Exploration and Colonization

Columbus's expedition of 1492, extending the voyages of discovery that preceded it, metaphorically and literally opened up a new world. Adventures on land and sea recounted the perils of the unknown and the courage of those who risked lives and fortunes to discover uncharted territory. Celebrating the restless human spirit, stories of exploration also demonstrate a callousness to indigenous people and their little-valued cultures.

Colonies in the new world led to the formation of new nation-states. As the American colonies moved inexorably to the break with their parent country, so did other colonies in South America, led by Simon Bolivar. In Europe, winds of democracy were fanned by the French Revolution. Further exploration in the East began to reveal political structures and culture in China and Japan and other Asian areas of significance.

A novel depicting the Revolutionary War period in Boston is Esther Forbes's classic, *Johnny Tremain* (1943). A young apprentice to a silversmith, Johnny meets the Sons of Liberty, led by Sam Adams, Paul Revere, and other patriots. His own quest for personal independence is mirrored in the new nation's struggle.

Elizabeth George Speare is another author of historical fiction with impeccable credentials as a researcher who re-creates scenes of historical veracity. Two of her outstanding books, *The Witch of Blackbird Pond* (1958) and *The Sign of the Beaver* (1983), illustrate what New England colonists faced in the severity of Puritan values and hard winters.

Recommended books of exploration and colonization

The True Confessions of Charlotte Doyle, Avi (1990) (U.S.)

Morning Girl, Michael Dorris (1992) (Native American)

Shadow in Hawthorn Bay, Janet Lunn (1986) (Canada)

Bartholomew Fair, Mary Stolz (1990) (England)

Western Expansion and Industrialization

In the United States, the nineteenth century saw the population expand toward western agricultural land while filling up eastern cities. Pioneers and immigrants demonstrated a love for personal freedom and a willingness to brave unfamiliar territory. A conviction that freedom was a right for every person led to the Civil War and the final abolition of slavery.

Advances in medicine, technology, communications, and transportation led to a better quality of life for many people. Education became possible for a greater percentage of the population.

The quintessential pioneer story depicting the American dream and spirit was told in the Little House books by Laura Ingalls Wilder. She was more than sixty years old when she wrote these seven books about her childhood and her family as they moved from territory to homestead in the years from 1860 to 1880. Each book is a separate adventure, but together they present a coherent portrait of pioneer life in slow-paced plots full of details of everyday life. The books are: *Little House in the Big Woods* (1932), *Little House on the Prairie* (1935), *On the Banks of Plum Creek* (1937), *By the Shores of Silver Lake* (1939), *The Long Winter* (1940), *Little Town on the Prairie* (1941), and *These Happy Golden Years* (1943).

Recommended books of westward expansion and industrialization

The Great Brain, John Fitzgerald (1967) (Utah)

Bells of Christmas, Virginia Hamilton (1989) (Ohio)

Sweetgrass, Jan Hudson (1989) (Canada/Native American)

The Early Twentieth Century

The world was caught up in two wars during the first half of this century. Global conflict replaced regional conflicts of previous eras. The literature of historical realism became the lens through which we saw scenes of combat, displacement of persons, and horrendous atrocities inflicted upon men, women, and children.

Other economic and social events included the collapse of world markets, known as the stock market crash of 1929, and the resulting Great Depression of the 1930s. Society became more mobile, as people immigrated from country to country and, in the United States, from state to state. The advent of television hastened a consciousness of a new world order.

Set in the early twentieth century, *Goodbye, Billy Radish* (Skurzynski, 1992) is a poignant story of friendship between two boys, one of whom is a newly immigrated Ukrainian. Against the backdrop of the steel mills in a Pennsylvania town and the approaching first World War, Henry and Billy explore differences and similarities in their lives and cultures.

A book representing the middle twentieth century is Lois Lowry's *Number the Stars* (1989). Set in Denmark during World War II, it recounts the heroism of two families, one Jewish and the other Christian, as they find hope in the midst of terror.

Recommended books of the early twentieth century

The Man from the Other Side, Uri Orlov (1991) (Poland/Holocaust)

Roll of Thunder, Hear My Cry, Mildred Taylor (1976) (Rural South/the Great Depression)

Journey to Topaz, Yoshiku Uchida (1971) (Japanese-American Internment in WW II)

EVALUATION OF HISTORICAL REALISTIC FICTION

Historical fiction must be credible, with all the elements working together to depict a genuine, believable story. Just as contemporary realism is evaluated by standards of good writing, appropriate theme, and insightful storytelling, so is historical realism held to those same standards. (See Figure 8.2, Evaluating Realistic Fiction.)

In historical fiction, however, accurate historical settings must be created with facts gleaned from careful research. Such research, from primary sources when possible, reveals details that are indispensable to a high quality of realism. Historical accuracy coupled with a riveting story should be the *sine qua non* of writing historical fiction for children. Unfortunately, this is not always the case. It is admittedly difficult to create an authentic scene from long ago; nevertheless, writers should strive for as much authenticity as possible and readers should read with a knowledgeable and critical eye.

BIBLIOGRAPHY OF INTERNATIONAL REALISM

Internationalism is a major trend in children's literature, the result of international boundaries breaking down due to population movement and the increased interdependence of global economies (Marshall, 1988). Translated books are becoming more numerous because of international publishing houses. The Mildred L. Batchelder Award, given to an American publisher by the American Library Association, recognizes outstanding translated books for children every year. Clearly a vital and healthy aspect of worldwide literacy efforts, internationalism promotes social awareness and multiculturalism through excellent fiction about children and their lives. (There was concern in 1993 because the Batchelder committee decided that the pool of translated books was too small to warrant the awarding of the prize. Obviously this is an aspect of publishing to watch closely.)

If you are unfamiliar with some of the relatively new books presenting multicultural and international realism, this list will point you to some sources. Please note that realism is the only genre represented here, with the exception of *AK*, a story set in an imaginary African country but very realistic in its depiction of a young boy who gives up his AK rifle, then reclaims it. Other chapters include multicultural folklore, poetry, and nonfiction. Titles were generally selected from the last five years, and the country is indicated in parentheses when it is not obvious from the title or the classification. In an effort to avoid duplication, these books will **not** be listed in References at the end of the chapter, as all publishing information is included here.

Africa
Dickinson, P. (1992). *AK*. New York: Delacorte. (Nagala)
Gordon, S. (1990). *Middle of Somewhere: A Story of South Africa*. New York: Orchard.
Sachs, M. (1989). *Beyond Safe Boundaries*. New York: Lodestar. (South Africa) (See also *Themba*, 1993.)

African American
Davis, O. (1992). *Just Like Martin*. New York: Simon and Schuster.
Hamilton, V. (1992). *Drylongso*. New York: Harcourt.
Stolz, M. (1992). *Stealing Home*. New York: HarperCollins.
Taylor, M. (1990). *Road to Memphis*. New York: Dial.

Asia
Baillie, A. (1992). *Little Brother*. New York: Viking. (Cambodia)
Chang, M. (1990). *In the Eye of War*. New York: Macmillan. (China)
Choi, S. N. (1991). *The Year of Impossible Goodbyes*. Boston: Houghton Mifflin. (Korea)
Hicyilmaz, G. (1992). *Against the Storm*. Boston: Little, Brown. (Turkey)
Laird, E. (1992). *Kiss the Dust*. New York: Dutton. (Iraq/Kurdistan)
Schami, R. (1990). *A Hand Full of Stars*. New York: Dutton. (Syria)
Staples, S. F. (1993). *Haveli*. New York: Knopf. (Pakistan)
Whelan, G. (1992). *Goodbye, Vietnam*. New York: Knopf. (Vietnam)

Asian American
Namioka, L. (1992). *Yang the Youngest and His Terrible Ear*. Boston: Joy Street/Little, Brown.
Okimoto, J. (1992). *Molly by Any Other Name*. New York: Scholastic.
Savin, M. (1992). *Moon Bridge*. New York: Scholastic.
Yep, L. (1991). *The Star Fisher*. New York: Morrow.

Australia and New Zealand
Mahy, M. (1992). *The Underrunners*. New York: Viking.
Mayne, W. (1993). *Low Tide*. New York: Delacorte.

Savage, D. (1992). *Stranger Calls Me Home*. Boston: Houghton Mifflin.
Wrightson, P. (1992). *The Sugar-Gum Tree*. New York: Viking.

Canada

Hudson, J. (1992). *Dawn Rider*. New York: Philomel. (Blackfoot)
Pearson, K. (1992). *Looking at the Moon*. New York: Viking. (English)

Caribbean

Berry, J. (1992). *Ajeemah and His Son*. New York: HarperCollins.
Hodge, M. (1993). *For the Life of Laetitia*. New York: Farrar, Straus & Giroux.
Powell, P. (1992). *Turtle Watchers*. New York: Viking.
Temple, F. (1992). *A Taste of Salt: A Story of Modern Haiti*. New York: Orchard.

Europe

Hesse, K. (1992). *Letters from Rifka*. New York: Holt, Rinehart & Winston. (Russia)
Lindenbaum, P. (1992). *Boodil, My Dog*. New York: Holt, Rinehart & Winston. (Sweden)
Magorian, M. (1992). *Not a Swan*. New York: HarperCollins. (England)
Oppenheim, S. L. (1992). *The Lily Cupboard*. New York: HarperCollins. (Holland) (a picture book)
Reuter, B. (1991). *Buster, the Sheikh of Hope Street*. New York: Dutton. (Denmark)

European American

Lingard, J. (1991). *Between Two Worlds*. New York: Lodestar/Dutton. (Latvia/Canada)
Winter, J. (1992). *Klara's New World*. New York: Knopf. (Sweden)

Hispanic

Soto, G. (1992). *The Skirt*. New York: Delacorte.
Temple, F. (1993). *Grab Hands and Run*. New York: Jackson/Orchard/Watts.

Native American

O'Dell, S., & Hall, E. (1992). *Thunder Rolling in the Mountains*. Boston: Houghton Mifflin. (Nez Percé)
Plain, F. (1992). *Little White Cabin*. Winnipeg, Canada: Pemmican. (Ojibway)
Roop, P. & C. (1992). *Ahyoka and the Talking Leaves*. New York: Lothrop, Lee & Shepard. (Cherokee)

● ● ● ● ●
SUMMARY

Realistic fiction, a very popular genre, draws its power from lifelike characters, setting, and conflict. Characters remind us of people we know; setting evokes emotional ties to times and places sometimes remembered and clearly recognized. Plots must be plausible, describing the unfolding of possible events.

In this chapter realistic fiction was explored from contemporary and historical points of view. Contemporary realism was defined as stories set from the 1960s to the present. Historical realism covered everything from the beginning of recorded time through the 1950s. Dividing realism into contemporary and historical eras should take into account the shorter life span of the primary audience of children's literature. What is historical to a child may be contemporary to an adult.

Subgenres of contemporary realism were first divided into Focus on Character and Focus on Plot. Modern books with a character focus included survival stories, animal realism, and family and school stories. Problem novels, a subgenre created by the new realism of previous decades, was subsumed under family and school stories because the emphasis is no longer so blatantly on a medical or societal problem—drugs, death, suicide, rape, incest, and so on.

Subgenres of historical realistic fiction represented historical eras: the Ancient World, the Medieval World, Exploration and Colonization, Westward Expansion and Industrialization, and the Twentieth Century. Stories from these eras exemplified the authenticity so necessary in evaluating historical realism.

The very nature of realistic fiction raises questions about how much reality or what kind of reality should be described in children's books. Should children be exposed to the sordid, very desperate reality that some people confront daily? Life is hard; it destroys innocence and causes despair. Does that kind of realism have a place in children's literature?

There are no easy answers to what is appropriate for today's child. What is appropriate is the freedom for authors to create and for readers to select the kinds of books that enlighten and enrich understanding. Each book, if controversial or subject to censorship, must be evaluated as a total work according to the purpose and audience for whom it is intended. Parents have a responsibility to monitor the reading of their children; they alone can restrict reading, but only for their own children.

Combating Censorship

The American Library Association, in its material on preserving intellectual freedom, outlines a procedure for libraries to combat censorship (American Library Association, 1989). Essentially, the procedure suggests that libraries, schools, and other groups promoting literature establish criteria for selection of books and materials. Then, when anyone questions why a certain book is available to children or adults, criteria can demonstrate the worth of its inclusion. Following this, if questions are still raised, the procedure suggests that libraries offer a form to be filled out by the challenger. After having read the entire work, the challenger must specify, in writing, why a book should be removed from circulation. (Too often, passages are taken out of context and their "unsavory" features are magnified.) Then a panel of people—librarians, challenger, and perhaps others—can decide if the judgment to remove the book is warranted. The procedure is important because it allows libraries and schools to establish criteria for all selections and to remove some of the emotionalism when charges are raised. Standards of community tolerance can be applied by the panel.

● ● ● ● ●

IMPLICATIONS FOR INSTRUCTION

First, *Reflections* contain questions related to ideas, concerns, and controversies identified in this chapter. You may want to react to these questions singly or in groups. Next, *Projects* will encourage your active involvement with the material. Reading, analyzing, creating bibliographies, evaluating, and discussing with others are examples of projects. Last, *Activities* for primary and intermediate and middle levels are described. Many of these activities have been classroom-tested, so try them in your classroom or with your group of children.

Reflections

1. Given parallels between realistic fiction and societal concerns, what do you predict will occur in children's books of the next decade? Will there be noticeable trends in publishing books about certain topics related to children's and adolescents' issues?

2. How "real" do you want children's books to be? Where is your personal line between acceptable and not acceptable? Given that children and adolescents see virtually any kind of topic realistically programmed on television, does it even matter what our standards for books are?

3. Realistic fiction provokes more censorship in libraries and schools than other genres. In what ways do we censor reading material for children? On what grounds? What do we do when others want to censor for us?

4. How do "isms" (like ageism, sexism, and racism) continue to affect children's books? Do we still find stereotypical characters projecting negative images of the elderly, women, and people of various racial and ethnic groups? Many would argue that this is still the case. What do you think? Do you have examples?

5. Popularity vs. Quality is an issue adults frequently face when children select books that do not have any redeeming literary value. On one hand, children need to have a freedom to select; on the other hand, selections are sometimes poor and haphazard. What will you do to ensure that a variety of quality literature is self-selected by your students?

6. **Bibliotherapy** is the practice of addressing an emotional problem by reading books in which a character with the same problem finds a solution. For example, if a child is coping with a death in the family, she or he is directed toward a book in which a character is coping with death. What are the ramifications of such a practice?

Projects

1. Compare a series book, a Nancy Drew for example, to *Missing May* (Rylant, 1992) or *Anastasia* (Lowry, 1991). Note differences in tone, style, structure, depth of emotional realism, and any other important factors.

2. Look back at the beginning of this chapter, where you identified a book that is memorable from your childhood or adolescent reading. Now recall who the author was, and find out something about that author. Did she or he write many more books? Why was that book important to you?

3. Select books with minority characters published in several past decades. Do you find portrayals of Native Americans and/or African Americans changing from early time periods to the current decade? Sex-role stereotyping is a similar issue; "An Analysis of Male and Female Roles in Two Periods of Children's Literature" (Hillman, 1974) demonstrates a method to compare characters from an earlier time period to a later one.

4. Develop an annotated bibliography of books focusing on a theme that would serve your purpose. You may select a subgenre, like humor or sports, or perhaps a special interest. For example, in the following books the main character has a sibling or a friend who is mentally retarded. The disabled person helps the main character become a better person through their relationship. All are recommended books.

   All Together Now, Sue Ellen Bridgers (1979)

   Summer of the Swans, Betsy Byars (1970)

   Take Wing, Jean Little (1968)

   Risk 'n Roses, Jan Slepian (1990)

5. Create a list of books that have been televised or filmed. You could start with classics such as *Heidi* or *Treasure Island* or begin with more recent titles, such as *Sarah Plain and Tall* (Maclachlan, 1985). Go to a video store and look for familiar titles, write television networks for information, and scan reviewing journals for examples. With your list, you can generate questions that will help children compare and contrast.

Activities for the Primary Level

1. Ramona Quimby is a delightful character in several Beverly Cleary novels appropriate for independent reading in second and third grades *(Ramona the Pest,* 1968; *Ramona the Brave,* 1975; *Ramona and Her Father,* 1977; *Ramona and Her Mother,* 1977; *Ramona Quimby, Age 8,* 1981). A recent public television series has also depicted Ramona's escapades. After children have read some of the books, or, in the case of kindergarten and first grade, listened to read-alouds, create a character cluster of Ramona. Although you will want to elicit ideas from the children, you could begin like this (see Figure 8.4).

2. To a class of second or third graders, read aloud *Morning Girl* (Dorris, 1992), a story about a Taino Indian family that takes place just prior to Columbus's arrival on their island in 1492. Chapters alternate—first in Morning Girl's voice, then in the voice of her younger brother, Starboy. While you are reading, or afterward, discuss the characters with the children, then have them

Figure 8.4   Character
Cluster of Ramona Quimby

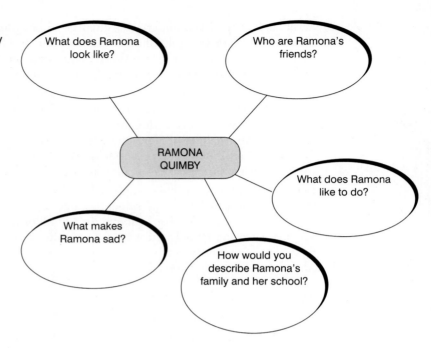

create some dialog that would give the characters and their parents additional development in the story. Children will enjoy writing some scenes, building on what the author has so convincingly portrayed.

3. You might use these transitional books to encourage independent silent reading by primary children. Each author has several titles, so explore your library for more.

   Elizabeth Levy, Something Queer at the . . . series

   Peggy Parrish, Amelia Bedelia series

   Louis Sachar, the Marvin Redpost series

   Jerry Spinelli, the Bathwater Gang series

   Cynthia Rylant, Henry and Mudge series

4. Using composition tools for Magic Slate II, a Wings for Learning/Sunburst computer program based on *Alexander and the Terrible, Horrible, No-Good, Very Bad Day* (Viorst, 1972), children in grades two and three can write their own realistic stories. Using this popular book as a springboard, many children have expanded their writing skills with this program, which is authored by Diane Schipper and Kim Vincent. *Storybook Theatre*, designed by Learningways, Inc., is another program that allows storymaking on a computer.

5. Two very moving stories to listen to, to dramatize, to illustrate, and to appreciate are *Stone Fox* (Gardiner, 1980) and *Red-Dirt Jessie* (Myers, 1992). Good readers in third and fourth grades can read them independently, and older reluctant readers will find them interesting. Both have young characters bent

on saving the family farm despite hardships while pulling a father or grandfather out of a severe depression. Both characters love a dog: Willy and the noble Searchlight, Jessie and the semi-wild Ring. Children will enjoy comparing these compelling stories, powerful characters, and historical settings.

Activities for the Intermediate and Middle Levels

1. Compare *The Incredible Journey* (Burnford, 1961) with its 1993 movie adaptation, *Homeward Bound*. (Actually, there is also an older movie version, so you could compare movies as well.)

2. After reading *The Sign of the Beaver* (Speare, 1983) and *Across Five Aprils* (Hunt, 1964), ask children to write simulated diary entries from Attean's point of view and from Jenny's. Using a minor character to reflect in a diary entry helps to learn another point of view, since the main character's point of view is often expressed literally. If children want a model for diary entries, see *A Gathering of Days* (Blos, 1979).

3. Characters Anastasia Krupnik and Bingo Brown can be compared when reading humorous stories. One way to note differences and similarities would be to use a Venn diagram like the one in Figure 8.5 to elicit ideas from children.

4. Family history is revealed by grandmothers in *My Daniel* (Conrad, 1989) and *The Night Journey* (Lasky, 1981). After children hear or read these books they could collect oral stories from their grandparents, or write a story about themselves and put it in a time capsule for a future reader. In addition, both books alternate past and present, Lasky's more obviously than Conrad's, thus providing an interesting format for children to try in their own writing.

5. Sometimes reluctant readers (and others) are intrigued by the format of "Choose Your Own Adventure" books. An example is *The Treasure of the Onyx Dragon* (Gilligan, 1990). After reading a few pages, the reader is instructed to choose alternatives, based on what he or she wants the plot to do, and turn to corresponding pages. Not much character development, but plenty of action propels the reader from one hazard to the next.

Figure 8.5 Comparing Anastasia Krupnik and Bingo Brown

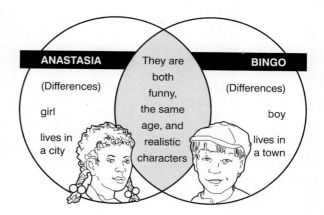

ANASTASIA — (Differences) girl / lives in a city

They are both funny, the same age, and realistic characters

BINGO — (Differences) boy / lives in a town

● ● ● ● ●
REFERENCES

Children's Works Cited

Alcock, V. (1992). *A kind of thief.* New York: Delacorte.

Anonymous. (1971). *Go ask Alice.* Clifton, NJ: Prentice Hall.

Avi. (1990). *The true confessions of Charlotte Doyle.* New York: Orchard.

Avi. (1991). *Nothing but the truth.* New York: Orchard.

Blos, J. (1979). *A gathering of days.* New York: Scribner's.

Blume, J. (1970). *Are you there, God? It's me, Margaret.* New York: Bradbury.

Bridgers, S. E. (1979). *All together now.* New York: Knopf.

Brennan, J. H. (1989). *Shiva: An adventure of the Ice Age.* New York: Lippincott.

Brooks, B. (1984). *Moves make the man.* New York: Harper & Row.

Brooks, B. (1992). *What hearts.* New York: HarperCollins.

Burnford, S. (1961). *The incredible journey.* Boston: Little, Brown.

Byars, B. (1970). *Summer of the swans.* New York: Viking.

Byars, B. (1990). *Bingo Brown, gypsy lover.* New York: Viking.

Christopher, M. (1989). *Tackle without a team.* Boston: Little, Brown.

Cleary, B. (1968). *Ramona the Pest.* New York: Morrow.

Cleary, B. (1975). *Ramona the Brave.* New York: Morrow.

Cleary, B. (1977). *Ramona and Her Father.* New York: Morrow.

Cleary, B. (1977). *Ramona and Her Mother.* New York: Morrow.

Cleary, B. (1981). *Ramona Quimby, Age 8.* New York: Morrow.

Cleary, B. (1983). *Dear Mr. Henshaw.* New York: Morrow.

Conrad, P. (1989). *My Daniel.* New York: Harper & Row.

Cormier, R. (1974). *The chocolate war.* New York: Pantheon.

Cresswell, H. (1989). *The Bagthorpes liberated.* New York: Macmillan.

Cross, G. (1991). *Wolf.* New York: Holiday.

DeAngeli, M. (1949). *A door in the wall.* New York: Doubleday.

Dorris, M. (1992). *Morning girl.* New York: Hyperion.

Duncan, L. (1989). *Don't look behind you.* New York: Delacorte.

Fitzgerald, J. (1967). *The great brain.* New York: Dial.

Fitzhugh, L. (1964). *Harriet the spy.* New York: Harper & Row.

Forbes, E. (1943). *Johnny Tremain.* Boston: Houghton Mifflin.

Gardiner, J. (1980). *Stone fox.* New York: Crowell.

George, J. C. (1972). *Julie of the wolves.* New York: Harper.

Gilligan, A. (1990). *The treasure of the onyx dragon.* New York: Bantam.

Hamilton, V.(1967). *Zeely.* New York: Macmillan.

Hamilton, V. (1989). *The bells of Christmas.* New York: Harcourt Brace Jovanovich.

Haugaard, E. C. (1963). *Hakon of Rogen's saga.* Boston: Houghton Mifflin.

Henry, M. (1948). *King of the wind.* New York: Rand.

Hill, K. (1990). *Toughboy and Sister.* New York: McElderry.

Hinton, S. E. (1967). *The outsiders.* New York: Viking.

Holland, I. (1990). *The unfrightened dark.* Boston: Little, Brown.

Holman, F. (1974). *Slake's limbo.* New York: Scribner's.

Hudson, J. (1989). *Sweetgrass.* New York: Philomel.

Hunt, I. (1964). *Across five Aprils.* New York: Follett.

Hunter, M. (1974). *The stronghold.* New York: Harper & Row.

Kelly, E.P. (1966). *The trumpeter of Krakow* (rev. ed.). New York: Macmillan. (Original work published in 1928).

Konigsberg, E. L. (1967). *From the mixed-up files of Mrs. Basil E. Frankweiler.* New York: Atheneum.

Lasky, K. (1981). *The night journey.* New York: Warne.

Lipsyte, R. (1967). *The contender.* New York: Harper & Row.

Lipsyte, R. (1991). *The brave.* New York: HarperCollins.

Little, J. (1968). *Take wing.* Boston: Little, Brown.

Lowry, L. (1989). *Number the stars.* Boston: Houghton Mifflin.

Lowry, L. (1991). *Anastasia at this address.* Boston: Houghton Mifflin.

Lunn, J. (1986). *Shadow in Hawthorn Bay.* New York: Scribner's.

Maclachlan, P. (1985). *Sarah plain and tall.* New York: Harper & Row.

Maclean, J. (1992). *When the mountain sings.* Boston: Houghton Mifflin.

Mahy, M. (1987). *Memory.* New York: McElderry.

McGraw, E. (1991). *The striped ships.* New York: McElderry.

Monson, A. (1992). *The deer stand.* New York: Lothrop, Lee & Shepard.

Myers, A. (1992). *Red-dirt Jessie.* New York: Walker.

Myers, W. D. (1992). *Somewhere in the darkness.* New York: Scholastic.

Naylor, P. R. (1991). *Shiloh.* New York: Atheneum.

O'Dell, S. (1960). *Island of the blue dolphins.* Boston: Houghton Mifflin.

Orlov, U. (1991). *The man from the other side.* Boston: Houghton Mifflin.

Parnall, P. (1991). *Marsh cat.* New York: Macmillan.

Paterson, K. (1977). *Bridge to Terabithia.* New York: Crowell.

Paterson, K. (1980). *Jacob have I loved.* New York: Crowell.

Paterson, K. (1991). *Lyddie.* New York: Dutton.

Paulsen, G. (1987). *Hatchet.* New York: Bradbury.

Rylant, C. (1992). *Missing May.* New York: Orchard.

Rylant, C. (1993). *Henry and Mudge and the wild wind.* New York: Bradbury.

Salinger, J. D. (1951). *Catcher in the rye.* Boston: Little, Brown.

Skurzynski, G. (1992). *Goodbye, Billy Radish.* New York: Bradbury.

Slepian, J. (1990). *Risk 'n roses.* New York: Putnam.

Slote, A. (1991). *Finding Buck McHenry.* New York: Harper & Row.

Sobol, D. (1982). *Encyclopedia Brown sets the pace.* New York: Scholastic.

Soto, G. (1991). *Taking sides.* New York: Harcourt Brace Jovanovich.

Speare, E. G. (1958). *The witch of Blackbird Pond.* Boston: Houghton Mifflin.

Speare, E. G. (1961). *The bronze bow.* Boston: Houghton Mifflin.

Speare, E. G. (1983). *The sign of the beaver.* Boston: Houghton Mifflin.

Steele, W. (1979). *The magic amulet.* New York: Harcourt Brace Jovanovich.

Stolz, M. (1990). *Bartholomew Fair.* New York: Greenwillow.

Sutcliff, R. (1978). *Song for a dark queen.* New York: Crowell.

Sutcliff, R. (1990). *The shining company.* New York: Farrar, Straus & Giroux.

Taylor, M. (1976). *Roll of thunder, hear my cry.* New York: Dial.

Uchida, Y. (1971). *Journey to Topaz.* New York: Scribner's.

Vanoosting, J. (1990). *Electing J.J.* New York: Farrar, Straus & Giroux.

Viorst, J. (1972). *Alexander and the terrible, horrible, no-good, very bad day.* New York: Atheneum.

Voigt, C. (1981). *Homecoming.* New York: Atheneum.

Voigt, C. (1982). *Dicey's song.* New York: Atheneum.

Walsh, J. P. (1978). *Children of the fox.* New York: Farrar, Straus & Giroux.

Wilder, L. I. (1932). *Little house in the big woods.* New York: Harper & Row.

Wilder, L. I. (1935). *Little house on the prairie.* New York: Harper & Row.

Wilder, L. I. (1937). *On the banks of Plum Creek.* New York: Harper & Row.

Wilder, L. I. (1939). *By the shores of Silver Lake.* New York: Harper & Row.

Wilder, L. I. (1940). *The long winter.* New York: Harper & Row.

Wilder, L. I. (1941). *Little town on the prairie.* New York: Harper & Row.

Wilder, L. I. (1943). *These happy golden years.* New York: Harper & Row.

Professional Works Cited

American Library Association. (1989). *Intellectual Freedom Manual* (3rd ed.). Chicago: ALA.

Carlson, J. (1970). *A comparison of the treatment of the Negro in children's literature in the periods 1929–1938 and 1959–1968.* Unpublished dissertation. Ann Arbor, MI: University Microfilms.

Egoff, S. (1980). The problem novel. In S. Egoff, G. T. Stubbs, & L. F. Ashley (Eds.), *Only connect* (2nd ed.) (pp. 356–369). Toronto: Oxford University Press.

Hillman, J. S. (1974). An analysis of male and female roles in two periods of children's literature. *Journal of Educational Research, 68,* 84–88.

Marshall, M. (1988). *An introduction to the world of children's books* (2nd ed.). Brookfield, VT: Gower.

Nodelman, P. (1992). *The pleasures of children's literature.* New York: Longman.

Sims, R. (1987). Whatever happened to the 'all-white' world of children's books? In B. Harrison & G. Maguire (Eds.), *Innocence and experience* (pp. 477–484). New York: Lothrop, Lee, & Shepard.

Smith, D. (1963). *Fifty years of children's books.* Champaign, IL: National Council of Teachers of English.

Soderburgh, P. (1980). The Stratemeyer strain: Educators and the juvenile series book, 1900–1980. In S. Egoff, G. T. Stubbs, & L. F. Ashley (Eds.), *Only connect* (2nd ed.) (pp. 63–73). Toronto: Oxford University Press.

Walsh, J. P. (1981). The art of realism. In B. Hearne & M. Kaye (Eds.), *Celebrating children's books* (pp. 35–36). New York: Lothrop, Lee & Shepard.

Watson, B. (1991). Tom Swift, Nancy Drew and pals all had the same dad. *The Smithsonian, Fall,* 50–61.

Wolf, V. (1975). Harriet the spy: Milestone, masterpiece? In F. Butler (Ed.), *Children's Literature Annual, 4* (pp. 120–126). Philadelphia: Temple University Press.

Additional Resources

Children's Book Clubs: *Scholastic* (P.O. Box 7502, Jefferson City, MO 65102); *Troll* (2 Lethbridge Plaza, Mahwah, NJ 07430); and *Trumpet* (P.O. Box 604, Holmes, PA 19043).
These book clubs provide inexpensive, popular paperback books to children in elementary schools.

Dreyer, S. S. (1989). *The bookfinder: A guide to children's literature about the needs and problems of youth aged 2–15.* Volumes I, II, III, and IV. Circle Pines, MN: American Guidance Service.
Titles are indexed according to a range of problems such as disabilities, parental absence, and so on. A second half of each volume provides a more in-depth annotation of each title.

Kruse, G. M., & Horning, K. T. (1991). *Multicultural literature for children and young adults: A selected listing of books 1980–1990 by and about people of color* (3rd ed.). Madison, WI: Wisconsin Dept. of Public Instruction.
Recent titles are annotated as well as a selection process and background of some authors and illustrators.

Meet the Newbery Author. Sound filmstrips from American School Publishers, SRA Division of Macmillan/McGraw Hill School Publishing Company, P.O. Box 543, Blacklick, OH 43004-0543.
Authors from this chapter include: Virginia Hamilton, Beverly Cleary, Katherine Paterson, Laurence Yep, and others. Especially commendable is the filmstrip of Laura Ingalls Wilder because of the detail.

Mill-Lachman, L. (1991). *Our family, our friends, our world: An annotated guide to significant multicultural books for children and teenagers.* New Providence, NJ: R. R. Bowker. *One thousand books, published from 1970 through 1990, are critically evaluated. Grade level indications are also given.*

National Council for the Social Studies, *Social Education.*
NCSS publishes a notable list of children's trade books every year in its journal, Social Education. *Although all genres are represented, historical realistic fiction is most frequently included. The Children's Book Council (568 Broadway, Suite 404, New York 10002) also disseminates this list, and single copies are available if a stamped, self-addressed envelope is sent.*

Wings for Learning and Sunburst Catalog, 1600 Green Hills Road, P.O. Box 660002, Scotts Valley, CA 95067-0002.
This catalog includes the composition tool for Magic Slate II, referred to earlier, as well as other computer programs related to literature.

Literature of Fact: Biography and Information

INTRODUCTION AND RESPONSE

In the last chapter, factual accuracy, especially in historical realism, was seen as an important feature in literature for children. In this chapter, accuracy becomes the foundation for narrative and expository prose. Whether writing about famous people, as in biography, or writing to inform, key features are accuracy, authenticity, and truth.

Like the last chapter, this one treats two genres of children's literature: **Biography** and **Information**. Both are *nonfiction*, which is defined as "writing that communicates knowledge based on verifiable facts." Biography has been an established genre for some time; *information* is a relatively new term in literature covering nonfiction about school subjects and other topics of interest to children. Both genres will be defined further, as recent and well-known examples are described, demonstrating the wide range of nonfiction that is available to children and youth. An evaluative scheme is presented for both, with the common aspect of accuracy providing the basis for selection. Notable authors of nonfiction are listed, the Summary reiterates high points of each genre, and then Implications for Instruction offers ideas for reflection and action.

As we focus on truth, on the accurate depiction of a person's life or information about a subject, begin to sift fact from fiction in your own life in this suggested writing exercise. Do you keep a journal? If so, read a few entries and then write an episode based on those entries for an audience of friends. If not, recall something that happened to you, an event that comes back to you with clarity, and write it for an audience. As you are composing your autobiographical sketch, think about the decisions you are making. Selecting facts, putting them in some order, and making the finished product interesting and readable is no easy task. How much invention is allowable? In your writing, will you make up dialogue, or enhance a scene with added description? A biographer walks a tightrope between fact and fiction in order to tell a truthful story. Enjoy your dilemma on the tightrope and share your story and insight with friends.

● ● ● ● ●
HISTORY OF CHILDREN'S NONFICTION

Even though *Orbis Pictus, or The World Illustrated* was considered a scientific book for children in the seventeenth century, nonfiction was a rare commodity at the bookseller's. Biographical accounts of exemplary lives of saints and martyrs were read by Puritan children, but generally nonfiction was neglected.

Biography, as a genre, gained recognition in the eighteenth century and developed into an art form epitomized by James Boswell's *Life of Samuel Johnson*. It was an age attuned to self-revelation, gossip, and confession, and everyone— actresses, murderers, statesmen, evangelists, and businessmen—wrote autobiographies or or were the subjects of biographies (Stauffer, 1941). However, these books were not written for children, nor considered appropriate for them, since the style was to recount every fact, every conversation, and every act with pedantic precision.

It is puzzling, though, to consider why the outpouring of notable children's books in the next century, considered the golden age of children's literature, did not include biographies or other nonfiction. Because of the lack of good nonfiction, children's literature grew to be closely associated with fiction, with imaginative adventures and fanciful stories seen as the "true" literature. A well-respected scholar of children's literature, Lillian Smith, expressed the point of view of many when she said "Informational books are infrequently literature and seldom do they survive the generation for which they are written" (1953, p. 180). The short period of up-to-date information, since knowledge was changing, expanding, and old ideas were proved invalid, worked against this genre in establishing a foothold in literature for children.

It wasn't until this century that nonfiction gained its literary place in the world of children's books. A notable event honored informational books in 1922 when the first Newbery Medal went to a history book, *The Story of Mankind* by Dr. Hendrik Van Loon. A few years later, in 1934, the award was given to *Invincible Louisa* by Cornelia Meigs, a biography of Louisa May Alcott. In ensuing years, biography has had its share of Newbery award winners and honor books, but informational books are woefully underrepresented.

Invincible Louisa was the first biography to present to children a contemporary look at a well-known person. The word *invincible* gives a clue as to how Cornelia Meigs selected facts to support her theme of Louisa's indomitable spirit in spite of grinding poverty and heavy family responsibilities. Closely following, another Newbery winner, *Daniel Boone* by James Daugherty, gave a sentimental portrait of the American frontiersman and has been justly criticized for romanticizing the past and glorifying the settlers' point of view at the expense of Native Americans.

Anne Frank's deeply moving autobiography, *Diary of a Young Girl* (1952), brought her story and the tragedy of the Holocaust to readers in a way no other form could match. This account of Anne's hiding to escape the terror of the Nazis during World War II galvanized sympathy and indignation at the injustices this horrifying war perpetuated. As literature moves hearts and minds, this autobiography gave evil a human face and still offered hope for the human ability to rise above it. (See Implications for Instruction for an opportunity to create a bibliography of holocaust literature or other antiwar themes.)

David Macaulay's superb informational books, *Cathedral: The Story of Its Construction* (1973) and *Castle* (1977), detail through fine line drawings the construction of these medieval edifices. Honored for artwork, these books and others by Macaulay demonstrate a successful blend of text and art and truly represent milestones in nonfiction for children.

Another milestone was Russell Freedman's *Lincoln: A Photobiography* (1987). Its spectacular use of archival photographs, integrated with a thoughtful text, brought this era and this man to life in the reader's mind. Popular and meritorious, *Lincoln* won the Newbery award when biographies and informational books had been forgotten for several years.

From *Lincoln: A Photobiography* by Russell Freedman, © 1987. By permission of the publisher, Houghton Mifflin Co.

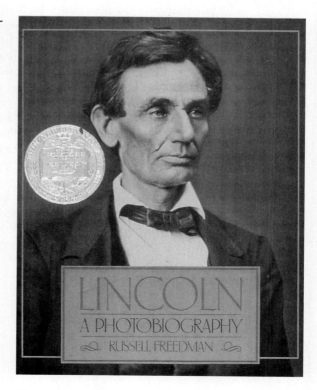

Milton Meltzer, a prominent biographer and historian, decried the lack of attention paid to nonfiction in prizes designed to honor literary work (1976). He also lamented the poor effort of reviewers evaluating nonfiction in major journals, a thought seconded by Seymour Simon, a prolific and well-respected writer of science books for children (DeLuca & Natov, 1982).

Because of the growing importance of nonfiction, its increased quantity and quality in book production, and a demand from school and public libraries for good biographies and current knowledge, these genres have become major forces in children's literature in the last decade. Libraries and bookstores today are replete with colorful, well-written, up-to-date nonfiction. Two prestigious awards for nonfiction (perhaps due in some part to Meltzer's call) were initiated in 1976 by the Boston Globe-Horn Book sponsorship, and in 1990 (the Orbis Pictus Award) by the National Council of Teachers of English.

A hopeful trend in biography for children has been noted by Ann Flowers, former editor of the *Horn Book Guide*. "Those who remember the earnest, carefully bowdlerized, extremely boring biographies of their childhoods must be happy with the advent of some glorious, carefully researched, handsomely presented, and fun-to-read biographies being published today" (Flowers, 1991, p. 215). She goes on to say that biographies now encompass a wide range of age groups, from picture books through young adult literature, and that a diversity of historical and contemporary persons, men and women, and people from many cultures and fields of endeavor are represented.

While there is a richness that is fairly new in biography, Flowers warns that there is also "a horrid proliferation of ill-conceived, poorly edited, and shoddily produced series books—usually but not always nonfiction" (Flowers, 1990, p. 19). A commonplace occurrence in publishing, series of biographies or informational books around a theme—women composers of the nineteenth century, for example—seem to generate a cookie-cutter approach to producing mass-market biographies and informational books. Nonfiction is particularly susceptible to superficial scholarship and uninspired writing. Probably because of the added demands of factual accuracy and verifiable authenticity, books of knowledge must be carefully evaluated and selected. Readers must have confidence in the veracity of what they are reading.

Important works of nonfiction from this brief history are listed here. You may want to explore some of these titles if you are unfamiliar with them. Because of the necessity to be up-to-date in knowledge, only the most recent books appear as examples in the subgenre sections that follow. These books, however, were catalysts in changing ideas and opinions of what nonfiction for children should be, and were forerunners of exciting new books mentioned later.

1657   *Orbis Pictus*

1921   *The Story of Mankind*

1933   *Invincible Louisa*

1952   *Diary of a Young Girl*

1973   *Cathedral: The Story of Its Construction*

1987   *Lincoln: A Photobiography*

• • • • •
DEFINING BIOGRAPHY

Biography is the written record of an individual's life. It is a record of events, conversations, and inferred thoughts and motives of a person interacting with circumstances in his or her world. An autobiography is a record of a person's life written by that person. Lives of people—famous or common—may become interesting stories in the hands of a competent biographer who can sift through the minutiae of daily living, find the essence of a life, and record it with imagination and wit.

Biography, as a genre, stands between the fiction of historical and contemporary realism and the facts of information books. Not altogether factual, but borrowing from illusion and inference, biographies are creative attempts to bring a person to life in literature. Philip Guedalla, a prominent biographer, said that biography is a region bounded on the north by history, on the south by fiction, on the east by obituary, and on the west by tedium (Boorstin, 1986).

In order to write, biographers must explore every known detail (somewhat tedious in practice, no doubt) and decide what is important and what can be tossed aside. Imposing a narrative structure on all these details gives shape to a biography, while the selection and integration of detail gives theme and point of view. A person's life is a story, but it takes a talented, meticulous writer with a knowledge of history and an interest in detective work to write a biography of candor and worth.

When writing for children, biographers have often felt the need to fictionalize. Facts that were not known were made up; facts thought to be unsuitable for children were changed. There are biographies based largely on fiction and, on the other hand, biographies in which most, if not all, facts are well documented. The amount of fiction included in biographies for children gives rise to terms that refer to this orientation: **authentic biography, fictionalized biography,** and **biographical fiction** (Huck, Hepler, & Hickman, 1993). *Authentic biography* is a term for carefully researched histories about people in which almost everything can be substantiated in fact. Authors do not create conversations, events, or scenes. Jean Fritz is a biographer who is well known for the authenticity of her biographies (and her autobiography, *Homesick: My Own Story,* 1982) for children. Others will be mentioned in subgenres that follow.

Fictionalized biography is a term that means the biography includes many aspects of invention, supposition, and inference. By necessity or in order to tell a good story, facts were omitted, or not known, or embroidered to make a point. F. N. Monjo is regarded as an author who uses biographical data convincingly in his fictionalized biographies.

Biographical fiction is, as the term denotes, fiction with a brief bow to accuracy. Many stories classified as historical fiction can be considered biographical fiction if a historical person figures prominently or even incidentally. These stories are really not biographies and should not be evaluated as such. They can be excellent stories, but their purpose is not to impart an accurate biographical sketch of someone. The fantasy *Ben and Me* (Lawson, 1951) is an example of biographical fiction.

In the last few years, a healthy trend toward authentic biographies for young people has been evident. As in other genres of children's literature, the new realism of the 1960s permeated biography. Facts that had been considered inappropriate, too adult, or unsuitable became acceptable and contributed their truth to more lifelike depictions of notable figures. Biographies now may portray people who grapple with life, make mistakes, and fall short of perfection. Critics insist that biographers strive for and maintain the same scholarly rigor when writing for children as when writing for adults.

Forms of children's biographies are basically these three: a complete life story, collections of several shorter biographies, and partial biographies in which the author concentrates on a particular time period, such as the childhood of a famous person. Quite often publishers will offer a series of biographies under a theme, such as the Women of Our Time series from Viking Penguin. Following (see Figure 9.1) is a short list demonstrating the kinds of series that are available

Figure 9.1 Examples of Series of Biographies

Grade Level	Title of Series	Publisher
k-3	Your Family Album	Twenty-First Century
k-3	Great African Americans	Enslow
k-3	Picture Book Biographies	Holiday House
4-6	Junior World Biography	Chelsea
4-6	Creative Minds	Carolrhoda
4-6	Achievers Series	Lerner
4-6	Olympic Gold	Blackbirch
4-6	People in Focus	Dillon
4-6	Sports Great	Enslow
4-6	Martial Arts for Peace	Atrium
7-9	Library of Biography	Chelsea
7-9	North American Indians of Achievement	Chelsea
7-9	Hispanics of Achievement	Chelsea
7-9	New Directions	Millbrook

today. Note that some publishing houses specialize in series of biographies, so there may be some houses that are new to you. This in no way exhausts series of biographies, but remains just a small sample.

Value of Biography for Children

Biographies present models of achievement, compassion, and heroism—people who have worked under difficult circumstances to create lives worth living and telling. Historical biographies provide glimpses into the past, where one can observe the realism of living conditions and childhood in a different time and place. Contemporary biographies show possible actions and attitudes in our world today, and tell of decisions that people made to better themselves. When the story of someone's life is written with magnetism, it enhances the drama of everyone's life.

EVALUATING BIOGRAPHY

Contemporary biographies, like other genres of children's literature, must combine a well-written story with a thorough foundation of authentic detail. All nonfiction writing based on research has four criteria for excellence: accuracy, judicious selectivity, organization, and imaginative and lively use of facts (Haviland, 1973, p. 297). In order to judge the worth of a particular book, begin with the questions listed in Figure 9.2.

Further selection criteria depend upon your purpose and your audience. Is the subject of this biography of interest to the children with whom you work? Does it

Figure 9.2   Evaluating Biography

Criteria	My Personal Response
Accuracy	Is scholarship or research evident? What are the biographer's credentials?
Selection of facts	How were the facts selected? Why did the biographer choose this subject?
Organization of facts	How well are facts integrated? Do the facts support theme and style? What was the biographer's point of view?
Imaginative and lively use of facts	Does it hold your interest? Are there insights and revelations? How does it challenge you to consider the subject differently?

fit into thematic units you envision in your curriculum planning? Are you going to read this biography aloud? Is the subject sufficiently meritorious or provocative to devote class time to reading and discussion? These evaluative questions should guide your selection as well.

One clue leading to a judgment about selection and organization of facts often lies in the subtitle of the biography. And since biographies frequently include subtitles, we can use the phrase to predict theme, style, or author's point of view. For example, in the title of Milton Meltzer's *Benjamin Franklin: A New American* (1988), the clue is "new American" and facts fit around aspects of Benjamin Franklin's life that led to his role as a revolutionary. As a contrast, Mary Pope Osborne's *The Many Lives of Benjamin Franklin* (1991) uses a broader selection of facts to underscore the "many lives" of this statesman—he was an inventor, a businessman, a writer and publisher, and a politician. Both biographies are excellent, and the titles help to send a message about how each one could be read.

● ● ● ● ●
SUBGENRES OF BIOGRAPHY

In this section biography will be divided into two subgenres: historical and contemporary. Biographies of historical figures will be discussed first, and examples will be drawn from books for older readers and books for younger readers (picture books and transitional books). Similarly, biographies of contemporary figures will be presented with examples of collections, autobiographies, people of color, women, and sports and entertainment figures. Meant to give a quick introduction to the range of biography available to children, this section encourages you to seek biographies of people you admire by visiting a library or bookstore and selecting some for your reading list.

Biographies of Historical Figures

As the premier representative of a biographer, Jean Fritz does not invent dialogue or idealize her subjects. Winner of the first *Orbis Pictus* award for nonfiction in 1990, she writes with a sense of humor and breathes life into her historical subjects. As she states, "We cannot afford to forget that the past is not just a series of events; it is *people* doing things" (Fritz, 1981, p. 86). The following sample of biographies attests to Fritz's range of knowledge and interests (asterisks indicate books for younger readers).

> *What's the Big Idea, Ben Franklin?* (1976)
>
> *Where Do You Think You're Going, Christopher Columbus?* (1980)
>
> *Make Way for Sam Houston* (1986)
>
> *The Great Little Madison* (1989)
>
> *Bully for You, Teddy Roosevelt* (1991)

F. N. Monjo has also been mentioned for his lighthearted fictionalized biographies. For younger readers, they impart a sense of history while looking at a famous person from someone else's point of view, as in *The One Bad Thing About Father* (1987), in which Father is President Theodore Roosevelt.

There are, of course, thousands of biographies of historical figures, from the founding fathers of the United States to internationally known figures. If you are new to this genre, start with some of the following examples. Also note that the asterisk denotes a picture book or transitional book.

Recommended biographies of historical figures

A Picture Book of Jesse Owens, David Adler (1992)

Calamity Jane, Doris Faber (1992)

Native American Doctor: The Story of Susan La Flesche Picotte, Jeri Ferris (1991)

Hiawatha, Messenger of Peace, Dennis Fradin (1992)

Against All Opposition: Black Explorers in America, Jim Haskins (1992)

Sojourner Truth: Ain't I a Woman? Patricia and Frederick McKissack (1992)

The Bard of Avon, Diane Stanley and P. Vennema (1992)

Mary Cassatt, Robyn M. Turner (1992)

Biographies of Contemporary Figures

From sports figures to political activists, subjects in contemporary biographies should be realistically depicted, including positive and negative facets of their lives. As evident in *A Twilight Struggle: The Life of John Fitzgerald Kennedy* (Harrison & Terris, 1992), a leader's mistakes, moral hesitancies, and character flaws may be described in realistic terms without detracting from qualities of charismatic leadership. Harrison and Terris showed many aspects of John Kennedy's life in vivid prose as well as extensive photographs. They also used oral history documentation and other audiovisual material to give a well-rounded, balanced account of Kennedy's life. In addition to the recommended books, Implications for Instruction describes several biographies that have been classroom tested.

Recommended biographies of contemporary figures

Bo Jackson: A Star for All Seasons, J. Devaney (1992)

Don't Explain: A Song of Billie Holiday, Alexis DeVeaux (1980)

Sandra Day O'Connor: Justice for All, B. Gherman (1991)

Showa: The Age of Hirohito, Dorothy and Thomas Hoobler (1990)

Malcolm X: By Any Means Necessary, Walter Dean Myers (1993)

*El Chino, Allen Say (1990)

Ryan White: My Own Story, by Ryan White and Ann Marie Cunningham (1991)

*Denotes picture or transitional book.

Multicultural Biographies

In addition to the ones just listed, here are several more historical and contemporary biographies representing four major cultural groups in the United States. Recommended and recent, the list also includes a few informational books. (Because all information is included here, these books are not referenced again in children's works cited at the end of this chapter.)

African American

Levine, E. (1993). *Freedom's Children: Young Civil Rights Activists Tell Their Own Stories.* New York: Putnam.

Lyons, M. (1990). *Sorrow's Kitchen: The Life and Folklore of Zora Neale Hurston.* New York: Scribner's.

*Marzollo, J. (1993). *Happy Birthday, Martin Luther King.* New York: Scholastic.

Morgan, B. (1992). *The Magic: Earvin Johnson.* New York: Scholastic.

Parks, R., & Haskins, J. (1992). *Rosa Parks: My Story.* New York: Dial.

Asian American

*Demi. (1991). *Chingis Khan*. New York: Holt, Rinehart & Winston.

Marrun, A. (1992). *Mao Tse Tung and His China*. New York: Viking.

Morey, J. N., & Dunn, W. (1992). *Famous Asian Americans*. New York: Cobblehill.

Say, A. (1993). *Grandfather's Journey*. Boston: Houghton Mifflin.

Hispanic

Conord, B. (1992). *Cesar Chavez*. New York: Chelsea.

Mohr, N. (1993). *All for the Better: A Story of El Barrio*. Milwaukee, WI: Raintree/Steck Vaughn.

Neimark, A. (1992). *Diego Rivera: Artist of the People*. New York: HarperCollins.

Turner, R. M. (1993). *Frida Kahlo*. Boston: Little, Brown.

Native American

Hoyt-Goldsmith, D. (1993). *Cherokee Summer*. New York: Holiday House.

Klausner, J. (1993). *Sequoyah's Gift: A Portrait of the Cherokee Leader*. New York: HarperCollins.

Lipsyte, R. (1993). *Jim Thorpe: Twentieth Century Jock*. New York: HarperCollins.

Scordato, E. (1992). *Sarah Winnemucca: Northern Paiute Writer and Diplomat*. New York: Chelsea.

*Denotes picture or transitional book.

● ● ● ● ●

INFORMATIONAL BOOKS

Informational books for children (and adults) cover almost every conceivable topic. New knowledge entering fields every day continually generates the need for additional material. An explosion of knowledge, increased use of informational books in schools, and a higher quality of book production pushes this genre to the top when one looks at the number of books published. When combined with biography, nonfiction, as a category, includes more than half of the books published each year. One can see the results of this proliferation in schools and public libraries. Although fiction usually gains the most attention from specialists in literature, nonfiction has equal if not more stature in the marketplace and in the classroom.

Children are curious. They demand answers to questions, and they want to figure things out, to discover why things work. They should be able to believe in the accuracy of their texts and trade books. The value of informational books lies in the curiosity of the human mind.

Books of information supplement and, in some cases, provide the basis for curricula in science and social studies. Teachers using topical approaches, thematic units, and innovative organizational structures (such as cooperative grouping) find that trade books offer the necessary variety and versatility to sustain these innovations.

In the past few years, books of information have appeared in increased quantity and, more importantly, in improved quality. Books are designed to invite the reader in, to make knowledge as accessible as possible. In keeping with the idea that visual literacy is a crucial skill for the television-reared child, much attention is paid to the careful preparation of graphic elements accompanying the text, especially in science books (Lauber, 1982).

In a critical evaluation of nonfiction for children, Margery Fisher (1972) pointed out that informational books may be used as propaganda. Information may be selectively offered, and it might reflect a tendency to persuade. Objectivity is essential, she asserted, to guard against an unhealthy use of selective information.

• • • • •
DESCRIPTION OF INFORMATIONAL BOOKS

Informational books transmit knowledge. They do not simply describe what happens, but explain why and how. They are usually written in an **expository** style, as contrasted with the narrative style associated with fiction. There are many types of informational books, with the most common ones described here.

1. Nonfiction chapter books: Books in which most of the information is organized into chapters and graphic material is included when necessary. Knowledge is primarily conveyed through the printed word. The intended audience is literate.

2. Illustrated informational books: Books that *show and tell.* Many scientific books, such as *Our Solar System* (Simon, 1992) are illustrated lavishly with diagrams, photos, charts, reproductions of computer screens, and so forth. Text and graphics are about equally important in conveying information.

3. Concept books: Books that explain a concept (see the Picture Book description of concept books in Chapter 5). The concept presented is singular, without complexity. For young readers/listeners, this is a picture book to be read to an audience. Usually text is minimal.

4. Photo essays: Much like illustrated informational books, photo essays use photos almost exclusively. There is about an equal balance between photos and text.

5. Fact books: These are books of text and minimal graphics, organized around topics such as how to use computers and other machines, driver's education, and hunting manuals. A popular book with most children, *The Guinness Book of World Records,* published annually by the Sterling Publishing Company, is an example.

Value of Informational Books

Because most informational books focus on a single subject, readers can hone in easily on interests and assignments. For example, the index in a book about the sea can provide exact information in an efficient format. Children (and adults) can satisfy curiosity, learn about far-flung places and topics, and probe new topics. With the abundance of subjects available, readers can find just about anything they need.

● ● ● ● ●
EVALUATING INFORMATIONAL LITERATURE

Writing in informational books should be clear, concise, and compelling. Graphics must also be clear, labeled properly, and balanced with text. Facts should be organized so that information is easily accessible and understandable. Generally, information should proceed from simple to complex, from general to specific.

In selecting nonfiction, two things should be avoided. First, objects should not be personified. When a human characteristic is imposed on a nonliving element, accuracy is compromised. For example, to give human emotions to a planet or a tree would be misleading, and would move the information from the realm of science into mythology. It is perfectly fine to mythologize plants or trees, but not under the rubric of scientific information. Second, if opinions are given as facts, readers are again misled. It is well to expect clear statements of conjecture, or theory, or to note the use of words like *may be* or *could be* instead of the emphatic *is*.

Figure 9.3 presents questions to ask while evaluating a work of nonfiction.

Figure 9.3 Evaluating Informational Books

Criteria	My Personal Response
Accuracy of facts	What are the author's credentials?
	What evidence is there of scholarship and research?
	How are opinions differentiated from facts?
Selection of facts	Are childlike analogies used to explain difficult concepts?
	Are concepts developed convincingly?
Organization of facts	Is the format attractive?
	Are graphics clear and labeled?
	Is there a framework, or overview, into which specifics fit?
Imaginative and lively use of facts	Does the writing challenge and stimulate the reader?
	What is the author's attitude toward the information?

• • • • •
SUBGENRES OF INFORMATIONAL LITERATURE

Roughly based on the Dewey decimal system of library classification, these five subgenres are drawn from categories of content readily found in school and public libraries: 1. general knowledge; 2. the social sciences; 3. science, technology, and mathematics; 4. the humanities; and 5. history and biography. These subgenres relate to curriculum planning as well. Each one will be described briefly, with an exemplary work and a list of recommended books following. Note authors and subjects, because if a specific book is unavailable in your search, there may be others that will substitute. These subgenres are meant to suggest divisions among all available information, but not to be rigid and mutually exclusive. Some categories may overlap, as knowledge among scientific fields is interrelated and multifaceted in many cases. Also, only recent books are recommended. Books for beginning readers are marked with an asterisk (*).

General Knowledge

General knowledge covers information about how to use resources such as libraries, newspapers, and museums. How to ask questions, how to study, and how to locate information are subjects of books in this subgenre. Truly "general knowledge," examples of these books are *The Guinness Book of World Records* and series from publishers such as Grosset's *The Kids Question and Answer Book* (Owl Magazine Editors, 1989).

Recommended books of general knowledge

Behind the Headlines: The Story of American Newspapers,
    Thomas Fleming (1989)

My Hometown Library, William Jaspersohn (1994)

**Let's Go to the Museum,* Lisl Weil (1989)

Social Science

Families, occupations, government and economics, social problems, including sexuality and substance abuse, customs, and holidays constitute some of the topics found in this subgenre. An example is *AIDS: What Does It Mean to You?* written by the well-respected author Margaret O. Hyde in collaboration with a medical doctor, Elizabeth H. Forsyth. Addressing myths associated with the disease, Hyde and Forsyth write in a matter-of-fact style for middle-level readers, using clear diagrams to explain how the virus works. Social issues are raised so that discussion is encouraged.

Recommended books of social science

Population: Too Many People? David Newton (1992)

Living with a Single Parent, Maxine Rosenberg (1992)

*Sisters and Brothers, Gretchen Super (1992)

Science, Technology, and Mathematics

From physical science to natural science, from medical technology to space, books in this subgenre provide current information to children and adults (but be sure the copyright is recent). Seymour Simon has been mentioned as an influential, highly respected, and prolific author of science books for children. He writes on many subjects and his books represent some of the best nonfiction that is available.

Recommended books of science, technology, and mathematics

To the Top of the World: Adventures with Arctic Wolves, Jim Brandenburg (1993)

Planets, Moons, and Meteors, John Gustafson (1992)

*Take a Look at Snakes, Betsy Maestro (1992)

Our Solar System, Seymour Simon (1992)

The Humanities

Music, the visual and performing arts, crafts, and games and hobbies are included in this subgenre. Books about orchestras, movies, and stamp-collecting and even joke books can be found in this section of the library. Photographic essays such as *A Very Young Musician* (Krementz, 1991) provide information by integrating photographs and text—in this case telling of a ten-year-old boy learning and practicing the trumpet. Krementz has several of these photo essays demonstrating children excelling in various fields.

Recommended books of the humanities

The Amazing Paper Cuttings of Hans Christian Andersen, Beth W. Brust (1994)

Talking with Artists, Pat Cummings (1992)

Lives of the Musicians: Good Times, Bad Times (and What the Neighbors Thought), Kathleen Krull (1992)

History and Biography

This area includes history, geography, and exploration, individual and collective biographies and autobiographies, and memoirs. Books of ancient and modern history, further subdivided into Europe, the Middle East, Africa, North and South America, and Australia represent this subgenre. Native Americans are also included. (Because biography was treated in the first part of this chapter, it will not be discussed here.)

An example of a well-researched, thoughtful presentation of information for fourth through sixth grades is *An Ancient Heritage: The Arab-American Minority* (Ashabranner, 1991). Written in clear prose, with photographs accompanying a balanced text, this is an eye-opening glimpse into the culture and attitudes of a little-known minority group. A bibliography and an index encourage further investigation. Another fine example, *Children of the Dust Bowl: The True Story of the School at Weed Patch Camp* (Stanley, 1992), shows how children of migrant laborers were treated in California in the late 1930s. Using personal interviews and a wide range of written sources, Stanley tells the story of a compassionate teacher who helped children build their own school when public education was denied them.

Recommended books of history

Navajo Code Talkers, Nathan Aaseng (1992)

*A Capital Capital City 1790–1814, Suzanne Hilton (1992)

Arctic Hunter, Diane Hoyt-Goldsmith (1992)

The Amazing Potato: A Story in Which the Incas, Conquistadors, Marie Antoinette, Thomas Jefferson, Wars, Famines, Immigrants, and French Fries All Play a Part, Milton Meltzer (1992)

Across America on an Emigrant Train, Jim Murphy (1993)

• • • • •
NOTABLE AUTHORS OF NONFICTION

In addition to the authors listed with examples in subgenres, here are some outstanding authors of nonfiction. In your search for a topic or biography of your choice, you may want to consult these.

Irving Adler	Leonard Everett Fisher	Dorothy Hinshaw Patent
Jim Arnosky	James Cross Giblin	Laurence Pringle
Isaac Asimov	Kathryn Lasky	Millicent E. Selsam
Rhoda Blumberg	Patricia Lauber	

• • • • •
SUMMARY

Nonfiction, as represented by the genres biography and information, was the focus of this chapter. Both genres demand accuracy of data, wise selection and organization of data, and an attractive format to appeal to children. Usually more specific and up-to-date than textbooks, these trade books are used extensively in school curricula.

Biography and information are fairly recent additions to genres of children's literature. Until this present century nonfiction was virtually ignored by scholars who defined and evaluated children's books. Considered often to be dull, tedious, and overloaded with facts, "literature of fact" had to prove itself by gaining credibility as literature. To do this, books of nonfiction had to become well written and well researched, and to be presented in attractive formats. Having gradually assumed these characteristics, the best nonfiction stands equally beside the best fiction now.

When the new realism permeated children's literature in the 1960s, biographies evidenced effects of changing attitudes. No longer were historical and contemporary figures pictured so heroically or so romantically. A more balanced account of a life story, combined with verifiable authenticity, began to appear in biography for children. Jean Fritz, Milton Meltzer, and a few others raised standards with authentic biographies based on fact.

Informational books, perhaps competing with television, began to be colorful, well organized, and pertinent to interesting topics in science, history, medicine, art, geography, and other subjects. The last decade has seen an unprecedented quality and quantity in these books. Seymour Simon, a writer of science books for children, represents this trend toward outstanding informational books.

As knowledge explodes exponentially, literature of fact is more and more necessary to fill gaps in school curricula. Accurate information is crucial to living responsibly and well. With over half of the children's books published annually today considered to be nonfiction, the popularity and the need for factual books seem firmly entrenched. However, with the popularity and sizable number of books produced comes the added responsibility of selecting the best for schools, homes, and libraries. Nonfiction, with its foundation of accuracy, must be judged by the strictest criteria for excellence. This is difficult to do, because those of us who know literature and children do not always have the knowledge that must be conveyed. Similarly, people who do have the knowledge, in medical technology, for example, do not always understand the audience for whom they are writing or have the talent for writing literate prose. The challenge of nonfiction is to combine the art of literature with the science of knowledge, a challenge that continually intrigues and entertains us as we prepare for the twenty-first century.

● ● ● ● ●
IMPLICATIONS FOR INSTRUCTION

In this section, questions allow you to reflect on some of the controversies and special issues related to biography and informational books for children. Generate some of your own questions as well, because there may be ideas in this chapter that you find provocative or with which you disagree. After *Reflections*, *Projects* are described that will allow you to explore some of the issues in a more active way, such as finding out about authors, comparing books, and applying criteria for evaluation, for example. Finally, *Activities* for primary, intermediate, and middle-level classrooms are suggested so that you can test some of your theories with children. Their response can guide you to further enjoyment in bringing children and books together.

Reflections

1. Generate the names of five people who should be subjects of a biography. They can be historical or contemporary. Who would you select to write about first? Why did you select that person? Are all these relatively unknown figures, or do biographies already exist about their lives?

2. Are you an avid reader of nonfiction? Do you enjoy biographies, how-to books, or informational books about science, history, or art? Reflect on why you would choose nonfiction, what kind of nonfiction you would choose, and how you might read it differently from fiction. (For example, do you read it cover to cover, in order, or do you skip around? Do the graphics get in your way, or do you enjoy the visual representation?)

3. Should a biographer like his or her subject, or should there be some emotional distance, or even antipathy, between them? What causes biographers to select one person to write about? When is it evident that the biographer's feelings are intruding? Can you cite an example of this?

4. Even nonfiction distorts the truth in its necessary act of reorganizing reality. The writing process ensures that facts are selected and interpreted as concepts are developed. How does this affect the way you approach nonfiction? Perry Nodelman, writing about nonfiction for children, says that nonfictional texts are never complete, never objective, and never wholly accurate (Nodelman, 1992). What is your response to this and what implications are there for using these books with children?

5. Do biographies and informational books have a potential propaganda value? Do they sometimes "sell" a point of view? In biography, for example, is it possible to revise history and make it more sympathetic to a person? Is this acceptable? In informational books on some aspect of technology, is it possible to present a view that this aspect of technology is inevitable, that it is crucial, regardless of cost or diminution of natural resources?

6. Do you think there is bias against nonfiction in children's literature? Is there a lack of attention, a disregard for nonfiction among reviewers or among those who are specialists in this field? Jo Carr (1982, p. ix) said there is a "consistent, if unconscious, denigration of nonfiction for children," which "contrasts sharply with the serious treatment of nonfiction for adults." Use this resource, *Beyond Fact: Nonfiction for Children and Young People,* to discover if you think nonfiction is neglected or not taken seriously.

7. How popular is biography? Do children seek out biographies? What kind of readers choose biographies for fun? And at what age do children begin to choose biographies for independent reading?

Projects

1. Compare several biographies about the same person so that different themes, points of view, and styles are obvious. Also look for discrepancies. Since

Christopher Columbus was a popular choice of biographers in celebration of the five hundredth anniversary of his first voyage, and because not everything is known about the man, he would be an interesting choice (see also activities for children). Here are three examples; after reading and comparing, which do you prefer?

Christopher Columbus: Voyager to the Unknown, Levinson
    (1990)

I, Columbus: My Journal 1492–3, Roop & Roop (1990)

Christopher Columbus: The Great Adventure and How We
    Know About It, West & West (1991)

2. It seems that lately many children's authors have written autobiographies or have been featured in biographies. See if one of your favorite authors has written about himself or herself, or has been the subject of a biography. Here is a brief list to get you started; maybe your favorite is here:

Anderson, W. (1992). *Laura Ingalls Wilder.*

Byars, B. (1992). *The Moon and I.*

Meltzer, M. (1988). *Starting from Home: A Writer's Beginnings.*

Naylor, P. R. (1987). *How I Came to Be a Writer.*

3. Select a topic that interests you and see how it is presented in some informational books. If you like space, dinosaurs, Wales, or maps, there are books for you. You can go to a library to survey the collection for your interest, or consult these reviewing sources to find nonfiction (as well as fiction):

Bulletin of the Center for Children's Books, Betsy Hearne (Ed.),
    University of Illinois Press, Champaign, IL 61820.

Choices, Kathleen T. Horning, Ginny Moore Kruse, and Merri
    V. Lindgren (Eds.), the Cooperative Children's Book
    Center, University of Wisconsin-Madison, 600 N. Park
    St., Madison, WI 53706.

The Horn Book Guide, 14 Beacon St., Boston, MA 02108.

4. Practice applying the criteria for evaluation of biography and informational books by choosing some books, then answering the questions in Figures 9.2 and 9.3. How do the criteria help you to make judgments?

5. How many works of nonfiction are represented in the Newbery award winners and honor books? Is nonfiction represented in the Caldecott list? Estimate a number or percentage, then find out how accurate your estimation is.

6. Literature of the Holocaust serves as a poignant reminder of our need to stop senseless destruction of life. Create a bibliography of themes of peace for your

needs with young children or middle-level children. It would be possible and powerful to combine fiction and nonfiction.

Activities for the Primary Level

1. Many biographies are now written for beginning readers (some have been marked with an asterisk in this chapter). Here are some transitional or easy-reader biographies. Use these books to elicit drama (scenes that can be acted out), to initiate writing exercises (for example, "what would you do if . . ."), or to discuss why this person was important.

   Fritz, J. (1992). *George Washington's Mother.*

   Giblin, J. C. (1992). *George Washington: A Picture Book Biography.*

   Thaxter, C. (1992). *Celia's Island Journey.*

   Also look for books in the Great African Americans Series from the Enslow Publishing Company, which are appropriate for K–3 classrooms.

2. From common classroom units on these subjects, themes related to ecology, the human body, the ocean, and many other topics can be explored when children create alphabet books on a subject. If you are studying the ocean, for example, an alphabet book might start: A Anemone, B Barracuda, and so on. Children would learn these words from the informational books read to them and read by them. They will want to illustrate their books, too.

3. Children can learn to compare two information books on the same topic. Looking at Gail Gibbons's *The Milk Makers* (1985) and Cynthia McFarland's *Cows in the Parlor* (1990) allows comparisons of several descriptions of how the milking process works on dairy farms.

4. Primary children can begin to write their life stories. One way to begin is to create a time line for each child. When was he or she born? Where did he or she live? What significant events happened? After enough events are placed on a time line, connect them in an autobiography. Parents will help to find pictures for a photobiography.

5. Combine some fantasy and some information by reading Joanna Cole's Magic School Bus stories, all illustrated by Bruce Degen, then create some magic bus rides with your class.

   The Magic School Bus at the Waterworks (1988)

   The Magic School Bus Inside the Earth (1987)

   The Magic School Bus Inside the Human Body (1989)

The Magic School Bus Lost in the Solar System (1990)
The Magic School Bus on the Ocean Floor (1992)

Activities for the Intermediate and Middle Levels

1. In middle-level reading periods, biographies of sports heroes can be compared to realistic fiction about the sport. Children could read *Finding Buck McHenry* (Slote, 1991) and then *Bo Jackson: A Star for All Seasons* (Devaney, 1992). Are the baseball aspects of Bo's career described from different points of view in each novel? Are there differences? What would happen if Bo saw Buck McHenry's team? What if the team went to see Bo play?

2. Biographies of the same person are rich in comparisons too. Different groups in a classroom could read *Benjamin Franklin: A New American* (Meltzer, 1988) and *The Many Lives of Benjamin Franklin* (Osborne, 1991). Information could be elicited and then compared on a character chart or a semantic web.

3. Dramatic scenes flourish in well-written biographies and middle-level readers enjoy acting out a "you are there" scenario. What would it be like to create the scene where Cornwallis surrenders to George Washington at Yorktown, or when Madame Curie presents her findings to skeptical scientists? See the unit, People of Destiny, in Chapter 10 for a more complete description of how to dramatize meetings of famous people.

4. Reading and writing imaginary conversations between two historical figures add insight to knowledge. William Shakespeare (see *The Bard of Avon*, Stanley, 1992) and Elizabeth I of England (see *Good Queen Bess*, Stanley, 1990) were contemporaries who probably met at some time. These two picture book biographies could be used to generate ideas for a conversation. Also, historical figures from different periods of time could have interesting conversations, sparked from the imagination of middle-level readers. (See the curriculum unit, People of Destiny, in the next chapter.)

5. Informational books usually contain graphic aids such as indexes, glossaries, charts, maps, photographs, and graphs. It is well to make sure students know how to read graphic information. Even good readers do not analyze information well when it is presented in unfamiliar contexts; find out what students know how to do and plan lessons directed toward what they do not know. All readers benefit from a careful preparation of study skill lessons.

6. Encourage children to create their own photobiographies. Most will have pictures from home and other "archival" material to add. Children may want to write about themselves; some may want to write about each other.

7. Children can evaluate the informational books they use. Questions like these will get them started: What are the author's credentials? Are the ideas presented clearly? How is the book organized? Is one book on the subject better than another? Why?

● ● ● ● ●
REFERENCES

Children's Works Cited

Aaseng, N. (1992). *Navajo code talkers.* New York: Walker.

Adler, D. (1992). *A picture book of Jesse Owens.* New York: Holiday.

Anderson, W. (1992). *Laura Ingalls Wilder.* New York: HarperCollins.

Ashabranner, D. (1991). *An ancient heritage: The Arab-American minority.* New York: HarperCollins.

Brandenburg, J. (1993). *To the top of the world: Adventures with arctic wolves.* New York: Walker.

Brust, B.W. (1994). *The amazing paper cuttings of Hans Christian Andersen.* New York: Ticknor & Fields.

Byars, B. (1992). *The moon and I.* New York: Messner.

Cole, J. (1987). *The magic school bus inside the earth.* New York: Scholastic.

Cole, J. (1988). *The magic school bus at the waterworks.* New York: Scholastic.

Cole, J. (1989). *The magic school bus inside the human body.* New York: Scholastic.

Cole, J. (1990). *The magic school bus lost in the solar system.* New York: Scholastic.

Cole, J. (1992). *The magic school bus on the ocean floor.* New York: Scholastic.

Cummings, P. (1992). *Talking with artists.* New York: Bradbury.

Devaney, J. (1992). *Bo Jackson: A star for all seasons.* New York: Walker.

DeVeaux, A. (1980). *Don't explain: A song of Billie Holiday.* New York: Harper & Row.

Faber, D. (1992). *Calamity Jane.* Boston: Houghton Mifflin.

Ferris, J. (1991). *Native American doctor: The story of Susan La Flesche Picotte.* Minneapolis, MN: Carolrhoda Books.

Fleming, T. (1989). *Behind the headlines: The story of American newspapers.* New York: Walker.

Fradin, D. (1992). *Hiawatha, messenger of peace.* New York: McElderry.

Frank, A. (1952). *Diary of a young girl.* New York: Doubleday.

Freedman, R. (1987). *Lincoln: A photobiography.* New York: Clarion.

Fritz, J. (1976). *What's the big idea, Ben Franklin?* New York: Coward.

Fritz, J. (1980). *Where do you think you're going, Christopher Columbus?* New York: Putnam.

Fritz, J. (1982). *Homesick: My own story.* New York: Putnam.

Fritz, J. (1986). *Make way for Sam Houston.* New York: Putnam.

Fritz, J. (1989). *The great little Madison.* New York: Putnam.

Fritz, J. (1991). *Bully for you, Teddy Roosevelt.* New York: Putnam.

Fritz, J. (1992). *George Washington's mother.* New York: Grosset.

Gibbons, G. (1985). *The milk makers.* New York: Macmillan.

Giblin, J.C. (1992). *George Washington: A picture book biography.* New York: Scholastic.

Gustafson, J. (1992). *Planets, moons, and meteors.* New York: Messner.

Harrison, B., & Terris, D. (1992). *A twilight struggle: The life of John Fitzgerald Kennedy.* New York: Lothrop.

Haskins, J. (1992). *Against all opposition: Black explorers in America.* New York: Walker.

Hilton, S. (1992). *A capital capital city 1790–1814.* New York: Atheneum.

Hoyt-Goldsmith, D. (1992). *Arctic hunter.* New York: Holiday.

Hoyt-Goldsmith, D. (1993). *Cherokee summer.* New York: Holiday House.

Hyde, M., & Forsyth, E. (1992). *AIDS: What does it mean to you?* New York: Walker.

Jaspersohn, W. (1994). *My hometown library.* Boston: Houghton Mifflin.

Krementz, J. (1991). *A very young musician.* New York: Simon & Schuster.

Krull, K. (1992). *Lives of the musicians: Good times, bad times (and what the neighbors thought).* New York: Harcourt.

Lawson, R. (1951). *Ben and me.* Boston: Little, Brown.

Levinson, N.S. (1990). *Christopher Columbus: Voyager to the unknown.* New York: Lodestar/Dutton.

Macaulay, D. (1973). *Cathedral: The story of its construction.* Boston: Houghton Mifflin.

Macaulay, D. (1977). *Castle.* Boston: Houghton Mifflin.

Maestro, B. (1992). *Take a look at snakes.* New York: Scholastic.

McFarland, C. (1990). *Cows in the parlor.* New York: Atheneum.

McKissack, P., & McKissack, F. (1992). *Sojourner Truth: Ain't I a woman?* New York: Scholastic.

Meltzer, M. (1988). *Benjamin Franklin: A new American.* New York: Watts.

Meltzer, M. (1988). *Starting from home: A writer's beginnings.* New York: Penguin.

Meltzer, M. (1992). *The amazing potato: A story in which the Incas, Conquistadors, Marie Antoinette, Thomas Jefferson, wars, famines, immigrants, and french fries all play a part.* New York: HarperCollins.

Monjo, F. N. (1987). *The one bad thing about Father.* New York: Harper & Row.

Murphy, J. (1993). *Across America on an emigrant train.* New York: Clarion.

Myers, W. D. (1993). *Malcolm X: By any means necessary.* New York: Scholastic.

Naylor, P. R. (1987). *How I came to be a writer.* New York: Aladdin.

Osborne, M. P. (1991). *The many lives of Benjamin Franklin.* New York: Dial.

Owl Magazine Editors. (1989). *The kid's question and answer book.* New York: Grosset.

Roop, P., & Roop, C. (Eds.). (1990). *I, Columbus: My journal 1492–3.* New York: Walker.

Rosenberg, M. (1992). *Living with a single parent.* New York: Bradbury.

Say, A. (1990). *El Chino.* Boston: Houghton Mifflin.

Simon, S. (1992). *Our solar system.* New York: Morrow.

Stanley, D., & Vennema, P. (1990). *Good Queen Bess: The story of Elizabeth I of England.* New York: Four Winds Press.

Stanley, D., & Vennema, P. (1992). *The Bard of Avon.* New York: Morrow.

Stanley, J. (1992). *Children of the dust bowl: The true story of the school at Weed Patch Camp.* New York: Crown.

Thaxter, C. (1992). *Celia's island journey.* Boston: Little, Brown.

Turner, R. (1992). *Mary Cassatt.* Boston: Little, Brown.

Weil, L. (1989). *Let's go to the museum.* New York: Holiday.

West, D., & West, J. (1991). *Christopher Columbus: The great adventure and how we know about it.* New York: Atheneum.

Professional Works Cited

Boorstin, D. (1986). Welcome. In J. Y. Cole (Ed.), *Biography and books.* Washington, DC: Library of Congress.

Carr, J. (1982). (Ed.). *Beyond fact: Nonfiction for children and young people* (p. ix). Chicago: American Library Association.

DeLuca, G., & Natov, R. (1982). Who's afraid of science books? An interview with Seymour Simon. *The Lion and the Unicorn, 6,* 10–27. Brooklyn, NY: Dept. of English.

Fisher, M. (1972). *Matters of fact: Aspects of nonfiction for children.* New York: Thomas Y. Crowell.

Flowers, A. (Ed.). (1990). Silver lining in a big, black cloud. *The Horn Book Guide 2,* 1, 19. Boston: Horn Book, Inc.

Flowers, A. (Ed.). (1991). Real people. *The Horn Book Guide, 2,* 2, 215. Boston: Horn Book, Inc.

Fritz, J. (1981). The very truth. In B. Hearne & M. Kaye, (Eds.), *Celebrating children's books* (p. 86). New York: Lothrop, Lee and Shepard.

Haviland, V. (1973). *Children and literature: Views and reviews* (p. 297). Glenview, IL: Scott, Foresman.

Huck, C., Hepler, S., & Hickman, J. (1993). *Children's literature in the elementary school* (5th ed.). New York: Harcourt Brace Jovanovich.

Lauber, P. (1982). What makes an appealing and readable science book? *The Lion and the Unicorn, 6,* 5–9. Brooklyn, NY: Dept. of English.

Meltzer, M. (1976). Where do all the prizes go? The case for nonfiction. *The Horn Book, LII,* 17–23.

Nodelman, P. (1992). *The pleasures of children's literature.* New York: Longmans.

Smith, L. (1953). *The unreluctant years* (p. 180). New York: Viking.

Stauffer, D. (1941). *The art of biography in eighteenth-century England.* Princeton, NJ: Princeton University Press.

Additional Resources

Barron, P. P., & Burley, J. Q. (Eds.). (1984). *Jump over the moon.* New York: Holt, Rinehart & Winston.
A book of selected professional readings, this volume contains five excellent articles about informational books. From "The Art of Nonfiction" (Betty Bacon) to "What do we do about Bad Biographies" (Jo Carr) these articles are provocative and timely.

Biography Today: Profiles of People of Interest to Young Readers. Omnigraphics, Inc., Penobscot Building, Detroit, MI 48226.
A monthly magazine for middle readers, Biography Today includes timely, short articles about people in the news as well as historical figures.

Kobrin, B. (1988). *EYEOPENERS! How to choose and use children's books about real people, places, and things.* New York: Viking.
A valuable handbook with a strong message attesting to the importance of nonfiction in classrooms, this book also includes a guide to more than 500 books with tips for use with children. Kobrin also publishes The Kobrin Newsletter, a monthly guide to nonfiction.

Leal, D. (1993). Storybooks, information books, and informational storybooks: An explication of the ambiguous grey genre. In *The New Advocate, 6,* 1 (Winter), 61–70.
Leal suggests that a "hybrid text" combining fiction and nonfiction is helpful in concept development of primary school children. She gives several examples of these informational storybooks, such as Joanna Cole's Magic Bus Ride . . . books (1986–92) listed in this chapter, and classroom uses for them.

Prelude Series from the Children's Book Council, Inc., 67 Irving Place, New York, New York 10003.
A series of audiotapes on different aspects of children's literature; some that are especially related to nonfiction are:

Paper Airplanes, Dinosaurs and Space: Science Books are the Real Thing, Seymour Simon, Series 7.

Trade Books and the Social Studies, Margaret Branson, Series 4.

Science Books and Young Children, Glenn O. Blough, Series 1.

Richardson, Selma. (1990). *Magazines for children.* Chicago: American Library Association.
Children's magazines are incredibly good resources of nonfiction. Here are some popular ones in different fields of interest. Most are for approximate ages 6 through 12.

Cobblestone: The history magazine for young people. Cobblestone Publications, 30 Grove St., Peterborough, NH 03458.

Cricket, P.O. Box 58342, Boulder, CO 80332.

National Geographic World. National Geographic Society, 17th and M Streets, N.W., Washington, DC 20036.

Ranger Rick. National Wildlife Federation, 8925 Leesburg Pike, Vienna, VA 22184.

Sports Illustrated for Kids. Time, Inc. Magazine Co., 1271 Avenue of the Americas, New York, New York 10020.

3 - 2 - 1 Contact. Children's Television Workshop, P.O. Box 53051, Boulder, CO 80322.

Chapter Ten

The Literacy-Literature Connection: Six Units

• • • • •
INTRODUCTION

Each of the preceding chapters dealt with a particular aspect of literature for children and youth. Most often a genre was presented with criteria for selection and several recommended books were listed. Throughout each chapter, implicit themes underscored the value of literature to empower listeners, readers, writers and speakers. When carefully selected for a single child or for a classroom of children, literature can inspire, entertain, and instruct.

It is now time to explore the instructional aspect of literature—its capacity to enliven the language arts curriculum. When literature-based approaches form the foundation of school reading programs, children and teachers "grow into a community of learners and view themselves as readers and writers" (Wepner & Feeley, 1993, p. 28). Within these communities, learners respond to books actively and passionately. They become literate through reading, writing, speaking, and listening.

By encouraging informal responses as well as creating structured activities, teachers use literature to develop the language and thinking abilities of their students. A natural connection between literacy, or the ability to read and write, and literature, the best of written work, sustains and motivates the learning community. This chapter capitalizes on the literacy-literature connection by proposing six thematic units, suitable for children from kindergarten through sixth grade. Themes play on basic interests, needs, and common topics of elementary school curricula. Additional resources at the end of the chapter will point you toward thematic units and teaching strategies for adolescents from seventh through twelfth grades.

There is no "response" to this introduction, and no "Implications for Instruction" at the close of this chapter. Instead, you are urged to imagine yourself in a classroom or other instructional setting, using these plans to teach children through literature. Better yet, actually try these units in classrooms, watching children respond to literature as they become literate. Field-tested in classrooms and identified in Chapter 1, the following six resource units show how a teacher selects and organizes resources, and then creates opportunities for children and preadolescents to enjoy and be instructed by the books chosen by them and for them.

> Kindergarten and Grade One: SINGING SONGS AND
>   STORIES
> Grades One and Two: WILD THINGS
> Grades Two and Three: UNEXPECTED FRIENDS
> Grades Three and Four: STARS: FACT AND FICTION
> Grades Four and Five: PEOPLE OF DESTINY
> Grades Five and Six: JOURNEYS

● ● ● ● ●
DESCRIBING LITERATURE UNITS

A literature unit is "a set of instructional activities linked by a unifying element" (Cox & Zarillo, 1993, p. 121). The unifying element may be a theme, a genre, an author or illustrator, or a school-related subject. For example, literature units may focus on journeys, poetry, Walter Dean Myers, or Protecting the Environment.

There is no single model for a literature unit; there is instead a varied pattern of activities coming from the purposes and objectives of the curriculum and the teacher, the needs and interests of the students, the resources available, and the time limits imposed by a school schedule. However, guiding principles to the formulation of units arise from beliefs about the value of literature and a conviction that children learn by interacting with text in myriad ways. Common features of literature-based programs typically include the following (deLapp, 1989):

1. Children are read to on a daily basis;
2. Children have time to read books of their own choosing;
3. Children discuss and reflect upon the books they read;
4. Children respond to books through writing, art, drama, music, and talk;
5. Children write on topics of their own choosing;

6. Children share their reading, writing, and art products with the whole class;

7. Children use a variety of good books as an essential part of any theme or unit of study; and

8. The daily schedule is flexible.

A literature-based classroom would find children being read to, children reading silently and aloud in pairs or small groups, all responding to literature holistically and analytically. Responses are seen in a variety of written work, as well as artwork, drama, three-dimensional constructions, musical productions, and lots of discussion. Reflecting a reader's authentic interpretation of story, essay, chapter, or poem, responses are valued because they show what and how children are thinking, not because they are "right" or "wrong." The transaction between the reader and the text creates the context for learning to occur (Rosenblatt, 1978).

How to Plan a Unit

Planning usually begins with the teacher, or the teacher and the students, identifying a theme or subject. Some themes are dictated by curriculum development; some may come from conversations, community happenings, or ideas from other teachers. Next, the teacher begins to gather resources—books and other print material, audiovisual and technological support (movies, computer software, etc.), and particular things relative to the theme (art supplies, science supplies). Guided by a careful perusal, the teacher then decides on activities and skills generated by the literature. Special projects may be developed. Finally, daily lesson plans are created and the unit is launched!

Occasionally, the theme may not come first; it may come after the teacher reads an especially compelling book and wants to use it with children. A theme might develop as a result of several books that seem to explore an issue or topic that fits into plans and purposes.

Cairney (1990) suggests that the most delicate aspect of creating literature units is the careful, thoughtful attention to selecting books, then allowing the power of literature to generate applications that call for authentic responses. Clearly, a careful selection of literature is the heart of successful literature-based instruction. Inherent in the selection process is a regard for the best possible match between book and reader.

● ● ● ● ●
THEMATIC UNITS

The following units were written to demonstrate some of the great variety and depth that literature can offer to a classroom. Each unit is appropriate for at least two grade levels, and conceivably could stretch to accommodate adjacent grade levels as well with a judicious selection of a few additional books. Each unit is projected into a week of five consecutive lessons, scheduled for approximately sixty to ninety minutes each, but a teacher could stretch some lessons and shorten others, depending on the time allotted to activities. A variety of lessons, or applications that call for varied responses, have been included; activities that follow each chapter could be consulted as well. These units do not presuppose an indepth knowledge of reading pedagogy, but are written so that people with some familiarity with children and schools could implement them.

The units are different, but they share common features that provide a predictable structure. Basically, each unit includes

- Reading aloud to children (or storytelling)
- Silent reading and shared book reading by children
- Reading and writing applications
- Bridging to other disciplines
- Opportunities for assessment

To elaborate, reading aloud to children usually begins the daily lesson, as it introduces or reintroduces the theme and signals a reading and language arts period. Reading aloud creates a setting for content and establishes the community feeling of the participants. Storytelling serves a similar function. It is crucial that teachers learn to read aloud well, to use their voices effectively to pull listeners into stories. Reading aloud should be pleasurable for both reader and listener.

Equally important, and following naturally, is silent reading and shared book reading. Silent reading is crucial to develop effective readers; shared book reading occurs when children select "book buddies" or form teams for "partner reading." They might read the same book silently side by side, or, after silent reading, read aloud to each other.

Reading and writing applications are responses to literature. These responses take as many forms as one can imagine in a busy classroom. Children may write in response journals; participate in discussions of theme, characterization, and plot; create poems, puppets, and plays; and develop story maps and story frames. Applications called for in the six units presented are charted in Figure 10.1.

Responses allow and, in fact, enable bridging to other disciplines. Informational books, available in abundant topics for a variety of grade levels, provide opportunities to bridge into the humanities, sciences, social sciences, and other fields. Equally so, fiction in fantasy, realism, and traditional stories sparks connections to art, music, philosophy, and many other disciplines. Figure 10.2 presents examples of how the six units bridge to other disciplines.

Additionally, applications allow the assessment of reading and writing abilities through the **process** of completing an activity and the ultimate **product**. Writing and other artistic samples of work are evaluated according to the teacher's criteria and are sometimes added to portfolios that document a child's development as a learner of language.

A note of caution is pertinent here, because an important part of each unit deals with children choosing books from a wide selection. Care must be taken in helping them choose appropriately. Too much direction from the teacher results

Figure 10.1 Reading and Writing Applications

UNITS	APPLICATIONS				
	Comparing elements in literature (themes, characters, plots, setting, style, etc.)	Writing responses and composing	Identifying story structure; creating story maps and webs	Developing vocabulary	Reading and writing poetry
SINGING SONGS AND STORIES	Comparing poems in *Mother Goose* to poems in *Jelly Belly*	Orally identifying favorite part of unit	Writing/illustrating "The Muffin Man"	Identifying words in recipes and rhymes	Listening to *Mother Goose, Sing to the Sun,* and others
WILD THINGS	Comparing *Where the Wild Things Are* to their personal stories	Composing personal stories	Creating a storyboard	Learning words to describe the "wild things"	Listening to *Wild Critters*
UNEXPECTED FRIENDS	Discussing stories with partners	Responding in journals		Learning words to describe friends	Sharing poems in *Best Friends*
STARS: FACTS AND FICTION	Comparing legends	Composing legends		Word-gathering "star" words	Listening to poems about stars
PEOPLE OF DESTINY	Comparing qualities of fame to self	Writing autobiographies, dialogues	Creating a time line	Learning and categorizing occupational words	
JOURNEYS	Comparing read-aloud book to choice book	Responding in journals	Creating a literary map and web of journeys	Learning place names	

Figure 10.2 Bridging to Other Disciplines

UNITS / DISCIPLINES	Music	Drama	Science and Mathematics	Art	History
SINGING SONGS AND STORIES	Singing, playing rhythm instruments	Movement to music and rhythm	Baking muffins, measuring ingredients	Illustrating "The Muffin Man"	Opportunity for history of Mother Goose rhymes
WILD THINGS	Opportunity to add music to the "wild rumpus"	Creating a "wild rumpus"	Opportunity to contrast *real* animals to imaginary wild things	Making paper-bag puppets	
UNEXPECTED FRIENDS		Pantomiming or dramatizing *Yo! Yes?*		Choosing among several art projects	Opportunity for historical setting in choice book
STARS: FACTS AND FICTION	Opportunity to find appropriate music for star myths and legends.		Recognizing constellations; learning facts about stars	Creating a constellation	Opportunity to learn history of stars, constellations
PEOPLE OF DESTINY	Reading biographies of musicians and other performers	Dramatizing a famous person's life in "Meeting of Minds"	Reading biographies of scientists and mathematicians	Reading biographies of artists	Learning about Shakespearian England and 15th-century France
JOURNEYS	Selecting music appropriate to the culture represented in the choice book	Dramatizing a scene from the journey	Measuring journeys in miles and kilometers	Choices of art projects: collage, diorama, etc.	Discussion of socio-historical reasons for journeys

in restricted choices; not enough direction results in mismatches and sometimes frustration for the child because of a text that is too demanding or too easy. The teacher must know the children and the books very well and be able to make subtle suggestions. It is best to trust children to make appropriate choices and then support them with effective instruction so that the literature is enjoyable and instructive.

Singing Songs and Stories   Audience: Ages 5–7 (Kindergarten and Grade One)

Overview: This unit introduces beginning readers to the joy of expression that literature evokes. These experiences with literature heighten an awareness of rhyming words and predictable language in words and plot, and provide opportunities for singing, movement, and artistic expression. From *Mother Goose* to *Jelly Belly,* and from traditional folk songs to newer American folk songs, combining literature and music celebrates life and imagination!

First Day: Read aloud selections from *Brian Wildsmith's Mother Goose* (1964). Choose some familiar ones and some not-so-familiar ones. After reading "Old Mother Hubbard" (p. 50) and "Girls and Boys Come Out to Play" (p. 60), encourage children to clap as the words are chanted rhythmically. Try some with children hopping, and use rhythm instruments such as sticks and wood blocks to emphasize the rhythm. Sing "Baa Baa Black Sheep" (p. 66).

There may be other tunes that are known or that could be learned: "Jack and Jill" and "Little Bo Peep," for example. A listening corner, with audiotapes and headphones available to several children at a time would enhance this unit. Examples of specific cassettes are:

Chapin, Tom. (1992). *Family Tree.* New York: Sony Music Entertainment.

Penner, Fred. (1991). *Happy Feet.* Don Mills, Ontario: Oak Street Music, distributed by Sony Music Canada.

Raffi. (1990). *Evergreen, Everblue.* Universal City, CA: Troubador Records.

Rosenshontz. (1984). *It's the Truth.* Brattleboro, VT: R S Records.

Sharon, Lois and Bram. (1984). *Mainly Mother Goose.* Toronto: Elephant Records.

For silent reading, allow children to select one of the following picture books with song texts, or cassettes from the listening center.

Aliki	*Go Tell Aunt Rhody*
Ed Emberley	*London Bridge Is Falling Down*
Paul Galdone	*Cat Goes Fiddle-I-Fee*

S. J. Hale	*Mary Had a Little Lamb*
E. J. Keats	*Over in the Meadow*
John Langstaff	*Frog Went a Courtin'; Oh A-Hunting We Will Go; Over in the Meadow*
Tracy Campbell Pearson	*Old MacDonald Had a Farm*
Glen Rounds	*Old MacDonald Had a Farm*
Peter Spier	*The Erie Canal; The Star-Spangled Banner; The Fox Went Out on a Chilly Night; London Bridge Is Falling Down*
Diane Stanley	*The Farmer in the Dell; Fiddle-I-Fee*

Second Day: Sing "Oh, Do You Know the Muffin Man" (Hart, 1982, p. 34), shown on p. 217, as well as the tunes from yesterday. Introduce the activity of baking muffins. (You will need an adult/child ratio of about one to four or five for this activity.) In small groups of four or five children, use easy muffin mixes and allocate a task for each child. Have the procedure written on large posters so that children can practice reading it with you. An example follows.

| Procedure | Crack an egg into the bowl. Beat it. Open the box and pour the mix into the bowl. Measure the milk. Add it to the mix. Spoon the mix into the muffin cups. Bake (at 350° for 20 minutes). Eat and enjoy! |

While the muffins are baking, provide for each child a large piece of paper (11" X 17") with the words to "Oh, Do You Know the Muffin Man" and space for a picture. Children may read the words silently and illustrate them.

Third Day: Read aloud *All God's Critters Got a Place in the Choir* (Staines, 1989). Assign children to the "critter" parts: the bullfrog, the cow, the hippopotamus, etc. Read again, stopping for the child who is that critter to make the appropriate sound. Sing the chorus and then teach the children to sing it. You can speak or sing the verses, with sound effects or not, and have everyone join in the chorus.

If you have time, allow the children to choose a song picture book for silent reading or the listening corner. These picture books, related to songs and musical performances, may be added to the possibilities:

Karen Ackerman	*Song and Dance Man*
Molly Bang	*The Paper Crane*
Ashley Bryan	*Sing to the Sun* (Poetry)
Tomie dePaola	*Sing, Pierrot, Sing* (wordless)
Jacob and Wilhelm Grimm	*The Bremen Town Musicians*
Rachel Isadora	*Ben's Trumpet*
Maryann Kovalski	*Take Me Out to the Ballgame*
Karla Kuskin	*The Philharmonic Gets Dressed* (informational)

This is the first verse to "Oh, Do You Know the Muffin Man?"

The Muffin Man

arr. J. Hillman

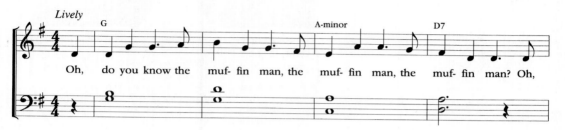

Vera Williams   *Music, Music for Everyone*
Etta Wilson   *Music in the Night*
Charlotte Zolotow   *The Song*

Fourth Day: Read aloud selections from *Jelly Belly*. Compare "There Was an Old Lady" (p. 14) to "Old Mother Hubbard" (from *Brian Wildsmith's Mother Goose*) and "Dirty Georgie" (p. 32) to "Georgy Porgy." Discuss similarities and differences in the words, the characters, and what the characters did (see Figure 10.3). Chant, clap, and move to some of the other delightful rhymes in *Jelly Belly*, such as "The Dinosaur Dinner" (p. 44) and "Up in North Ontario" (p. 60).

Allow children to choose picture books for silent reading.

Fifth Day: Read aloud selections from *Sing to the Sun*. Allow children to compare these poems with others they've heard throughout the week. Select songs from *Gonna Sing My Head Off, Diane Goode's Book of Silly Stories and Songs*, or *All Night, All Day*. Use rhythm instruments to punctuate the beat, if you wish. After enjoying, ask a number of children, or each child, to identify his or her favorite part of the unit and describe why it was best. These short vignettes, printed on large paper or typed into the computer, then printed, provide an example of the child's language for him or her to read, to illustrate, and to remember.

Figure 10.3   Comparing
"There Was an Old Lady" to
"Old Mother Hubbard"

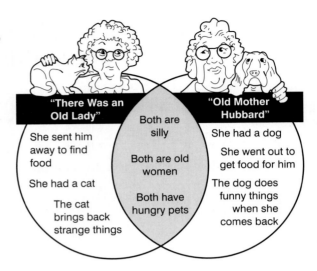

"There Was an
Old Lady"

"Old Mother
Hubbard"

Both are
silly

Both are old
women

Both have
hungry pets

She sent him
away to find
food

She had a cat

The cat
brings back
strange things

She had a dog

She went out to
get food for him

The dog does
funny things
when she
comes back

Bibliography for Singing Songs and Stories

Ackerman, K. (1988). *Song and dance man*. New York: Knopf.
Aliki. (1974). *Go tell Aunt Rhody*. New York: Macmillan.
Bang, M. (1985). *The paper crane*. New York: Greenwillow.
Bryan, A. (1991). *All night, all day: A child's first book of African-American spirituals*. New York: Atheneum.
Bryan, A. (1992). *Sing to the sun*. New York: HarperCollins.
dePaola, T. (1983). *Sing, Pierrot, sing*. New York: Harcourt Brace Jovanovich.
Emberley, E. (1967). *London bridge is falling down*. Boston: Little, Brown.
Galdone, P. (1985). *Cat goes fiddle-i-fee*. New York: Clarion.
Goode, D. (1992). *Diane Goode's book of silly stories and songs*. New York: Dutton.
Grimm, J., & Grimm, W. (1980). *The Bremen Town musicians*. New York: Greenwillow.
Hale, S. J. (1984). *Mary had a little lamb*. New York: Holiday House.
Hart, J. (comp.) (1982). *Singing bee: A collection of favorite children's songs* (p. 34). New York: Lothrop, Lee & Shepard.
Isadora, R. (1979). *Ben's trumpet*. New York: Greenwillow.
Keats, E. J. (1971). *Over in the meadow*. New York: Scholastic.
Kovalski, M. (1993). *Take me out to the ballgame*. New York: Scholastic.
Krull, K. (1992). *Gonna sing my head off*. New York: Knopf.
Kuskin, K. (1982). *The Philharmonic gets dressed*. New York: Harper.
Langstaff, J. (1955). *Frog went a courtin'*. New York: Harcourt Brace Jovanovich.
Langstaff, J. (1967). *Over in the meadow*. New York: Harcourt Brace Jovanovich.
Langstaff, J. (1977). *Oh a-hunting we will go*. New York: Atheneum.
Lee, D. (1983). *Jelly belly*. Toronto: Macmillan of Canada.
Pearson, T. C. (1984). *Old MacDonald had a farm*. New York: Dial.
Rounds, G. (1989). *Old MacDonald had a farm*. New York: Holiday.
Spier, P. (1961). *The fox went out on a chilly night*. New York: Doubleday.
Spier, P. (1967). *London bridge is falling down*. New York: Doubleday.
Spier, P. (1970). *The Erie Canal*. New York: Doubleday.
Spier, P. (1973). *The star-spangled banner*. New York: Doubleday.
Staines, B. (1989). *All God's critters got a place in the choir*. New York: Puffin Unicorn.
Stanley, D. Z. (1978). *The farmer in the dell*. New York: Little, Brown.
Stanley, D. Z. (1978). *Fiddle-i-fee*. New York: Little, Brown.

Wildsmith, B. (1964). *Brian Wildsmith's Mother Goose.* New York: Franklin Watts.
Williams, V. (1984). *Music, music for everyone.* New York: Greenwillow.
Wilson, E. (1993). *Music in the night.* New York: Cobblehill.
Zolotow, C. (1982). *The song.* New York: Greenwillow.

Additional Resources

Cohn, A. L. (comp.) (1993). *From sea to shining sea.* New York: Scholastic.
Lamme, L. L. (1990). Exploring the world of music through picture books. *Reading Teacher, 44,* 294–300.
Jarnow, J. (1991). *All ears: How to choose and use recorded music for children.* New York: Viking Penguin.
Sale, L. (1992). *Growing up with music: A guide to the best recorded music for children.* New York: Avon.

Wild Things
Audience: Ages 6–8 (Grades One and Two)

Overview: Using *Where the Wild Things Are* (Sendak, 1963) as a focal point, children will create wild things of their own. They will explore descriptive vocabulary words (adjectives) as they make puppets, draw, write, and dramatize their own stories, prompted by Maurice Sendak's book.

First Day: Before reading aloud *Where the Wild Things Are,* activate prior knowledge by asking these purpose-setting questions: Why does Max's mother call him a "wild thing"? When Max meets the wild things, what are they like? Tell the children that you are going to read the book to them, and challenge them to think of some words to describe the wild things.

After the reading, elicit responses to the questions above and ask which words might describe "wild things." Write these words with colorful markers on a large piece of paper in the front of the class so that everyone can see. (You may have words like *scary, kind, funny, weird,* etc.) Remind the children that Max tames the wild things by using a magic trick, and ask, "Do you remember what that trick was?" (Staring into their eyes without blinking once and saying "Be still.")

Tell the children that these are imaginary wild things—wild creatures created by a storyteller. Give them a chance to create their own wild things as they make paper-bag puppets to represent large, but friendly, wild things, capturing the character type they choose. With the help of the descriptive words they gave, try to help each child create a character type—shy, sporty, ferocious, whatever. (You will need large paper bags, crayons or markers, ribbons, yarn, construction paper, scissors, and stapler or masking tape.) Fit the paper bag over each child's head and lightly mark a pencil dot where the eyes should go. Take the bag off and assist the child, if necessary, to cut holes for the eyes. From that point, the mouth and other appendages, such as ears, horns, hair, warts, feathers, teeth, and eyelashes can be added or attached. The ferocious wild things will be used tomorrow in the children's own stories.

Second Day: Read aloud *Where the Wild Things Are*. Have the children imagine, as they listen to the story, how their own wild thing would have acted in the story, especially during the wild rumpus. Say: "Today, after reading, we'll act out some of the wild rumpus, with our own puppet wild things on our heads, and then we'll begin to write our own story of wild happenings." (You will want to control the level of this activity so that chaos does not ensue. Establish a signal with the children by asking what Max did when it was time for the wild rumpus to stop. He said "Stop." You can say "stop," or, if you have music as a background to the rumpus, stopping the music could be a signal for activity to cease.)

When the children have had the opportunity to join in the wild rumpus, introduce the Storyboard activity (see Figure 10.4).

Give each child a big copy of the storyboard. His or her task is to draw three scenes from an imaginary story with his or her character in it. Help children think of a beginning by asking "Who would your character meet first? Maybe this person would send it on a journey or ask it to do something." For the middle, have the children think of what their characters would like to do—perhaps have a wild rumpus, or play in a band, or meet the queen. The last picture will be the end. Ask, "Would your character come back home? Or would your character stay and live happily ever after in a new place?" Pictures should reflect a story. Most of the stories will be quite similar to *Where the Wild Things Are,* and that's fine. Say to the children that tomorrow we'll write our stories, using the storyboard to give us ideas. Some children will begin to write as they label pictures, and some will be able to write sentences.

Figure 10.4   Storyboard for *Where the Wild Things Are*

Draw a picture of the beginning of your story.	Draw something that happens in the middle of your story.	Draw the end of your story.
Beginning	Middle	End

Third Day: If you think the children need to hear *Where the Wild Things Are* again, read it aloud. If not, begin by giving them a chance to talk about the drawings on their storyboards and to recall the story that started to form in their minds yesterday. Discuss beginning, middle, and end. Some children will want to tell the story orally, using the storyboards. After time for discussion, each child will write a story. Some will describe each picture, some will use words very sparingly, and some will elaborate until a complete story is written. Encourage them to use their adjectives from the first day's experience. Allow invented spelling so that children are not searching for precise spellings of words. (Correct spellings can be supplied later.)

Fourth Day: Select two or three of the children's stories to read aloud to the group, or ask for volunteers. Have the children listen for similarities and differences among the stories. Praise and enjoy each story. Ask the children if the storyboards helped them organize their thoughts for the story. As a prelude to reading aloud *Wild Critters* (Jones, 1992), tell the children that you are going to read some poems that their own wild things might enjoy (and they will too!). These poems are about wild animals in Alaska. (You may want to distinguish between their imaginary wild things and the realistic wild critters.) Select in advance poems that interest you, and read several aloud. Suggestions include "Caribou Carrie" (p. 12), "Determined Ermine" (p. 34), or "Pfine Pfeathered Pfashion" (p. 36).

If there is time, these poems may inspire some poetry writing about their wild things. See Chapter 6 for some ideas.

Fifth Day: Read aloud *Where the Wild Things Are* and have the children read along with you. Notice how many sight words some children are beginning to recognize. Call attention to predictable words, such as *wild things* and *wild rumpus.*

You may want to compare some of the personal stories of the children with the structure or vocabulary of the book. There will be noticeable similarities and differences.

Finally, ask the children what they learned from this literature unit. Help them recall what they learned from the puppet-making, reading, drawing, and writing they did.

Bibliography for Wild Things

Jones, T. (1992). *Wild critters*. Fairbanks, AL: Epicenter Press.
Sendak, M. (1963). *Where the wild things are*. New York: Harper & Row.

Unexpected Friends   Audience: Ages 7–9 (Grades Two and Three)

Overview: This unit introduces children to multicultural and multigenerational books that explore unexpected friendships. Through reading and writing, children examine what qualities are important in friendship, how to become a good friend, and how to look in unexpected places for people and animals that become connected to us through friendship.

First Day: Introduce the concept of friendship by asking children to finish the sentence, "A friend is someone who. . . ." Write their responses on a large paper with markers. When six or seven have volunteered, continue on another sheet by asking "Who can be a friend?" and elicit ideas such as a pet, a person like me, a relative, and so on.

Direct attention to the book and activate prior knowledge by saying, "At first the two characters in this story are not friendly to each other. But listen and see what happens." Read aloud *Yo! Yes?* (Raschka, 1993). (Two boys, one white and one black, carry on a conversation of monosyllables until a friendship develops.) After reading, discuss what might be happening. Ask two children to pantomime or dramatize the making of new friends while you read aloud again. If there is time, allow other children to participate in the dramatization. Elicit other words that might be used in an exchange. Ask the children to write in their response journals, describing friends that they have or would like to have. (Provide a **Response Journal**, or a small blank book, for each child.)

Second Day: Ask children what they think is the most important quality in a friend. Have them listen for this quality as you read aloud *The Lemonade Babysitter* (Waggoner, 1992). (In this story, a young girl and her babysitter, an elderly man, grow to like each other.) Discuss with children the idea of friends who are different ages. Can one become friends with someone older? And younger? Ask for oral vignettes from children who would like to describe friendships with older/younger, same sex/different sex, same color/different color friends. Ask the children to write in their journals about an older person or someone different who might be a good friend.

Third Day: Begin by recalling the two books read previously and the idea that friends can be of different cultures or age groups. Read aloud *Now One Foot, Now the Other* (dePaola, 1981). (A young boy learns from his grandfather, but after his grandfather has a stroke, the young boy becomes the teacher.) For shared book reading, organize the children into pairs. Each pair will read the same book, silently first, then aloud to each other. (Have enough copies of the books so that each child is holding his or her own.) Help children read to discover what kind of friendship is described in their books—between similar people or between different, unexpected people? (Following is a list of easy readers, unless otherwise noted, that most second and third graders will be able to enjoy. However, your children may require books at either end of the spectrum, from very easy to reasonably difficult, and so you may need to supplement this list.)

Mary Blount Christian	*Penrod's Party*
Lee Bennett Hopkins	*Best Friends* (poetry)
Johanna Hurwitz	*The Hot and Cold Summer; The Cold and Hot Winter; The Up and Down Spring.*

Arnold Lobel	*Frog and Toad Are Friends*
Philip Mendez	*The Black Snowman*
Dav Pilkey	*A Friend for Dragon*
Cynthia Rylant	*Henry and Mudge and the Wild Wind*
Louis Sachar	*Marvin Redpost: Why Pick on Me?*
Jerry Spinelli	*The Bathwater Gang Gets Down to Business*
Mary Stolz	*Go Fish**
Mildred Taylor	*The Friendship**
Margaret Wild	*The Very Best of Friends* (picture book)
Vera Williams	*A Chair for My Mother* (picture book)
Elizabeth Winthrop	*Luke's Bully*

*More difficult than easy readers

Fourth Day: Begin by asking the children what kind of friendship was demonstrated in the books they read yesterday. How would they define *friendship* now? Are their ideas similar to what was expressed on the first day? What did some of the characters (e.g., Marvin Redpost, Henry, etc.) say or do to become a friend? In *The Hot & Cold Summer* two boys learn to like and trust a girl in spite of their earlier reluctance. How did that happen? After discussing the books, encourage the children to choose an activity to illustrate their book's depiction of friendship. They may:

Make a bookmark that shows their book's characters acting friendly

Write a dialogue between their characters

Make a diorama of their favorite part of the book

Write a newspaper article describing the friendship

Make a time line that shows important points in the friendship

Design a new cover for the book (and a new title)

Choose from other activities stemming from the books.

Fifth Day: The children will share their projects or activities. (You may want to allot more time for the activities, depending upon how detailed children will be in their depictions of friendship.) Encourage each child to describe his or her creation, and connect it to previous discussions about friendship.

Bibliography for Unexpected Friends

Christian, M. B. (1990). *Penrod's party.* New York: Macmillan.
dePaola, T. (1981). *Now one foot, now the other.* New York: Putnam.
Hurwitz, J. (1984). *The hot and cold summer.* New York: Morrow.
Hurwitz, J. (1988). *The cold and hot winter.* New York: Morrow.
Hurwitz, J. (1993). *The up and down spring.* New York: Morrow.

Lobel, A. (1970). *Frog and toad are friends.* New York: Harper & Row.
Mendez, P. (1989). *The black snowman.* New York: Scholastic.
Pilkey, D. (1991). *A friend for dragon.* New York: Orchard.
Raschka, C. (1993). *Yo! yes?* New York: Jackson/Orchard.
Rylant, C. (1993). *Henry and Mudge and the wild wind.* New York: Bradbury. (The twelfth
    Henry and Mudge book.)
Sachar, L. (1993). *Marvin Redpost: Why pick on me?* New York: Random House. (The sec-
    ond Marvin Redpost book.)
Spinelli, J. (1992). *The bathwater gang gets down to business.* Boston: Little, Brown.
Stolz, M. (1991). *Go fish.* New York: HarperCollins.
Taylor, M. (1987). *The friendship.* New York: Dial.
Waggoner, K. (1992). *The lemonade babysitter.* New York: Joy Street/Little.
Wild, M. (1990). *The very best of friends.* New York: Harcourt Brace Jovanovich.
Williams, V. (1982). *A chair for my mother.* New York: Greenwillow.
Winthrop, E. (1990). *Luke's bully.* New York: Viking.

Stars: Fact and Fiction   Audience: Ages 8–10 (Grades Three and Four)

Overview: This unit explores the night sky through fiction and nonfiction. Children will learn to recognize some constellations, create and name a constellation,
enjoy a poem, and increase vocabulary through reading and writing.

First Day: Introduce the read-aloud book, *How the Stars Fell into the Sky*
(Oughton, 1992), by saying "Listen to this Navajo legend that explains how stars
got into the sky. When we're finished, each of you will create a legend that
explains how the stars got into the sky or why stars twinkle. Have you ever won-
dered about stars? Why there are so many, what they're made of, and how they
got so high? Here is one explanation."

This poem in haiku form was
written by a fourth grader as
she participated in Stars: Fact
and Fiction.

Stars

A beautiful star
So bright in the night, shining
In the galaxy.

by
Emily Hillman

Read the story aloud, then encourage a brief discussion about First Woman's plan for an ordered sky and Coyote's impatience with her deliberate placement of stars. (Coyote tricked First Woman into letting him help, and then simply threw stars into the night sky.)

Help children get started with their legends by asking "Where would stars come from? What on earth might be thrown up into the sky (diamonds, bright hopes, good deeds, wishes, sand, and whatever else children think of)? Some children might want to think about why stars twinkle. Some will be very literal; some will more easily slip into metaphorical thinking.

Second Day: Ask children to share legends. Introduce the concept constellation (it will appear in some of the legends). Remind children that legends may explain scientific phenomena in a fictional way, while informational books explain nature in a factual way. Using *The Stars* (Rey, 1980), read aloud about the Big Dipper (p. 30) and other familiar constellations. Make the connection between the stars and the names and shapes people (sometimes from ancient times) gave them. Give the children black construction paper and chalk, and have each student create a constellation. Or build a three-dimensional constellation, which is explained in *Stars, Clusters, and Galaxies* (Gustafson, 1992, p. 37).

Third Day: Each child presents his/her constellation and it is mounted on the ceiling so that a night sky is replicated. Ask the children what they know about stars, and listen for vocabulary such as *sun, galaxy, nebula, Milky Way, shooting star, Orion, black hole, quasar,* and other words concerning the solar system. List these words on a large piece of paper or the chalkboard. Introduce *Stars* (Simon, 1986) by saying that many of the terms the children already know and some unfamiliar ones as well will be explained in this book. Suggest that they listen for familiar words, and remember a new one for discussion after the reading. Read aloud *Stars,* then check to see which new terms are listed or remembered.

Allow children to choose books about stars for silent reading. Emphasize that some of the books are factual, and some are fiction. You might want to give a brief one- or two-sentence description of the books to help children make choices.

Necia Apfel	*Nebulae: The Birth and Death of Stars*
Franklyn Branley	*The Big Dipper; Shooting Stars* (picture book)
Eric Carle	*Draw Me a Star* (picture book)
John Gustafson	*Stars, Clusters, and Galaxies*
Lenny Hort	*How Many Stars in the Sky?* (picture book)
X. J. Kennedy	*Knock at a Star* (poetry)
Patricia Lauber	*Lost Star: The Story of Amelia Earhart*
Riki Levinson	*Watch the Stars Come Out*
Lois Lowry	*Number the Stars*
Ellen McKenzie	*Stargone John*
Gretchen Will Mayo	*Star Tales: North American Indian Stories about the Stars*

F. N. Monjo	*The Drinking Gourd*
Scott O'Dell	*Black Star, Bright Dawn*
Deborah Ray	*Stargazing Sky* (picture book)
H. Rey	*The Stars*
R. Schami	*A Hand Full of Stars*
Seymour Simon	*Stars; Galaxies*
Rose Wyler	*The Starry Sky* (picture book)

Fourth Day: Introduce *Follow the Drinking Gourd* (Winter, 1988) by saying, "The Big Dipper is a constellation that had special significance for African Americans who followed the underground railway prior to the Civil War. Listen to this story to see how the Big Dipper, which they called the Drinking Gourd, was important in their escape to freedom. After I read, you will be able to read your books silently."

Read aloud *Follow the Drinking Gourd*. Because this is such a compelling story, the students will probably be anxious to discuss it.

Fifth Day: Begin by reading aloud "The Falling Star" by Sara Teasdale (see p. 126). You might also read star poems from pages 22–23, 26–27, 33, 39, and 76 in *The Random House Book of Poetry for Children* (Prelutsky, 1983). Say, "The stars have inspired writers, poets, and scientists for centuries. Think about how we use the word *star* to mean a famous person or something that's special. In the book you are reading, how is the word *star* used? After silent reading today, write in your response journal about what *star* means in your book, or compose a poem about stars if you'd rather."

Children continue with their books in silent reading. (Those who chose picture books may want to select again.)

A trip to a planetarium would be a great capstone for this unit. If such an opportunity arises, activities should be oriented toward preparing children for the trip.

Bibliography for Stars: Fact and Fiction

Apfel, N. (1988). *Nebulae: The birth and death of stars.* New York: Lothrop.

Branley, F. (1962). *The big dipper.* New York: HarperCollins. (reissued in 1991).

Branley, F. (1989). *Shooting stars.* New York: Crowell.

Carle, E. (1992). *Draw me a star.* New York: Philomel.

Gustafson, J. (1992). *Stars, clusters, and galaxies.* New York: Messner.

Hort, L. (1991). *How many stars in the sky?* New York: Tambourine.

Kennedy, X. J. (1982). *Knock at a star.* Boston: Little, Brown.

Lauber, P. (1988). *Lost star: The story of Amelia Earhart.* New York: Scholastic.

Levinson, R. (1985). *Watch the stars come out.* New York: Dutton.

Lowry, L. (1989). *Number the stars.* Boston: Houghton Mifflin.

Mayo, G. W. (retold and ill.). (1987). *Star tales: North American Indian stories about the stars.* New York: Walker.

McKenzie, E. (1990). *Stargone John.* New York: Holt, Rinehart & Winston.

Monjo, F. N. (1970). *The drinking gourd.* New York: Harper & Row.

O'Dell, S. (1988). *Black star, bright dawn.* Boston: Houghton Mifflin.

Oughton, J. (1992). *How the stars fell into the sky*. Boston: Houghton Mifflin.
Prelutsky, J. (comp.) (1983). *The Random House book of poetry for children*. New York: Random House.
Ray, D. (1991). *Stargazing sky*. New York: Crown.
Rey, H. A. (1980). *The stars* (enlarged worldwide edition). Boston: Houghton Mifflin.
Schami, R. (1990). *A hand full of stars*. New York: Dutton.
Simon, S. (1986). *Stars*. New York: Morrow/Mulberry.
Simon, S. (1988). *Galaxies*. New York: Morrow/Mulberry.
Winter, J. (1988). *Follow the drinking gourd*. New York: Knopf.
Wyler, R. (1989). *The starry sky*. New York: Messner.
Yep, L. (1991). *The star fisher*. New York: Morrow.

People of Destiny

Audience: Ages 9–11 (Grades Four and Five)

Overview: The purpose of this unit is to acquaint children with biographical literature. Biographies allow children to identify with a famous person or someone close to that person, and to understand the life and times of notable figures.

First Day: Present a partially completed bulletin board with the phrase *People of Destiny* at the top, *You* in the center, and a few words such as *athletes* and *inventors* (see Figure 10.5).

Ask questions to encourage discussion: What is destiny? Who do you think are people of destiny? What makes a person "special"? What qualities do people of destiny have? What kind of contributions to society (or to family) make a person famous? What are some occupations that will help us find people of destiny?

Figure 10.5 Bulletin Board for People of Destiny

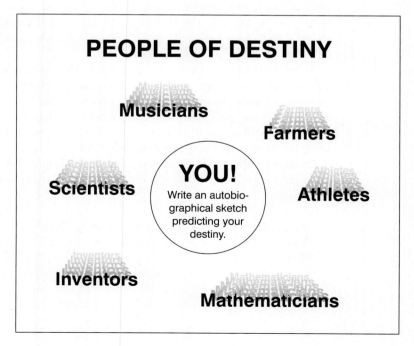

Try to elicit from the children that many ordinary people do extraordinary things, and that we have capacities and talents within us to be heroic just like other famous people in history. From the children's ideas of who some famous people are and some of your own ideas, categorize professions so that more labels can be added to the bulletin board. Examples might be: politicians, poets, scientists, artists, and so on. When children have generated many ideas, tell them that this week they will be exploring the lives of famous people through biographies. But before they think about the qualities or character traits that create the destiny for that famous person, they can think about personal qualities that they have within themselves. Say "Write an autobiographical sketch in your response journal about your destiny. What do you want to be or do? What special qualities do you have—dedication, perseverance, or courage—that will help you reach your potential? After considering your special traits, you will choose a person to read about who may be like you, or may be someone entirely different."

Second Day: Review with the children what qualities are important in people of destiny, and how these qualities help to make people successful in all careers. Ask if anyone would like to share their autobiographical sketches from response journals. (These may be too personal for some children to read aloud.)

Prior to matching children to biographies, tell them that after today, each day this week will begin with a read-aloud, followed immediately by a response activity. After that, each person will read silently in his or her biography and then complete a response activity similar to the one completed all together. Say to the group: "The purpose of reading these biographies is for you to get to know the subject of your biography very well. At the end of the week, we'll have a 'Meeting of Minds' (Lathlaen, 1993) and you'll become the person you've been reading about. You'll hear more about 'Meeting of Minds' as the week progresses. Now let's choose some interesting books."

It is important to have enough biographies so that each child may have some choice. Also, the range of independent reading abilities will be wide, so there are easy biographies (marked with an *) and more difficult ones in the following list. You must know enough about the children so that you can help them make successful decisions about what to read. If two or more children want to read the same book, multiple copies will be necessary.

Prepare short (two or three sentences) booktalks about your biographies. Examples may come from the list below; also consult the multicultural biographies from Chapter 9.

David Adler	*A Picture Book of Jesse Owens*
John Devaney	*Bo Jackson: Star for all Seasons*
Alexis DeVeaux	*Don't Explain: A Song of Billie Holiday*
Doris Faber	*Calamity Jane*
Jeri Ferris	*Native American Doctor: The Story of Susan LaFlesche Picotte*

Jean Fritz	*What's the Big Idea, Ben Franklin?; *Where do you think you're going, Columbus?; Make Way for Sam Houston; The Great Little Madison; Bully for you, Teddy Roosevelt; The Double Life of Pocahontas; Homesick, My Own Story; and others.
Dennis Fradin	Hiawatha: Messenger of Peace
Beverly Gherman	Sandra Day O'Connor: Justice for All
Barbara Harrison and Daniel Terris	A Twilight Struggle: The Life of John Fitzgerald Kennedy
Patricia and Frederick McKissack	Sojourner Truth: Ain't I A Woman
Milton Meltzer	Benjamin Franklin: A New American
F.N. Monjo	Grand Papa and Ellen Aroon, Letters to Horseface, One Bad Thing about Father, Poor Richard in France
Walter Dean Myers	Malcolm X: By Any Means Necessary
Mary Pope Osborne	The Many Lives of Benjamin Franklin
Allan Say	El Chino
Robyn Turner	Mary Cassatt
Ryan White and Ann Marie Cunningham	Ryan White: My Own Story

Third Day: Say "Today we'll look at two people in history and imagine that they met and conversed." Ask the children what they know about William Shakespeare and Queen Elizabeth I. After several ideas have been expressed, read aloud *The Bard of Avon* (Stanley, 1992) and *Good Queen Bess: The Story of Elizabeth I of England* (Stanley, 1990). You may want to have the children write a dialogue in their response journals or dramatize an interchange. Tell them that this is what they'll do on the last day in a "Meeting of Minds" when they become their characters and converse with other characters. Perhaps the people of destiny will be from different periods of history, unlike Shakespeare and the queen, so remind the children to pay attention to the time period as they read today. Say "After reading, write an imaginary dialogue between you and your subject in your response journal. What would you like to know about your subject? And what will he or she tell you? Perhaps he or she will ask you questions about your life today."

Fourth Day: To initiate a grand discussion, refer back to the bulletin board by having children create more categories of "people of destiny." Have them tell what role their subject played, then add his or her name to the bulletin board. Introduce *Beyond the Myth: The Story of Joan of Arc* (Brooks, 1990) by asking the children if they have heard of Joan of Arc. You may need to confirm that she was a mystic, a woman-warrior who lived about 550 years ago in France. She was persuaded to help her king, Charles VII, drive the English from French soil. A peasant girl, she had great faith in God and proved to be a charismatic figure who could rally troops to fight for her cause, unheard of for a woman of her time. After reading aloud the first chapter, present this time line of Joan of Arc (see Figure 10.6):

After silent reading, ask each child to construct a time line of his or her subject, using information from the biography he or she is reading. Some may prefer to use *TimeLiner* (Snyder & Kaemmer, 1988), a software program that creates time lines from information typed into a keyboard.

Remind the children that tomorrow they should have their biographies finished and that they may bring a costume to wear for the "Meeting of Minds."

Fifth Day: You may want to display time lines around the room. After the children have finished their biographies, have them meet in groups of four. They may rehearse for a period of time, then stage their conversation for the whole group. A typical group might consist of Sam Houston, Wolfgang Amadeus Mozart, Mary Cassatt, and John Fitzgerald Kennedy.

Each person begins by telling something about himself or herself, then questions are asked by a moderator (teacher). Questions can be about characters' common experiences in childhood, relationships with parents and siblings, or issues pertinent to their achievement or their qualities. (For example, "What was it like to be so different?")

As a wrap-up to the experience, children should be encouraged to evaluate their own depth of understanding of the person they became in their response journals, and to evaluate their reading and activities. You might want to create a checklist so that the children can judge themselves, or provide a more open-ended questionnaire asking for their evaluations.

Bibliography for People of Destiny

Adler, D. (1992). *A picture book of Jesse Owens*. New York: Holiday.
Brooks, P. S. (1990). *Beyond the myth: The story of Joan of Arc*. New York: Lippincott.
Devaney, J. (1992). *Bo Jackson: A star for all seasons*. New York: Walker.
DeVeaux, A. (1980). *Don't explain: A song of Billie Holiday*. New York: Harper & Row.
Faber, D. (1992). *Calamity Jane*. Boston: Houghton Mifflin.
Ferris, J. (1991). *Native American doctor: The story of Susan LaFlesche Picotte*. Minneapolis, MN: Carolrhoda Books.

Figure 10.6   Time Line of Joan of Arc

Born	Age 13	Age 17	Age 17	Age 17	Age 18	Age 19
1412? in Domrémy, France	(1425) Experiences mystical visions telling her to save France	(January 1429) Began to raise an army	(April 1429) Victory at Orléans	(July 1429) Saw Charles VII crowned King of France	(May 1430) Was captured by the English	(May 1431) Accused of witchcraft and burned at the stake

Fradin, D. (1992). *Hiawatha: Messenger of peace.* New York: McElderry.

Freedman, R. (1987). *Lincoln: A photobiography.* New York: Clarion.

Fritz, J. (1980). *Where do you think you're going, Christopher Columbus?* New York: Putnam.

Fritz, J. (1982). *What's the big idea, Ben Franklin?* New York: Coward.

Fritz, J. (1982). *Homesick: My own story.* New York: Putnam.

Fritz, J. (1986). *Make way for Sam Houston.* New York: Putnam.

Fritz, J. (1987). *The double life of Pocahontas.* New York: Puffin.

Fritz, J. (1989). *The great little Madison.* New York: Putnam.

Fritz, J. (1991). *Bully for you, Teddy Roosevelt.* New York: Putnam.

Fritz, J. (1992). *George Washington's mother.* New York: Grosset.

Giblin, J. (1992). *George Washington: A picture book.* New York: Scholastic.

Harrison, B., & Terris, D. (1992). *A twilight struggle: The life of John Fitzgerald Kennedy.* New York: Lothrop.

Levinson, N. S. (1990). *Christopher Columbus: Voyager to the unknown.* New York: Lodestar/Dutton.

Lipsyte, R. (1993). *Jim Thorpe: Twentieth century jock.* New York: HarperCollins.

McKissack, P., & McKissack, F. (1992). *Sojourner Truth: Ain't I a woman?* New York: Scholastic.

Meltzer, M. (1988). *Benjamin Franklin: A new American.* New York: Watts.

Monjo, F. N. (1970). *The one bad thing about Father.* New York: Harper & Row.

Monjo, F. N. (1973). *Poor Richard in France.* New York: Dell.

Monjo, F. N. (1974). *Grandpapa and Ellen Aroon.* New York: Dell.

Monjo, F. N. (1975). *Letters to Horseface.* New York: Puffin.

Myers, W. D. (1993). *Malcolm X: By any means necessary.* New York: Scholastic.

Osborne, M. P. (1991). *The many lives of Benjamin Franklin.* New York: Dial.

Say, A. (1990). *El chino.* Boston: Houghton Mifflin.

Snyder, T., & Kaemmer, D. (1988). *TimeLiner.* Cambridge, MA: Tom Snyder Productions. (software)

Stanley, D. (1990). *Good Queen Bess: The story of Elizabeth I of England.* New York: Four Winds.

Stanley, D. (1992). *The bard of Avon.* New York: Morrow.

Turner, R. (1992). *Mary Cassatt.* Boston: Little, Brown.

Additional Resources

Lathlaen, P. (1993). A meeting of minds: Teaching using biographies. *Reading Teacher, 46,* 529–531.

Journeys   Audience: Ages 10–12 (Grades Five and Six)

Overview: In this unit, children are asked to explore literary journeys through fiction and nonfiction. Historical journeys to a new world, survival journeys through war-torn countries, and fantastic journeys to another time and place allow readers to experience vicariously the drama of moving. Sadness, joy, curiosity, and wonder are all part of these journeys into a new life. Literature makes the journeys relevant to our own lives.

If you are planning for approximately twenty-five children, you will need five copies each of *The Remarkable Journey of Prince Jen* (Alexander, 1991), *Year of Impossible Goodbyes* (Choi, 1991), *A Wrinkle in Time* (L'Engle, 1962), *Journey*

(Maclachlan, 1991), and *Grab Hands and Run* (Temple, 1993). Most of these are in paperback, so multiple copies are not too expensive.

First Day: In order to focus on journeys, create a web with the class. Using an overhead projector and transparency, begin with a circle in the middle of the page and write *JOURNEY* inside it (see Figure 10.7).

Elicit from the children what kinds of journeys occur in books. If they are familiar with *Sarah Plain and Tall* (Maclachlan, 1985), for example, you can remind them that Sarah went west to find a new husband and family. Add ideas that children offer to the web, such as "to the west," "to freedom," "to the city," or "to a new stepparent." Point out that sometimes the main character discovers something about himself or herself, and the journey is a personal one to self-discovery and personal insight.

Continue to activate prior knowledge by saying, "In the next few days we'll be reading about journeys that occur in books. We'll discover why the journey is important to the character, and how he or she feels about it. We'll be reading aloud about a journey taken by a twelve-year-old girl from Russia to the United States in 1919 in a book called *Letters from Rifka* (Hesse, 1992). Right now, though, here are the five books about journeys, and after hearing about them, each of you will choose to be in a group."

Booktalk these five books. Booktalks are oral presentations by teachers or librarians; their purpose is to stimulate students' interest in the book and motivate them to read it. They are not reports, analyses, or opinions, but offer just enough enticing information to pique curiosity. Usually, a brief synopsis of the beginning of the book is given, with dramatic portions read aloud. Only a brief synopsis is given below.

Figure 10.7   Brainstorming Web for Journeys

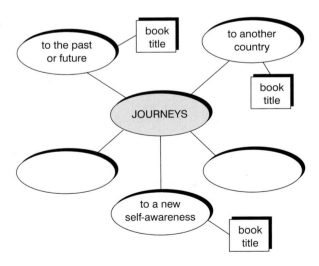

The Remarkable Journey of Prince Jen, by Lloyd Alexander
Bearing six unusual gifts, young Prince Jen embarks on a perilous quest and emerges triumphantly. In this fantasy (which is, however, filled with rich details of a past Chinese culture), Prince Jen journeys between self-doubt and courage.

Year of Impossible Goodbyes, by Sook Nyul Choi
A young Korean girl survives the oppressive Japanese and Russian occupation of North Korea during the 1940s, and makes a harrowing journey to freedom in South Korea in this work of historical realistic fiction.

A Wrinkle in Time, by Madeleine L'Engle
Interplanetary travel through dimensions of time allows Meg Murry, her brother Charles Wallace, and her friend Calvin to find her father. The children battle an evil shadow threatening to envelop earth with the help of otherworldly creatures.

Journey, by Patricia Maclachlan
When their mother goes away, leaving Journey and his older sister, Cat, with their grandparents, they feel their past has been erased until Grandfather uses photography to restore it. In this work of contemporary realism, Journey's path to understanding (his mother) and love (his grandfather) is a difficult one.

Grab Hands and Run, by Frances Temple
Two children and their mother escape from El Salvador in the midst of the recent civil war. Walking to Canada, they experience many hardships for political freedom.

After giving the booktalks, elicit first and second choices from the children. Form groups, and give this purpose-setting statement to begin silent reading. "Read to find out who the characters are and what their journey is or might be."

Second Day: Introduce *Letters from Rifka* (Hesse, 1992) with a booktalk, or use the author's note on page ix. "In this book Rifka writes letters about her journey. After your reading today, write a letter from your main character to another character in the story. Perhaps it's a letter of explanation, or a letter asking why the situation is so perilous. In the meantime, enjoy Rifka's letters as she explains her situation."

Read aloud about thirty minutes. (If you plan to finish the book this week, you will need to read about thirty-seven pages per day.) After reading, ask the children to read silently (for about thirty minutes), then write letters as instructed earlier. The letters may be written in their response journals or written for others in the group. You may want the group to compose a letter, if cooperation is a goal of the unit.

Third Day: "As Rifka journeys, we will construct a map that shows how extensive her journey is. Today, after your reading, begin to plot on a literary map the journey of your main character or characters."

Read aloud for about thirty minutes, then trace Rifka's journey so far on a map of Eastern Europe in 1919, or on a more informal drawing of your own.

Allow children to read for about thirty minutes, then begin work on their own maps.

Fourth Day: "After reading *Rifka,* we'll discuss her character and create a character web" (see Figure 10.8). This can be done on the overhead projector, with a large sheet of paper and markers, or on the chalkboard. After reading aloud, elicit Rifka's character traits, and ask if any of the characters from books the children are reading have similar ones.

Tell children that after their silent reading, they should construct a character web for the main character in their books.

Fifth Day: Finish *Letters from Rifka.* Give children these choices for responding to their own books:

Artistically   Create a collage to represent the main theme of the book; make illustrations for three to five important events; create a miniature scene from the book in a shoebox; complete a literary map of the journey; or make a model of the main character out of soap, clay, Plasticine, papier-mâché, or some other substance.

Writing   Rewrite the ending, adding a twist or unexpected event that you think fits the story; find or write poems that represent the theme of the book and the main character's traits; create a time line for the story; write to the author, describing your reactions to the story.

Other ways of responding   Interview someone in the community who is knowledgeable about some aspect of your book; cook a food described in or related to the book and eat it; compare your book to *Rifka* on a poster; find and select some music appropriate to the culture represented by your book and play

Figure 10.8   Character Web for Rifka

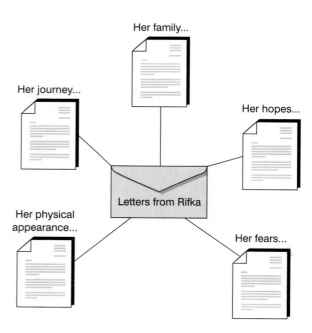

From Sook Nyul Choi's *Year of Impossible Goodbyes,* copyright © 1991. By permission of the publisher, Houghton Mifflin Company.

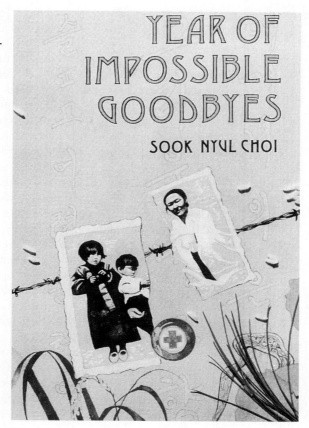

it for the class, describing how it fits character and theme; dramatize a particularly dramatic section of journeying (ask a friend or another member of the group to help you); research the time in which your story takes place and produce a written report; write a newspaper story about your characters and their plight.

If time permits, plan to have the children share their final responses with each other or with parents.

Bibliography for Journeys

Alexander, L. (1991). *The remarkable journey of Prince Jen.* New York: Dutton.
Choi, S. N. (1991). *Year of impossible goodbyes.* Boston: Houghton Mifflin.
Hesse, K. (1992). *Letters from Rifka.* New York: Holt, Rinehart & Winston.
L'Engle, M. (1962). *A wrinkle in time.* New York: Farrar, Straus & Giroux.
Maclachlan, P. (1985). *Sarah plain and tall.* New York: Harper & Row.
Maclachlan, P. (1991). *Journey.* New York: Delacorte.
Temple, F. (1993). *Grab hands and run.* New York: Orchard.

• • • • •
SUMMARY

In this concluding chapter, six thematic units demonstrated how to use literature in classrooms. Each unit was slightly different, as audiences, activities, and structure varied so that each one could become a prototype for others.

Singing Songs and Stories, appropriate for kindergartners and first graders, used language, melody, and rhythm to reinforce important emerging reading and writing skills. Traditional Mother Goose, folk songs, and contemporary verses provided the basis for children to enjoy and learn from the combined power of story and song.

Wild Things focused on Maurice Sendak's classic, *Where the Wild Things Are,* and demonstrated how a single book could generate reading, writing, and artistic skills. Children explored vocabulary and made puppets, and with the help of a storyboard wrote an original story for their puppet. The storyboard concretized basic story structure—beginning, middle, and end.

Unexpected Friends drew on cross-generational and multicultural books to explore friendships that develop over time. Through discussions children were expected to probe ideas about what qualities a good friend has and how to be a good friend. Partner-reading of literature considered to be transitional, or easy chapter books, reinforced the message of the unit—that friends do things together.

Stars: Fact and Fiction used traditional literature and informational literature to teach concepts about the night sky. Children in third and fourth grades were encouraged to think metaphorically in their rendition of a legend about stars, and to write, draw, construct, and enjoy the panorama of a starry sky. Choices of literature included contemporary and historical realism, as well as informational books.

The unit, People of Destiny, for fourth and fifth graders, reinforced self-esteem by beginning with each child's hopes and visions of his or her future. Biographical literature provided a wide view of possible choices and the destinies of famous people —athletes, inventors, and many others. Activities stemming from the biographies encouraged children to consider qualities of leadership and the development of skills and talents. A "Meeting of Minds" culminated this unit; readers became the subjects of their biographies and participated in round-table discussions, moderated by the teacher, demonstrating knowledge of their subjects' life and times.

Journeys allowed readers to travel vicariously to the past, to the future, and through danger and suspense with characters in compelling stories. As a metaphor for their own journey into adolescence, fifth and sixth graders first explored the different kinds of journeys literature offers, then chose a book in which a strong main character faced the hardships of change. Silent reading, creating literary maps and character webs, and listening to a read-aloud were the primary activities used to elicit critical thinking about journeying and making decisions.

While the units were all different in structure and content, they shared commonalities related to a philosophy of literature-based instruction, a philosophy that rests on the natural connection between literacy and literature. Simply stated, in order to learn to read, to become literate, children must be exposed to books of high quality. Exposure means many opportunities for listening, reading, talking about literature, and writing personal as well as analytical pieces based on feelings and knowledge. In each of the units the teacher read aloud to the children, and the children read silently and sometimes aloud to each other, usually books of their choice. Reading and writing applications revolved around significant aspects of literature, such as Who are the characters? Why are they important? How are they like you and me? Applications sprang from what literature does best: portraying the human condition and allowing imagination to flourish.

In the beginning of this text, you embarked on a journey of your own—a scholarly journey to discover the intricacies of children's literature. After establishing your goals, you read widely, evaluated, selected, and used books in whatever capacity you could. You now have completed the discoveries that this text offers, but the journey continues. Children's literature is a growing field, with many books published each year in a worldwide market. As long as there are children, as long as society values literacy and literature, each year will bring exciting new works of fiction and nonfiction. These new discoveries await you, the discoverer.

REFERENCES

(Children's books are referenced at the end of each unit.)

Professional Works Cited

Cairney, T. (1990). *Other worlds: The endless possibilities of literature.* Portsmouth, NH: Heinemann.

Cox, C., & Zarillo, J. (1993). *Teaching reading with children's literature* (p. 121). New York: Merrill/Macmillan.

deLapp, S. (1989). Administrative support for literature-based reading programs. In J. Hickman & B. Cullinan (Eds.), *Children's literature in the classroom: Weaving Charlotte's web* (pp. 221–229). Norwood, MA: Christopher Gordon.

Rosenblatt, L. (1978). *The reader, the text, the poem: The transactional theory of the literary work.* Carbondale, IL: SIU Press.

Wepner, S., & Feeley, J. (1993). *Moving forward with literature: Basals, books, and beyond* (p. 28). New York: Merrill/Macmillan.

Additional Resources

Resources with Units and Teaching Strategies for Adolescents

Bushman, J. H., & Bushman, K. P. (1993). *Using young adult literature in the English classroom.* New York: Merrill/Macmillan.

Moffett, J., & Wagner, B. J. (1992). *Student-centered language arts, K–12* (4th ed.). Portsmouth, NH: Heinemann.

Nilsen, A. P., & Donelson, K. L. (1993). *Literature for today's young adults* (4th ed.). New York: HarperCollins.

Probst, R. (1988). *Response and analysis: Teaching literature in junior and senior high school.* Portsmouth, NH: Heinemann.

Tompkins, G. E., & McGee, L. M. (1993). *Teaching reading with literature: Case studies to action plans.* New York: Merrill/Macmillan.

General Resources

Chambers, A. (1983). *Introducing books to children* (2nd ed.). Boston: Horn Book.

Moss, J. (1990). *Focus on literature: A context for literacy learning.* Katonah, NY: Richard C. Owen.

Rudman, M. (Ed.). (1993). *Children's literature: Resource for the classroom* (2nd ed.). Norwood, MA: Christopher Gordon.

Newbery and Caldecott Award Books

Each year the Children's Services Division of the American Library Association selects one children's book to be honored with the Newbery Medal and a children's picture book to be honored with the Caldecott Medal. These awards represent the highest honors in publishing in the United States. They celebrate significant contributions to children's literature by notable people: John Newbery, a noted British bookseller in the eighteenth century; and Randolph Caldecott, the British artist of the nineteenth century who raised the picture book to an art form.

The Newbery Award books and Honor books are listed first, followed by the Caldecott Award winners and Honor books. The Caldecott Medal is earned by the illustrator, not the author (although often the author is also the illustrator). The date on the left indicates the year of the award; all books were published in the preceding year.

Newbery Award Winners and Honor Books

1922   *The Story of Mankind,* Hendrik Willem van Loon, Liveright.

HONOR BOOKS: *The Great Quest,* Charles Hawes, Little, Brown; *Cedric the Forester,* Bernard Marshall, Appleton; *The Old Tobacco Shop: A True Account of What Befell a Little Boy in Search of Adventure,* William Bowen, Macmillan; *The Golden Fleece and the Heroes Who Lived before Achilles,* Padraic Colum, Macmillan; *Windy Hill,* Cornelia Meigs, Macmillan.

1923 *The Voyages of Doctor Dolittle,* Hugh Lofting, Lippincott.
HONOR BOOKS: no record.

1924 *The Dark Frigate,* Charles Hawes, Atlantic/Little, Brown.
HONOR BOOKS: no record.

1925 *Tales from the Silver Lands,* Charles Finger, Doubleday.
HONOR BOOKS: *Nicholas: A Manhattan Christmas Story,* Anne Carroll Moore, Putnam; *Dream Coach,* Anne Parrish, Macmillan.

1926 *Shen of the Sea,* Arthur Bowie Chrisman, Dutton.
HONOR BOOK: *Voyagers: Being Legends and Romances of Atlantic Discovery,* Padraic Colum, Macmillan.

1927 *Smoky, the Cowhorse,* Will James, Scribner.
HONOR BOOKS: no record.

1928 *Gayneck, the Story of a Pigeon,* Dhan Gopal Mukerji, Dutton.
HONOR BOOKS: *The Wonder Smith and His Son: A Tale from the Golden Childhood of the World,* Ella Young, Longmans; *Downright Dencey,* Caroline Snedeker, Doubleday.

1929 *The Trumpeter of Krakow,* Eric P. Kelly, Macmillan.
HONOR BOOKS: *Pigtail of Ah Lee Ben Loo,* John Bennett, Longmans; *Millions of Cats,* Wanda Gag, Coward-McCann; *The Boy Who Was,* Grace Hallock, Dutton; *Clearing Weather,* Cornelia Meigs, Little, Brown; *Runaway Papoose,* Grace Moon, Doubleday; *Tod of the Fens,* Elinor Whitney, Macmillan.

1930 *Hitty, Her First Hundred Years,* Rachel Field, Macmillan.
HONOR BOOKS: *Daughter of the Seine: The Life of Madame Roland,* Jeanette Eaton, HarperCollins; *Pran of Albania,* Elizabeth Miller, Doubleday; *Jumping-off Place,* Marian Hurd McNeely, Longmans; *Tangle-Coated Horse and Other Tales,* Ella Young, Longmans; *Vaino: A Boy of New England,* Julia Davis Adams, Dutton; *Little Blacknose,* Hildegarde Swift, Harcourt Brace Jovanovich.

1931 *The Cat Who Went to Heaven,* Elizabeth Coatsworth, Macmillan.
HONOR BOOKS: *Floating Island,* Anne Parrish, HarperCollins; *The Dark Star of Itze: The Story of a Pagan Princess,* Alida Malkus, Harcourt Brace; *Queer Person,* Ralph Hubbard, Doubleday; *Mountains Are Free,* Julia Davis Adams, Dutton; *Spice and the Devil's Cave,* Agnes Hewes, Knopf; *Meggy Macintosh,* Elizabeth Janet Gray, Doubleday; *Garram the Hunter: A Boy of the Hill Tribes,* Herbert Best, Doubleday; *Ood-Le-Uk the Wanderer,* Alice Lide and Margaret Johansen, Little, Brown.

1932   *Waterless Mountain,* Laura Adams Armer, Longmans.

HONOR BOOKS: *The Fairy Circus,* Dorothy P. Lathrop, Macmillan; *Calico Bush,* Rachel Field, Macmillan; *Boy of the South Seas,* Eunice Tietjens, Coward-McCann; *Out of the Flame,* Eloise Lownsbery, Longmans; *Jane's Island,* Marjorie Allee, Houghton Mifflin; *Truce of the Wolf and Other Tales of Old Italy,* Mary Gould Davis, Harcourt Brace.

1933   *Young Fu of the Upper Yangtze,* Elizabeth Foreman Lewis, Winston.

HONOR BOOKS: *Swift Rivers,* Cornelia Meigs, Little, Brown; *The Railroad to Freedom: A Story of the Civil War,* Hildegarde Swift, Harcourt Brace; *Children of the Soil: A Story of Scandinavia,* Nora Burglon, Doubleday.

1934   *Invincible Louisa: The Story of the Author of 'Little Women,'* Cornelia Meigs, Little, Brown.

HONOR BOOKS: *The Forgotten Daughter,* Caroline Snedeker, Doubleday; *Swords of Steel,* Elsie Singmaster, Houghton Mifflin; *ABC Bunny,* Wanda Gag, Coward-McCann; *Winged Girl of Knossos,* Eric Berry, Appleton; *New Land,* Sarah Schmidt, McBride; *Big Tree of Bunlahy: Stories of My Own Countryside,* Padraic Colum, Macmillan; *Glory of the Seas,* Agnes Hewes, Knopf; *Apprentice of Florence,* Ann Kyle, Houghton Mifflin.

1935   *Dobry,* Monica Shannon, Viking.

HONOR BOOKS: *Pageant of Chinese History,* Elizabeth Seeger, Longmans; *Davy Crockett,* Constance Rourke, Harcourt Brace; *Day on Skates: The Story of a Dutch Picnic,* Hilda Van Stockum, HarperCollins.

1936   *Caddie Woodlawn,* Carol Ryrie Brink, Macmillan.

HONOR BOOKS: *Honk, the Moose,* Phil Stong, Dodd, Mead; *The Good Master,* Kate Seredy, Viking; *Young Walter Scott,* Elizabeth Janet Gray, Viking; *All Sail Set: A Romance of the Flying Cloud,* Armstrong Sperry, Winston.

1937   *Roller Skates,* Ruth Sawyer, Viking.

HONOR BOOKS: *Phoebe Fairchild: Her Book,* Lois Lenski, Stokes; *Whistler's Van,* Idwal Jones, Viking; *Golden Basket,* Ludwig Bemelmans, Viking; *Winterbound,* Margery Bianco, Viking; *Audubon,* Constance Rourke, Harcourt Brace; *The Codfish Musket,* Agnes Hewes, Doubleday.

1938   *The White Stag,* Kate Seredy, Viking.

HONOR BOOKS: *Pecos Bill,* James Cloyd Bowman, Little, Brown; *Bright Island,* Mabel Robinson, Random House; *On the Banks of Plum Creek,* Laura Ingalls Wilder, HarperCollins.

1939 *Thimble Summer,* Elizabeth Enright, Rinehart.

   HONOR BOOKS: *Nino,* Valenti Angelo, Viking; *Mr. Popper's Penguins,* Richard and Florence Atwater, Little, Brown; *'Hello the Boat!'* Phyllis Crawford, Holt; *Leader by Destiny: George Washington, Man and Patriot,* Jeanette Eaton, Harcourt Brace; *Penn,* Elizabeth Janet Gray, Viking.

1940 *Daniel Boone,* James Daugherty, Viking.

   HONOR BOOKS: *The Singing Tree,* Kate Seredy, Viking; *Runner of the Mountain Tops: The Life of Louis Agassiz,* Mabel Robinson, Random House; *By the Shores of Silver Lake,* Laura Ingalls Wilder, Harper-Collins; *Boy with a Pack,* Stephen W. Meader, Harcourt Brace.

1941 *Call It Courage,* Armstrong Sperry, Macmillan.

   HONOR BOOKS: *Blue Willow,* Doris Gates, Viking; *Young Mac of Fort Vancouver,* Mary Jane Carr, Crowell; *The Long Winter,* Laura Ingalls Wilder, HarperCollins; *Nansen,* Anna Gertrude Hall, Viking.

1942 *The Matchlock Gun,* Walter D. Edmonds, Dodd, Mead.

   HONOR BOOKS: *Little Town on the Prairie,* Laura Ingalls Wilder, Harper-Collins; *George Washington's World,* Genevieve Foster, Scribner; *Indian Captive: The Story of Mary Jemison,* Lois Lenski, Lippincott; *Down Ryton Water,* Eva Roe Gaggin, Viking.

1943 *Adam of the Road,* Elizabeth Janet Gray, Viking.

   HONOR BOOKS: *The Middle Moffat,* Eleanor Estes, Harcourt Brace; *Have You Seen Tom Thumb?* Mabel Leigh Hunt, Lippincott.

1944 *Johnny Tremain,* Esther Forbes, Houghton Mifflin.

   HONOR BOOKS: *The Happy Golden Years,* Laura Ingalls Wilder, Harper-Collins; *Fog Magic,* Julia Sauer, Viking; *Rufus M.,* Eleanor Estes, Harcourt Brace; *Mountain Born,* Elizabeth Yates, Coward-McCann.

1945 *Rabbit Hill,* Robert Lawson, Viking.

   HONOR BOOKS: *The Hundred Dresses,* Eleanor Estes, Harcourt Brace; *The Silver Pencil,* Alice Dalgliesh, Scribner; *Abraham Lincoln's World,* Genevieve Foster, Scribner; *Lone Journey: The Life of Roger Williams,* Jeanette Eaton, Harcourt Brace Jovanovich.

1946 *Strawberry Girl,* Lois Lenski, Lippincott.

   HONOR BOOKS: *Justin Morgan Had a Horse,* Marguerite Henry, Rand; *The Moved-Outers,* Florence Crannell Means, Houghton Mifflin; *Bhimsa, the Dancing Bear,* Christine Weston, Scribner; *New Found World,* Katherine Shippen, Viking.

1947   *Miss Hickory,* Carolyn Sherwin Bailey, Viking.

HONOR BOOKS: *Wonderful Year,* Nancy Barnes, Messner; *Big Tree,* Mary and Conrad Buff, Viking; *The Heavenly Tenants,* William Maxwell, HarperCollins; *The Avion My Uncle Flew,* Cyrus Fisher, Appleton; *The Hidden Treasure of Glaston,* Eleanor Jewett, Viking.

1948   *The Twenty-One Balloons,* William Pene du Bois, Viking.

HONOR BOOKS: *Pancakes-Paris,* Claire Hutchet Bishop, Viking; *Li Lun: Lad of Courage,* Carolyn Treffinger, Abingdon; *The Quaint and Curious Quest of Johnny Longfoot, the Shoe-King's Son,* Catherine Besterman, Bobbs-Merrill; *The Cow-Tail Switch, and Other West African Stories,* Harold Courlander, Holt, Rinehart & Winston; *Misty of Chincoteague,* Marguerite Henry, Rand McNally.

1949   *King of the Wind,* Marguerite Henry, Rand McNally.

HONOR BOOKS: *Seabird,* Holling C. Holling, Houghton Mifflin; *Daughter of the Mountains,* Louise Rankin, Viking; *My Father's Dragon,* Ruth S. Gannett, Random House; *Story of the Negro,* Arna Bontemps, Knopf.

1950   *The Door in the Wall,* Marguerite de Angeli, Doubleday.

HONOR BOOKS: *Tree of Freedom,* Rebecca Caudill, Viking; *The Blue Cat of Castle Town,* Catherine Coblentz, Longmans Green; *Kildee House,* Rutherford Montgomery, Doubleday; *George Washington,* Genevieve Foster, Scribner; *Song of the Pines: A Story of Norwegian Lumbering in Wisconsin,* Walter and Marion Havighurst, Winston.

1951   *Amos Fortune, Free Man,* Elizabeth Yates, Aladdin.

HONOR BOOKS: *Better Known as Johnny Appleseed,* Mabel Leigh Hunt, Lippincott; *Ghandi, Fighter Without a Sword,* Jeanette Eaton, Morrow; *Abraham Lincoln, Friend of the People,* Clara Ingram Judson, Follett; *The Story of Appleby Capple,* Anne Parrish, HarperCollins.

1952   *Ginger Pye,* Eleanor Estes, Harcourt Brace Jovanovich.

HONOR BOOKS: *Americans Before Columbus,* Elizabeth Baity, Viking; *Minn of the Mississippi,* Holling C. Holling, Houghton Mifflin; *The Defender,* Nicholas Kalashnikoff, Scribner; *The Light at Tern Rock,* Julia Sauer, Viking; *The Apple and the Arrow,* Mary and Conrad Buff, Houghton Mifflin.

1953   *Secret of the Andes,* Ann Nolan Clark, Viking.

HONOR BOOKS: *Charlotte's Web,* E. B. White, HarperCollins; *Moccasin Trail,* Eloise McGraw, Coward-McCann; *Red Sails to Capri,* Ann Weil, Viking; *The Bears on Hemlock Mountain,* Alice Dalgliesh, Scribner; *Birthdays of Freedom,* Vol. 1, Genevieve Foster, Scribner.

1954 *. . . and Now Miguel,* Joseph Krumgold, Crowell.

HONOR BOOKS: *All Alone,* Claire Hutchet Bishop, Viking; *Shadrach,* Meindert DeJong, HarperCollins; *Hurry Home Candy,* Meindert DeJong, HarperCollins; *Theodore Roosevelt, Fighting Patriot,* Clara Ingram Judson, Follett; *Magic Maize,* Mary and Conrad Buff, Houghton Mifflin.

1955 *The Wheel on the School,* Meindert DeJong, HarperCollins.

HONOR BOOKS: *The Courage of Sarah Noble,* Alice Dalgliesh, Scribner; *Banner in the Sky,* James Ullman, Lippincott.

1956 *Carry On, Mr. Bowditch,* Jean Lee Latham, Houghton Mifflin.

HONOR BOOKS: *The Secret River,* Marjorie Kinnan Rawlings, Scribner; *The Golden Name Day,* Jennie Linquist, HarperCollins; *Men, Microscopes, and Living Things,* Katherine Shippen, Viking.

1957 *Miracles on Maple Hill,* Virginia Sorensen, Harcourt Brace Jovanovich.

HONOR BOOKS: *Old Yeller,* Fred Gipson, HarperCollins; *The House of Sixty Fathers,* Meindert DeJong, HarperCollins; *Mr. Justice Holmes,* Clara Ingram Judson, Follett; *The Corn Grows Ripe,* Dorothy Rhoads, Viking; *Black Fox of Lorne,* Marguerite de Angeli, Doubleday.

1958 *Rifles for Watie,* Harold Keith, Crowell.

HONOR BOOKS: *The Horsecatcher,* Mari Sandoz, Westminister; *Gone-away Lake,* Elizabeth Enright, Harcourt Brace Jovanovich; *The Great Wheel,* Robert Lawson, Viking; *Tom Paine, Freedom's Apostle,* Leo Gurko, Crowell.

1959 *The Witch of Blackbird Pond,* Elizabeth George Speare, Houghton Mifflin.

HONOR BOOKS: *The Family Under the Bridge,* Natalie Savage Carlson, HarperCollins; *Along Came a Dog,* Meindert DeJong, HarperCollins; *Chucaro: Wild Pony of the Pampa,* Francis Kalnay, Harcourt Brace Jovanovich; *The Perilous Road,* William O. Steele, Harcourt Brace Jovanovich.

1960 *Onion John,* Joseph Krumgold, Crowell.

HONOR BOOKS: *My Side of the Mountain,* Jean George, Dutton; *America Is Born,* Gerald W. Johnson, Morrow; *The Gammage Cup,* Carol Kendall, Harcourt Brace Jovanovich.

1961 *Island of the Blue Dolphins,* Scott O'Dell, Houghton Mifflin.

HONOR BOOKS: *America Moves Forward,* Gerald W. Johnson, Morrow; *Old Ramon,* Jack Schaefer, Houghton Mifflin; *The Cricket in Times Square,* George Selden, Farrar, Straus & Giroux.

1962 *The Bronze Bow,* Elizabeth George Speare, Houghton Mifflin.

HONOR BOOKS: *Frontier Living,* Edwin Tunis, World; *The Golden Goblet,* Eloise McGraw, Coward-McCann; *Belling the Tiger,* Mary Stolz, Harper-Collins.

1963 *A Wrinkle in Time,* Madeleine L'Engle, Farrar, Straus & Giroux.

HONOR BOOKS: *Thistle and Thyme: Tales and Legends from Scotland,* Sorche Nic Leodhas, Holt, Rinehart & Winston; *Men of Athens,* Olivia Coolidge, Houghton Mifflin.

1964 *It's Like This, Cat,* Emily Cheney Neville, HarperCollins.

HONOR BOOKS: *Rascal,* Sterling North, Dutton; *The Loner,* Ester Wier, McKay.

1965 *Shadow of a Bull,* Maia Wojciechowska, Atheneum.

HONOR BOOK: *Across Five Aprils,* Irene Hunt, Follett.

1966 *I, Juan de Pareja,* Elizabeth Borten de Trevino, Farrar, Straus & Giroux.

HONOR BOOKS: *The Black Cauldron,* Lloyd Alexander, Holt, Rinehart & Winston; *The Animal Family,* Randall Jarrell, Pantheon; *The Noonday Friends,* Mary Stolz, HarperCollins.

1967 *Up a Road Slowly,* Irene Hunt, Follett.

HONOR BOOKS: *The King's Fifth,* Scott O'Dell, Houghton Mifflin; *Zlateh the Goat and Other Stories,* Isaac Bashevis Singer, HarperCollins; *The Jazz Man,* Mary H. Weik, Atheneum.

1968 *From the Mixed-Up Files of Mrs. Basil E. Frankweiler,* E. L. Konigsberg, Atheneum.

HONOR BOOKS: *Jennifer, Hecate, Macbeth, William McKinley, and Me, Elizabeth,* E. L. Konigsberg, Atheneum; *The Black Pearl,* Scott O'Dell, Houghton Mifflin; *The Fearsome Inn,* Isaac Bashevis Singer, Scribner; *The Egypt Game,* Zilpha Keatley Snyder, Atheneum.

1969 *The High King,* Lloyd Alexander, Holt, Rinehart & Winston.

HONOR BOOKS: *To Be a Slave,* Julius Lester, Dial; *When Shlemiel Went to Warsaw and Other Stories,* Isaac Bashevis Singer, Farrar, Straus & Giroux.

1970 *Sounder,* William Armstrong, HarperCollins.

HONOR BOOKS: *Our Eddie,* Sulamith Ish-Kishor, Pantheon; *The Many Ways of Seeing: An Introduction to the Pleasures of Art,* Janet Gaylord Moore, World; *Journey Outside,* Mary O. Steele, Viking.

1971   *Summer of the Swans,* Betsy Byars, Viking.

HONOR BOOKS: *Kneeknock Rise,* Natalie Babbitt, Farrar, Straus & Giroux; *Enchantress from the Stars,* Sylvia Louise Engdahl, Atheneum; *Sing Down the Moon,* Scott O'Dell, Houghton Mifflin.

1972   *Mrs. Frisby and the Rats of NIMH,* Robert C. O'Brien, Atheneum.

HONOR BOOKS: *Incident at Hawk's Hill,* Allan W. Eckert, Little, Brown; *The Planet of Junior Brown,* Virginia Hamilton, Macmillan; *The Tombs of Atuan,* Ursula LeGuin, Atheneum; *Annie and the Old One,* Miska Miles, Atlantic/Little, Brown; *The Headless Cupid,* Zilpha Keatley Snyder, Atheneum.

1973   *Julie of the Wolves,* Jean Craighead George, HarperCollins.

HONOR BOOKS: *Frog and Toad Together,* Arnold Lobel, HarperCollins; *The Upstairs Room,* Johanna Reiss, Crowell; *The Witches of Worm,* Zilpha Keatley Snyder, Atheneum.

1974   *The Slave Dancer,* Paula Fox, Bradbury.

HONOR BOOK: *The Dark Is Rising,* Susan Cooper, Atheneum.

1975   *M. C. Higgins, the Great,* Virginia Hamilton, Macmillan.

HONOR BOOKS: *Figgs and Phantoms,* Ellen Raskin, Dutton; *My Brother Sam Is Dead,* James Lincoln Collier and Christopher Collier, Four Winds; *The Perilous Gard,* Elizabeth Marie Pope, Houghton Mifflin; *Philip Hall Likes Me, I Reckon Maybe,* Bette Greene, Dial.

1976   *The Grey King,* Susan Cooper, Atheneum.

HONOR BOOKS: *The Hundred Penny Box,* Sharon Bell Mathis, Viking; *Dragonwings,* Laurence Yep, HarperCollins.

1977   *Roll of Thunder, Hear My Cry,* Mildred D. Taylor, Dial.

HONOR BOOKS: *Abel's Island,* William Steig, Farrar, Straus & Giroux; *A String in the Harp,* Nancy Bond, Atheneum.

1978   *Bridge to Terabithia,* Katherine Paterson, Crowell.

HONOR BOOKS: *Ramona and Her Father,* Beverly Cleary, Morrow; *Anpao: An American Indian Odyssey,* Jamake Highwater, Lippincott.

1979   *The Westing Game,* Ellen Raskin, Dutton.

HONOR BOOK: *The Great Gilly Hopkins,* Katherine Paterson, Crowell.

1980   *A Gathering of Days: A New England Girl's Journal 1830–1832,* Joan Blos, Scribner.

HONOR BOOK: *The Road from Home: The Story of an Armenian Girl,* David Kherdian, Greenwillow.

1981   *Jacob Have I Loved*, Katherine Paterson, Crowell.

HONOR BOOKS: *The Fledgling*, Jane Langton, HarperCollins; *A Ring of Endless Light*, Madeleine L'Engle, Farrar, Straus & Giroux.

1982   *A Visit to William Blake's Inn: Poems for Innocent and Experienced Travelers*, Nancy Willard, Harcourt Brace Jovanovich.

HONOR BOOKS: *Ramona Quimby, Age 8*, Beverly Cleary, Morrow; *Upon the Head of a Goat: A Childhood in Hungary 1939–1944*, Aranka Siegel, Farrar, Straus & Giroux.

1983   *Dicey's Song*, Cynthia Voigt, Atheneum.

HONOR BOOKS: *Blue Sword*, Robin McKinley, Morrow; *Dr. DeSoto*, William Steig, Farrar, Straus & Giroux; *Graven Images*, Paul Fleischman, HarperCollins; *Homesick: My Own Story*, Jean Fritz, Putnam; *Sweet Whispers, Brother Rush*, Virginia Hamilton, Philomel.

1984   *Dear Mr. Henshaw*, Beverly Cleary, Morrow.

HONOR BOOKS: *The Sign of the Beaver*, Elizabeth George Speare, Houghton Mifflin; *A Solitary Blue*, Cynthia Voigt, Atheneum; *The Wish Giver*, Bill Brittain, HarperCollins.

1985   *The Hero and the Crown*, Robin McKinley, Greenwillow.

HONOR BOOKS: *Like Jake and Me*, Mavis Jukes, Knopf; *Sugaring Time*, Kathryn Lasky, Macmillan; *The Moves Make the Man*, Bruce Brooks, HarperCollins; *One-Eyed Cat*, Paula Fox, Bradbury.

1986   *Sarah, Plain and Tall*, Patricia MacLachlan, HarperCollins.

HONOR BOOKS: *Commodore Perry in the Land of the Shogun*, Rhoda Blumberg, Lothrop, Lee & Shepard; *Dogsong*, Gary Paulsen, Bradbury.

1987   *The Whipping Boy*, Sid Fleishman, Greenwillow.

HONOR BOOKS: *A Fine White Dust*, Cynthia Rylant, Bradbury; *On My Honor*, Marion Dane Bauer, Clarion; *Volcano*, Patricia Lauber, Bradbury.

1988   *Lincoln: A Photobiography*, Russell Freedman, Clarion.

HONOR BOOKS: *After the Rain*, Norma Fox Mazer, Morrow; *Hatchet*, Gary Paulsen, Bradbury.

1989   *Joyful Noise: Poems for Two Voices*, Paul Fleischman, HarperCollins.

HONOR BOOKS: *In the Beginning: Creation Stories from Around the World*, Virginia Hamilton, Harcourt Brace Jovanovich; *Scorpions*, Walter Dean Myers, HarperCollins.

1990   *Number the Stars,* Lois Lowry, Houghton Mifflin.

HONOR BOOKS: *Afternoon of the Elves,* Janet Taylor Lisle, Orchard; *Shabanu, Daughter of the Wind,* Susan Fisher Staples, Knopf; *The Winter Room,* Gary Paulsen, Orchard.

1991   *Maniac Magee,* Jerry Spinelli, Little, Brown.

HONOR BOOK: *The True Confessions of Charlotte Doyle,* Avi, Orchard.

1992   *Shiloh,* Phyllis Reynolds Naylor, Atheneum.

HONOR BOOKS: *Nothing But the Truth,* Avi, Orchard; *The Wright Brothers,* Russell Freedman, Holiday.

1993   *Missing May,* Cynthia Rylant, Orchard.

HONOR BOOKS: *The Dark Thirty: Southern Tales of the Supernatural,* Patricia McKissack, Knopf; *Somewhere in the Darkness,* Walter Dean Myers, Scholastic; *What Hearts,* Bruce Brooks, HarperCollins.

1994   *The Giver,* Lois Lowry, Houghton Mifflin.

HONOR BOOKS: *Crazy Lady,* Jane Leslie Conly, HarperCollins; *Eleanor Roosevelt,* Russell Freedman, Clarion; *Dragon's Gate,* Laurence Yep, HarperCollins.

Caldecott Award Winners and Honor Books

1938   *Animals of the Bible,* Helen Dean Fish, ill. by Dorothy P. Lathrop, Stokes.

HONOR BOOKS: *Seven Simeon: A Russian Tale,* Boris Artzybasheff, Viking; *Four and Twenty Blackbirds: Nursery Rhymes of Yesterday Recalled for Children of Today,* Helen Dean Fish, ill. by Robert Lawson, Stokes.

1939   *Mei Li,* Thomas Handforth, Doubleday.

HONOR BOOKS: *The Forest Pool,* Laura Adams Armer, Longmans; *Wee Gillis,* Munro Leaf, ill. by Robert Lawson, Viking; *Snow White and the Seven Dwarfs,* Wanda Gag, Coward-McCann; *Barkis,* Clare Newberry, HarperCollins; *Andy and the Lion: A Tale of Kindness Remembered or the Power of Gratitude,* James Daugherty, Viking.

1940   *Abraham Lincoln,* Ingri and Edgar Parin d'Aulaire, Doubleday.

HONOR BOOKS: *Cock-A-Doodle Doo: The Story of a Little Red Rooster,* Berta and Elmer Hader, Macmillan; *Madeline,* Ludwig Bemelmans, Simon & Schuster; *The Ageless Story,* Lauren Ford, Dodd, Mead.

1941   *They Were Strong and Good,* Robert Lawson, Viking.

HONOR BOOK: *April's Kittens,* Clare Newberry, HarperCollins.

1942   *Make Way for Ducklings,* Robert McCloskey, Viking.

HONOR BOOKS: *An American ABC,* Maud and Miska Petersham, Macmillan; *In My Mother's House,* Ann Nolan Clark, ill. by Velino Herrera, Viking; *Paddle-to-the-Sea,* Holling C. Holling, Houghton Mifflin; *Nothing at All,* Wanda Gag, Coward-McCann.

1943   *The Little House,* Virginia Lee Burton, Houghton Mifflin.

HONOR BOOKS: *Dash and Dart,* Mary and Conrad Buff, Viking; *Marshmallow,* Clare Newberry, HarperCollins.

1944   *Many Moons,* James Thurber, ill. by Louis Slobodkin, Harcourt Brace.

HONOR BOOKS: *Small Rain: Verses from the Bible,* Jessie Orton Jones, ill. by Elizabeth Orton Jones, Viking; *Pierre Pigeon,* Lee Kingman, ill. by Arnold E. Bare, Houghton Mifflin; *The Mighty Hunter,* Berta and Elmer Hader, Macmillan; *A Child's Good Night Book,* Margaret Wise Brown, ill. by Jean Charlot, Scott, Foresman; *Good Luck Horse,* Chih-Yi Chan, ill. by Plato Chan, Whittlesey.

1945   *Prayer for a Child,* Rachel Field, ill. by Elizabeth Orton Jones, Macmillan.

HONOR BOOKS: *Mother Goose: Seventy-Seven Verses with Pictures,* ill. by Tasha Tudor, Walck; *In the Forest,* Marie Hall Ets, Viking; *Yonie Wondernose,* Marguerite de Angeli, Doubleday; *The Christmas Anna Angel,* Ruth Sawyer, ill. by Kate Seredy, Viking.

1946   *The Rooster Crows . . . ,* ill. by Maud and Miska Petersham, Macmillan.

HONOR BOOKS: *Little Lost Lamb,* Golden MacDonald, ill. by Leonard Weisgard, Doubleday; *Sing Mother Goose,* Opal Wheeler, ill. by Marjorie Torrey, Dutton; *My Mother Is the Most Beautiful Woman in the World,* Becky Reyher, ill. by Ruth Gannett, Lothrop, Lee & Shepard; *You Can Write Chinese,* Kurt Wiese, Viking.

1947   *The Little Island,* Golden MacDonald, ill. by Leonard Weisgard, Doubleday.

HONOR BOOKS: *Rain Drop Splash,* Alvin Tresselt, ill. by Leonard Weisgard, Lothrop, Lee & Shepard; *Boats on the River,* Marjorie Flack, ill. by Jay Hyde Barnum, Viking; *Timothy Turtle,* Al Graham, ill. by Tony Palazzo, Viking; *Pedro, the Angel of Olvera Street,* Leo Politi, Scribner; *Sing in Praise: A Collection of the Best Loved Hymns,* Opal Wheeler, ill. by Marjorie Torrey, Dutton.

1948   *White Snow, Bright Snow,* Alvin Tresselt, ill. by Roger Duvoisin, Lothrop, Lee & Shepard.

HONOR BOOKS: *Stone Soup: An Old Tale,* Marcia Brown, Scribner; *McElligot's Pool,* Dr. Seuss, Random House; *Bambino the Clown,* George Schreiber, Viking; *Roger and the Fox,* Lavinia Davis, ill. by Hildegard Woodward, Doubleday; *Song of Robin Hood,* Anne Malcolmson (ed.), ill. by Virginia Lee Burton, Houghton Mifflin.

1949   *The Big Snow,* Berta and Elmer Hader, Macmillan.

HONOR BOOKS: *Blueberries for Sal,* Robert McCloskey, Viking; *All Around the Town,* Phyllis McGinley, ill. by Helen Stone, Lippincott; *Juanita,* Leo Politi, Scribner; *Fish in the Air,* Kurt Weise, Viking.

1950   *Song of the Swallows,* Leo Politi, Scribner.

HONOR BOOKS: *America's Ethan Allen,* Stewart Holbrook, ill. by Lynd Ward, Houghton Mifflin; *The Wild Birthday Cake,* Lavinia Davis, ill. by Hildegard Woodward, Doubleday; *The Happy Day,* Ruth Krauss, ill. by Marc Simont, HarperCollins; *Bartholomew and the Oobleck,* Dr. Seuss, Random House; *Henry Fisherman,* Marcia Brown, Scribner.

1951   *The Egg Tree,* Katherine Milhous, Scribner.

HONOR BOOKS: *Dick Whittington and His Cat,* Marcia Brown, Scribner; *The Two Reds,* William Lipkind, ill. by Nicholas Mordvinoff, Harcourt Brace; *If I Ran the Zoo,* Dr. Seuss, Random House; *The Most Wonderful Doll in the World,* Phyllis McGinley, ill. by Helen Stone, Lippincott; *T-Bone, the Babysitter,* Clare Newberry, HarperCollins.

1952   *Finders Keepers,* William Lipkind, ill. by Nicholas Mordvinoff, Harcourt Brace.

HONOR BOOKS: *Mr. T. W. Anthony Wood: The Story of a Cat and a Dog and a Mouse,* Marie Hall Ets, Viking; *Skipper John's Cook,* Marcia Brown, Scribner; *All Falling Down,* Gene Zion, ill. by Margaret Bloy Graham, HarperCollins; *Bear Party,* William Pene du Bois, Viking; *Feather Mountain,* Elizabeth Olds, Houghton Mifflin.

1953   *The Biggest Bear,* Lynd Ward, Houghton Mifflin.

HONOR BOOKS: *Puss in Boots,* Charles Perrault, ill. and tr. by Marcia Brown, Scribner; *One Morning in Maine,* Robert McCloskey, Viking; *Ape in a Cape: An Alphabet of Odd Animals,* Fritz Eichenberg, Harcourt Brace; *The Storm Book,* Charlotte Zolotow, ill. by Margaret Bloy Graham, HarperCollins; *Five Little Monkeys,* Juliet Kepes, Houghton Mifflin.

1954   *Madeline's Rescue,* Ludwig Bemelmans, Viking.

HONOR BOOKS: *Journey Cake, Ho!* Ruth Sawyer, ill. by Robert McCloskey, Viking; *When Will the World Be Mine?* Miriam Schlein, ill. by Jean Charlot, Scott, Foresman; *The Steadfast Tin Soldier,* Hans Christian Andersen, ill. by Marcia Brown, Scribner; *A Very Special House,* Ruth Krauss, ill. by Maurice Sendak, HarperCollins; *Green Eyes,* A. Birnbaum, Capitol.

1955   *Cinderella, or the Little Glass Slipper,* Charles Perrault, ill. and tr. by Marcia Brown, Scribner.

HONOR BOOKS: *Book of Nursery and Mother Goose Rhymes,* ill. by Marguerite deAngeli, Doubleday; *Wheel on the Chimney,* Margaret Wise

Brown, ill. by Tibor Gergely, Lippincott; *The Thanksgiving Story,* Alice Dalgliesch, ill. by Helen Sewell, Scribner.

1956   *Frog Went A-Courtin',* ed. by John Langstaff, ill. by Feodor Rojankovsky, Harcourt Brace Jovanovich.

HONOR BOOKS: *Play with Me,* Marie Hall Ets, Viking; *Crow Boy,* Taro Yashima, Viking.

1957   *A Tree Is Nice,* Janice May Udry, ill. by Marc Simont, HarperCollins.

HONOR BOOKS: *Mr. Penny's Race Horse,* Marie Hall Ets, Viking; *1 Is One,* Tasha Tudor, Walck; *Anatole,* Eve Titus, ill. by Paul Galdone, McGraw-Hill; *Gillispie and the Guards,* Benjamin Elkin, ill. by James Daugherty, Viking; *Lion,* William Pene du Bois, Viking.

1958   *Time of Wonder,* Robert McClosky, Viking.

HONOR BOOKS: *Fly High, Fly Low,* Don Freeman, Viking; *Anatole and the Cat,* Eve Titus, ill. by Paul Galdone, McGraw-Hill.

1959   *Chanticleer and the Fox,* adapted from Chaucer and ill. by Barbara Cooney, Crowell.

HONOR BOOKS: *The House That Jack Built: A Picture Book in Two Languages,* Antonio Frasconi, Harcourt Brace Jovanovich; *What Do You Say, Dear?* Sesyle Joslin, ill. by Maurice Sendak, Scott, Foresman; *Umbrella,* Taro Yashima, Viking.

1960   *Nine Days to Christmas,* Marie Hall Ets and Aurora Labastida, ill. by Marie Hall Ets, Viking.

HONOR BOOKS: *Houses from the Sea,* Alice E. Goudey, ill. by Adrienne Adams, Scribner; *The Moon Jumpers,* Janice May Udry, ill. by Maurice Sendak, HarperCollins.

1961   *Baboushka and the Three Kings,* Ruth Robbins, ill. by Nicolas Sidjakov, Parnassus.

HONOR BOOK: *Inch by Inch,* Leo Lionni, Obolensky.

1962   *Once a Mouse . . . ,* Marcia Brown, Scribner.

HONOR BOOKS: *The Fox Went Out on a Chilly Night: An Old Song,* Peter Spier, Doubleday; *Little Bear's Visit,* Else Holmelund Minarik, ill. by Maurice Sendak, HarperCollins; *The Day We Saw the Sun Come Up,* Alice E. Goudey, ill. by Adrienne Adams, Scribner.

1963   *The Snowy Day,* Ezra Jack Keats, Viking.

HONOR BOOKS: *The Sun Is a Golden Earring,* Natalia M. Belting, ill. by Bernarda Bryson, Holt, Rinehart & Winston; *Mr. Rabbit and the Lovely Present,* Charlotte Zolotow, ill. by Maurice Sendak, HarperCollins.

1964   *Where the Wild Things Are,* Maurice Sendak, HarperCollins.

HONOR BOOKS: *Swimmy,* Leo Lionni, Pantheon; *All in the Morning Early,* Sorche Nic Leodhas, ill. by Evaline Ness, Holt, Rinehart & Winston; *Mother Goose and Nursery Rhymes,* ill. by Philip Reed, Atheneum.

1965   *May I Bring a Friend?,* Beatrice Schenk de Regniers, ill. by Beni Montresor, Atheneum.

HONOR BOOKS: *Rain Makes Applesauce,* Julian Scheer, ill. by Marvin Bileck, Holiday; *The Wave,* Margaret Hodges, ill. by Blair Lent, Houghton Mifflin; *A Pocketful of Cricket,* Rebecca Caudill, ill. by Evaline Ness, Holt, Rinehart & Winston.

1966   *Always Room for One More,* Sorche Nic Leodhas, ill. by Nonny Hogrogian, Holt, Rinehart & Winston.

HONOR BOOKS: *Hide and Seek Fog,* Alvin Tresselt, ill. by Roger Duvoisin, Lothrop, Lee & Shepard; *Just Me,* Marie Hall Ets, Viking; *Tom Tit Tot,* Evaline Ness, Scribner.

1967   *Sam, Bangs, and Moonshine,* Evaline Ness, Holt, Rinehart & Winston.

HONOR BOOK: *One Wide River to Cross,* Barbara Emberley, ill. by Ed Emberley, Prentice Hall.

1968   *Drummer Hoff,* Barbara Emberley, ill. by Ed Emberley, Prentice Hall.

HONOR BOOKS: *Frederick,* Leo Lionni, Pantheon; *Seashore Story,* Taro Yashima, Viking; *The Emperor and the Kite,* Jane Yolen, ill. by Ed Young, World.

1969   *The Fool of the World and the Flying Machine,* Arthur Ransome, ill. by Uri Shulevitz, Farrar, Straus & Giroux.

HONOR BOOK: *Why the Sun and the Moon Live in the Sky: An African Folktale,* Elphinstone Dayrell, ill. by Blair Lent, Houghton Mifflin.

1970   *Sylvester and the Magic Pebble,* William Steig, Windmill.

HONOR BOOKS: *Goggles!* Ezra Jack Keats, Macmillan; *Alexander and the Wind-Up Mouse,* Leo Lionni, Pantheon; *Pop Corn and Ma Goodness,* Edna Mitchell Preston, ill. by Robert Andrew Parker, Viking; *The Friend, Obadiah,* Brinton Turkle, Viking; *The Judge: An Untrue Tale,* Harve Zemach, ill. by Margot Zemach, Farrar, Straus & Giroux.

1971   *A Story—A Story: An African Tale,* Gail Haley, Atheneum.

HONOR BOOKS: *The Angry Moon,* William Sleator, ill. by Blair Lent, Atlantic-Little; *Frog and Toad Are Friends,* Arnold Lobel, HarperCollins; *In the Night Kitchen,* Maurice Sendak, HarperCollins.

1972   *One Fine Day,* Nonny Hogrogian, Macmillan.

HONOR BOOKS: *If All the Seas Were One Sea,* Janina Domanska, Macmillan; *Moja Means One: Swahili Counting Book,* Muriel Feelings, ill. by Tom Feelings, Dial; *Hildilid's Night,* Cheli Duran Ryan, ill. by Arnold Lobel, Macmillan.

1973   *The Funny Little Woman,* retold by Arlene Mosel, ill. by Blair Lent, Dutton.

HONOR BOOKS: *Anansi the Spider: A Tale for the Ashanti,* adapted by Gerald McDermott, Holt, Rinehart & Winston; *Hosie's Alphabet,* Hosea Tobias and Lisa Baskin, ill. by Leonard Baskin, Viking; *Snow White and the Seven Dwarfs,* tr. by Randall Jarrell, ill. by Nancy Ekholm Burkert, Farrar, Straus & Giroux; *When Clay Sings,* Byrd Baylor, ill. by Tom Bahti, Scribner.

1974   *Duffy and the Devil,* Harve Zemach, ill. by Margot Zemach, Farrar, Straus & Giroux.

HONOR BOOKS: *Three Jovial Huntsmen,* Susan Jeffers, Bradbury; *Cathedral: The Story of Its Construction,* David Macaulay, Houghton Mifflin.

1975   *Arrow to the Sun,* adapt. and ill. by Gerald McDermott, Viking.

HONOR BOOK: *Jambo Means Hello: A Swahili Alphabet Book,* Muriel Feelings, ill. by Tom Feelings, Dial.

1976   *Why Mosquitoes Buzz in People's Ears,* retold by Verna Aardema, ill. by Leo and Diane Dillon, Dial.

HONOR BOOKS: *The Desert Is Theirs,* Byrd Baylor, ill. by Peter Parnall, Scribner; *Strega Nona,* retold and ill. by Tomie de Paola, Prentice Hall.

1977   *Ashanti to Zulu: African Traditions,* Margaret Musgrove, ill. by Leo and Diane Dillon, Dial.

HONOR BOOKS: *The Amazing Bone,* William Steig, Farrar, Straus & Giroux; *The Contest,* retold and ill. by Nonny Hogrogian, Greenwillow; *Fish for Supper,* M. B. Goffstein, Dial; *The Golem: A Jewish Legend,* Beverly Brodsky McDermott, Lippincott; *Hawk, I'm Your Brother,* Byrd Baylor, ill. by Peter Parnall, Scribner.

1978   *Noah's Ark,* Peter Spier, Doubleday.

HONOR BOOKS: *Castle,* David Macaulay, Houghton Mifflin; *It Could Always Be Worse,* retold and ill. by Margot Zemach, Farrar, Straus & Giroux.

1979   *The Girl Who Loved Wild Horses,* Paul Goble, Bradbury.

HONOR BOOKS: *Freight Train,* Donald Crews, Greenwillow; *The Way to Start a Day,* Byrd Baylor, ill. by Peter Parnall, Scribner.

1980   *Ox-Cart Man,* Donald Hall, ill. by Barbara Cooney, Viking.

HONOR BOOKS: *Ben's Trumpet,* Rachel Isadora, Greenwillow; *The Treasure,* Uri Shulevitz, Farrar, Straus & Giroux; *The Garden of Abdul Gasazi,* Chris Van Allsburg, Houghton Mifflin.

1981   *Fables,* Arnold Lobel, HarperCollins.

HONOR BOOKS: *The Bremen-Town Musicians,* Ilse Plume, Doubleday; *The Grey Lady and the Strawberry Snatcher,* Molly Bang, Four Winds; *Mice Twice,* Joseph Low, Atheneum; *Truck,* Donald Crews, Greenwillow.

1982   *Jumanji,* Chris Van Allsburg, Houghton Mifflin.

HONOR BOOKS: *A Visit to William Blake's Inn: Poems for Innocent and Experienced Travelers,* Nancy Willard, ill. by Alice and Martin Provensen, Harcourt Brace Jovanovich; *Where the Buffaloes Begin,* Olaf Baker, ill. by Stephen Gammell, Warner; *On Market Street,* Arnold Lobel, ill. by Anita Lobel, Greenwillow; *Outside Over There,* Maurice Sendak, HarperCollins.

1983   *Shadow,* Blaise Cendrars, ill. by Marcia Brown, Scribner.

HONOR BOOKS: *When I Was Young in the Mountains,* Cynthia Rylant, ill. by Diane Goode, Dutton; *A Chair for My Mother,* Vera B. Williams, Morrow.

1984   *The Glorious Flight: Across the Channel with Louis Bleriot,* Alice and Martin Provensen, Viking.

HONOR BOOKS: *Ten, Nine, Eight,* Molly Bang, Greenwillow; *Little Red Riding Hood,* retold and ill. by Trina Schart Hyman, Holiday House.

1985   *St. George and the Dragon,* retold by Margaret Hodges, ill. by Trina Schart Hyman, Little, Brown.

HONOR BOOKS: *Hansel and Gretel,* retold by Rika Lesser, ill. by Paul O. Zelinsky, Dodd, Mead; *Have You Seen My Duckling?* Nancy Tafuri, Greenwillow; *The Story of Jumping Mouse,* John Steptoe, Lothrop, Lee & Shepard.

1986   *The Polar Express,* Chris Van Allsburg, Houghton Mifflin.

HONOR BOOKS: *King Bidgood's in the Bathtub,* Audrey Wood, ill. by Don Wood, Harcourt Brace Jovanovich; *The Relatives Came,* Cynthia Rylant, ill. by Stephen Gammell, Bradbury.

1987   *Hey, Al,* Arthur Yorinks, ill. by Richard Egielski, Farrar, Straus & Giroux.

HONOR BOOKS: *Alphabatics,* Suse MacDonald, Bradbury; *Rumpelstiltskin,* retold and ill. by Paul O. Zelinsky, Dutton; *The Village of Round and Square Houses,* Ann Grifalconi, Little, Brown.

1988   *Owl Moon,* Jane Yolen, ill. by John Schoenherr, Philomel.

HONOR BOOK: *Mufaro's Beautiful Daughters: An African Tale,* John Steptoe, Lothrop, Lee & Shepard.

1989   *Song and Dance Man,* Karen Ackerman, ill. by Stephen Gammell, Knopf.

HONOR BOOKS: *The Boy of the Three-Year Nap,* Dianne Stanley, ill. by Allen Say, Houghton Mifflin; *Free Fall,* David Wiesner, Lothrop, Lee & Shepard; *Goldilocks and the Three Bears,* ad. and ill. by James Marshall, Dial; *Mirandy and Brother Wind,* Patricia McKissack, ill. by Jerry Pinkney, Knopf.

1990   *Lon Po Po: A Red Riding Hood Story from China,* ad. and ill. by Ed Young, Philomel.

HONOR BOOKS: *Bill Peet: An Autobiography,* Bill Peet, Houghton Mifflin; *Color Zoo,* Lois Ehlert, Lippincott; *Herschel and the Hanukkah Goblins,* Eric Kimmel, ill. by Trina Schart Hyman, Holiday; *The Talking Eggs,* Robert D. San Souci, ill. by Jerry Pinkney, Dial.

1991   *Black and White,* David Macaulay, Houghton Mifflin.

HONOR BOOKS: *Puss in Boots,* Charles Perrault, tr. by Malcolm Arthur, ill. by Fred Marcellino, Farrar, Straus & Giroux; *"More More More,"* *Said the Baby,* Vera B. Williams, Greenwillow.

1992   *Tuesday,* David Wiesner, Clarion.

HONOR BOOK: *Tar Beach,* Faith Ringgold, Crown.

1993   *Mirette on the High Wire,* Emily Arnold McCully, Putnam.

HONOR BOOKS: *Seven Blind Mice,* Ed Young, Philomel; *The Stinky Cheese Man and Other Fairly Stupid Tales,* Jon Scieszka, ill. by Lane Smith, Viking; *Working Cotton,* Sherley Anne Williams, ill. by Carole Byard, Harcourt Brace Jovanovich.

1994   *Grandfather's Journey,* Allen Say, Houghton Mifflin.

HONOR BOOKS: *Peppe the Lamplighter,* Elisa Bartone, ill. by Ted Lewin, Lothrop, Lee & Shepard; *In the Small, Small Pond,* Denise Fleming, Holt, Rinehart & Winston; *Owen,* Kevin Henkes, Greenwillow; *Raven: A Trickster Tale from the Pacific Northwest,* Gerald McDermott, Harcourt Brace Jovanovich; *Yo! Yes?* Christopher Raschka, Jackson/Orchard.

For a complete listing of awards and honored books in children's literature, see *Children's Books: Awards and Prizes,* 1993 edition, compiled and edited by the Children's Book Council, Inc., 568 Broadway, New York, NY 10012. This six-part volume is available in hard cover and paperback, and includes international and multinational awards.

Glossary

Allegory   A prose or poetry narrative in which persons or objects represent general concepts or abstractions.

Alliteration   Repetition of initial consonant sounds in words.

Allusion   An indirect reference to a well-known person or event.

Antagonist   Character or force that opposes the main character (the protagonist) in a literary work.

Archetype   Universal images, situations, plots, characters, and themes found in traditional literature and repeated in modern literature, either consciously or unconsciously.

Authentic biography   A biography in which almost every fact is documented. There are no invented characters, scenes, or events.

Autobiography   A factual account of someone's life written by that person.

Ballad   A narrative poem in short stanzas with or without music.

Battledore   A large piece of heavy paper folded in thirds, printed with the alphabet, numerals, and little ditties, or phonograms. Popular in the 1700s, they contained early reading lessons for children and were cheaply produced.

Bibliotherapy   The use of books to promote emotional healing in an individual.

Biographical fiction   A realistic or fanciful story that includes some biographical (factual) material.

Biography   A written factual account of someone's life.

Blank verse   Unrhymed iambic pentameter such as that used by William Shakespeare in his dramas.

Booktalks   Brief oral presentations (not reports, analyses, or critiques) about books; teachers and librarians use them to stimulate and motivate children to read and to generate interest in the book and the topic.

Canon   A list of literary works that are especially meritorious.

Chapbook   Cheaply made story booklets that were crudely illustrated with wood-cuts; they were popular from the fifteenth through the seventeenth centuries.

Character   A person, or a personified animal or object, creating a role in literature.

Cinquain   A five-line poem that does not rhyme, but follows a pattern that defines each line.

Cliffhanger   Unresolved suspense that concludes a chapter.

Climax   The high point of a story when tension breaks and conflict begins to be resolved.

Collage   A design that is made by pasting nonpainterly materials on a surface.

Concrete poetry   A poem written to represent visually the shape or the meaning of the poem.

Conflict   Tension between two opposing forces.

Couplet   Two lines that end in rhyming words.

Cross-hatching   A technique in which artists cover a drawing with fine black lines. Cross-hatching can be light or heavy; it is used to add depth and texture to a picture.

Cubism   A style of art in which paintings of the human figure and landscape are represented by geometrical shapes, often cubes.

Diamante   A seven-line poem, shaped like a diamond, that follows a pattern for each line.

Didactic   Primarily intended to teach a moral lesson, with any entertainment or amusement value remaining secondary.

Double-page spread   The design or drawing spreads over both pages when a book is opened. Also, double-spread.

Dynamic   A character who changes as a result of the story.

Endpapers   The paper sheets immediately inside the front and back covers of a book.

Explicit theme   A stated, obviously articulated, unifying idea.

Expository prose   Written material of a factual, informative nature such as that found in textbooks or encyclopedias.

Expressionism   Art that leans toward abstraction, expressing the emotional subjectivity of objects.

Fable   A brief narrative with a pointed moral that takes abstract ideas of behavior and makes them concrete through the actions of animal characters.

Fantasy   A genre of modern literature; it includes an impossible element.

Fictionalized biography   A biography based on fact; it includes a significant amount of fiction.

Figurative language   The use of words out of their literal meaning to add beauty or force.

First person   The point of view of a character using "I" to tell a story.

Flashback   Looking back at a previous event, out of chronological order.

Flat character   A character who has very few traits.

Foil   Character who has contrasting traits with those of the main character.

Folklore   The traditional beliefs, legends, customs, etc., of a community or society.

Folktale   A story passed down the generations through the oral tradition.

Foreshadowing   A hint of an upcoming event.

Free verse   Poetry free of the usual or "formal" traditional metrical and stanzaic patterns.

Genre   A large category of literary works that has a set of similar characteristics.

Haiku   Japanese lyric verse form in three unrhymed lines with counted syllables; the syllable counts for the lines are five, seven, and five.

High fantasy   A subgenre of fantasy that has the characteristics of a romance.

Hornbook   A wooden paddle about 2 ¾ by 5 inches, on which was pasted a lesson sheet of vellum or parchment. The sheet began with a cross, followed by the alphabet, syllables, and prayers. This was covered with a thin layer of transparent horn and bound along the edges with strips of brass. It was sometimes worn around the neck, suspended by a leather thong strung through a hole in the handle.

Implicit theme   A unifying idea that is not directly stated.

Impressionism   Relying on the play of light on an object or scene, impressionism hints at and suggests reality. A dreamlike quality is often achieved.

Information   A genre of children's literature that refers to factual writing about school subjects.

Intaglio   A process of engraving used in the production of early picture books.

Internal rhyme   Words that rhyme inside a line of verse.

Irony   Deliberately saying the opposite of what one means; insinuating the opposite theme throughout a literary work.

Limerick   A humorous poem of five lines; it follows the rhyme scheme: a, a, b, b, a.

Lithography   A printing method in which pictures are drawn with oil-based chalk or paint on a limestone plate. After the plate is submerged in water, ink adheres to the chalk or paint; when heavy pressure is applied to paper, the design prints.

Lyrical poetry   Poetry that is descriptive and personal and follows no prescribed form or pattern. It can be set to music.

Metaphor   An implied comparison.

Montage   The combination of several distinct pictures to make a composite picture.

Mood   A subjective emotional state created by setting and other elements.

Motif   A recurring pattern of imagery or action.

Multicultural literature   Literature coming from a cultural group that is usually seen as out of the mainstream of political and economic power.

Myth   A story originating in folk belief; myths often show supernatural forces operating.

Narrative poetry   A poem that tells a story; narrative poems typically have no refrain and are quite long.

Omniscient   An all-knowing point of view using third person; an author tells the story in third person.

Onomatopoeia   The use of words that sound like their meanings, such as *buzz* or *hiss*.

Parable   A brief narrative that takes abstract ideas and makes a point through the actions of one-dimensional characters.

Personification   Giving human traits to animals or objects.

Picture book   A book in which artwork and text are equally important; in some cases, the artwork is more important. Also, a genre of children's literature.

Picture storybook   A picture book that tells a story. *Picture storybook* is a term sometimes used synonymously with *picture book;* it sometimes just refers to fictional picture books such as contemporary and historical realistic fiction, traditional literature, and fantasy picture books.

Plot   The order of events in a story.

Poetry   A genre of literature with well-defined forms that include, but are not restricted to, rhythm and rhyme.

Point of view   The narrative direction from which a story is written.

Primary world   The realistic world as a setting for fiction (realism and fantasy).

Problem   An event or task that begins the action, conflict, or tension in a story.

Protagonist   The principal character in a literary work.

Realism   A genre of literature in which stories mirror reality.

Representational, or **realistic, art**   Art that imitates reality in shape, color, proportion, and so on.

Response journal   A journal in which the reader writes his or her reactions to ideas in books. Usually personal (but sometimes directed by a teacher), these responses encourage critical thinking about story, plot, character, or identification with some element in literature.

Rhyme scheme   A pattern created by the rhyming words of a stanza or poem.

Romance   A particular kind of literature based on medieval imagery and codes of behavior.

Round character   A well-developed character, one with many traits.

Science-fiction fantasy   A subgenre of Fantasy; stories are set in a future time and rely on imaginary technological inventions or extensions of today's technology.

Setting   The time and place in which the action occurs.

Simile   An explicit comparison using *like* or *as.*

Sonnet   A poem of fourteen lines, usually in iambic pentameter. A sonnet typically has the rhyme scheme abab cdcd efef gg.

Static character   A character who does not change over time.

Stereotype   A person who possesses only the expected traits of a group.

Stock character   Flat character with little or no development.

Story grammar   The linear pattern of the events in a story.

Story structure   The linear, circular, or episodic pattern of events in a story, from introduction to resolution.

Style   Aspects of language that create a total effect.

Stylistic language   Words used in patterns that become familiar over time, such as "Once upon a time."

Subgenre   A part of a larger genre, or category, of literature. For example, alphabet books constitute a subgenre of picture books.

Surrealistic art   Artwork that distorts and plays with images, juxtaposing reality with absurdity.

Symbol   Someone or something that stands for something else.

Theme   Unifying idea that permeates a literary work.

Third person   A point of view from "above" the action, sometimes called omniscient. The author can project a story from any person's thoughts or by description.

Tone   The attitude that permeates a written piece.

Touchstone   A book that represents the "best" or highest quality; a book that is used to evaluate other books by comparison.

Trade book   A book such as that sold in bookstores or found in libraries—*not* a textbook.

Traditional literature   Stories, proverbs, rhymes, and other linguistic expressions coming from the oral tradition. The names of the authors or originators have been lost in time.

Verse   (1) One line of poetry; (2) a stanza, particularly with refrain (the verse of a song); (3) poetry in general; (4) light poetry as opposed to serious.

Wordless picture book, or **wordless book**   A subgenre of picture books in which no text (or minimal text) is used, and the story is told through the artwork.

About the Author

Dr. Judith Hillman, an associate professor of education at Saint Michael's College, Colchester, Vermont, teaches reading and language arts courses and literature for children and youth to graduate and undergraduate students. She has initiated graduate courses in children's literature which now lead to a specialization on the master's level.

Before entering college teaching, Dr. Hillman taught vocal music in junior high schools and elementary grades in Missouri, then earned a Ph.D. in the teaching of English from the University of Nebraska-Lincoln. She has served as state officer and state coordinator for the International Reading Association and presently fulfills the vice-presidency of the New England Reading Association, assuming the presidency in 1996.

In her work as a supervisor of student teachers, Dr. Hillman visits elementary and secondary classrooms almost daily, always eliciting and enjoying responses to literature from children and adolescents. Also chair of the Dorothy Canfield Fisher (DCF) State Book Award Committee, she reads approximately 350 children's books yearly, then leads the committee to formulate the DCF list of best books. (Children vote for their favorite each spring.)

Dr. Hillman has been a tireless advocate for literacy through literature throughout her teaching career. Conducting workshops, speaking and demonstrating to teachers, and writing articles and reviews, she presents the many enjoyable and instructive uses of books for children and adolescents.

Index